Teaching Character Education through Literature

This book demonstrates how secondary (and post-secondary) teachers of literature can help students become more responsive to the ethical themes and questions that emerge from the narratives they study. It assists teachers in integrating character education into classroom instruction. Instead of focussing primarily on the formal analysis of plot, symbol, mood and irony, the author illustrates a variety of ways to draw instructive insights from fictional life narratives. The case studies and questions throughout are designed to awaken students' moral imagination and prompt ethical reflection on four protagonists' motivations, aspirations and choices.

The book is divided into two parts. Part I, 'Narrative and Moral Agency', provides a theoretical basis for this new approach to teaching character education through literature. Part II, 'Case Studies in Character', demonstrates how this approach can be applied to the study of four literarure characters:

Sydney Carton from Charles Dickens' *Tale of Two Cities*
Jay Gatsby from F. Scott Fitzgerald's *Great Gatsby*
Elizabeth Bennet from Jane Austen's *Pride and Prejudice*
Janie Crawford from Zora Neale Hurston's *Their Eyes Were Watching God*

The questions, ideas, and approaches used in these case studies can be applied as well to protagonists from other narratives works in the curriculum.

In a nutshell, this approach to teaching literature respects the integrity of the story, embraces the complexity of each character's moral growth and responds to the developmental readiness of young adult readers.

Karen E. Bohlin is head of school at Montrose School in Natick, MA, one of the few schools in the USA to earn the distinction of National School of Character in 1999. She is also a senior scholar at the Center for the Advancement of Ethics and Character and · ̵ ̵ t Boston University.

Teaching Character Education through Literature

Awakening the moral imagination
in secondary classrooms

Karen E. Bohlin

RoutledgeFalmer
Taylor & Francis Group

LONDON AND NEW YORK

Simultaneously published in the USA and Canada
by RoutledgeFalmer
270 Madison Ave, New York, NY 10016

First published 2005 by RoutledgeFalmer
2 Park Square, Milton Park, Abingdon, Oxon OX14 4RN

RoutledgeFalmer is an imprint of the Taylor & Francis Group

© 2005 Karen E. Bohlin

Typeset in Sabon and Gill by
BC Typesetting Ltd, Bristol
Printed and bound in Great Britain by
TJ International Ltd, Padstow, Cornwall

British Library Cataloguing in Publication Data
A catalogue record for this book is available from the British Library

Library of Congress Cataloging in Publication Data
A catalog record for this book has been requested

ISBN 0–415–32202–2 (pbk)
ISBN 0–415–32201–4 (hbk)

Contents

Acknowledgments

This book is the fruit of several years of teaching and research, ongoing collaboration with English teachers, and sustained dialogue with colleagues in education, literature, and philosophy from Boston University and universities around the world. The students, colleagues, and mentors who have made an imprint on this book are too numerous to mention here. These pages have been written with them in mind as well as all the future English teachers they may know.

I am grateful to Kevin Ryan, who recognized the importance of this book to educators and urged me to pursue this project several years ago. The spirited intellectual support of Steven S. Tigner, Linda Wells, and Brian Jorgensen helped me to shape an earlier incarnation of this work and bring it to the next level. I owe a special thanks to James Arthur from Canterbury Christ Church University College who offered sage insights on character education in England and feedback on early chapters. I am grateful to Jon Davison from the University of North London for his important recommendations on how this book could promote "classrooms as a discursive village" as he puts it in his very fine book, *Issues in English Teaching*, and for his kind Foreword. Wayne Booth's scholarship, particularly *The Company We Keep: An Ethics of Fiction*, has served as one of the original inspirations for this book, and I am indebted to him for his generous support, early criticisms, and excellent Foreword. William Kilpatrick's work on narrative has also been helpful to me. I am grateful for his careful reading of the draft manuscript and excellent suggestions. Thomas Lickona deserves special thanks for his early endorsement of this project and his commitment to pursuing excellence in character education at the secondary level. His forthcoming research report written with Matthew Davidson (Templeton Press: 2004) *Smart and Good: Developing Performance Character and Moral Character in America's High Schools* addresses the wider range of approaches and best practices in character education in high school.

I would also like to thank a number of colleagues who provided incisive feedback or comment on early chapters. Megan Black Uy, Allison Dalton, and Alison Reichert from the Center for the Advancement of Ethics and

Character deserve special mention. I would also like to acknowledge Kelly O'Leary, Joan and Terrance Earls, Bernice Lerner, Samuel Driver, Arthur J. Schwartz, Cathleen Stutz, Moira Walsh, Emily Marcucci, and Marie Oates. I am grateful to Molly Marsh, my research assistant at the outset of this project, for her meticulous work and commitment. Theresa Madison and Pat O'Donovan brought their combined forty plus years of English teaching experience, dedicated support, and wonderful sense of humor to their careful review and commentary on the manuscript and its usefulness to teachers. Their incisive editorial feedback enabled me to bring this project across the finish line. I am also indebted to Melissa Moschella for her unflagging assistance and help on multiple fronts. To Virginia Roberts Holt and Mary Anne Presberg I owe special thanks for their gift from the Full Circle Family Foundation enabling me to secure the teaching release time I needed to complete the lion's share of writing. I am also thankful to Anna Clarkson from RoutledgeFalmer in London whose enthusiasm and support of this project has made this book possible. Finally, I would like to thank my family who have been enormously gracious and flexible while I have been immersed in this project. Their love and support have most certainly helped to school my desire.

American Foreword

The past two decades have exhibited an impressive revival of ethical criticism of fiction. Through much of the last century most critics either ignored or condemned ethical questions, as if they were no better than crude intrusions on the "aesthetic" or "beautiful." Only recently have more and more critics acknowledged that authors and readers cannot—indeed must not—avoid engaging in ethical discourse, as an essential part of their joining in any serious narrative encounter.

Karen Bohlin's case studies in her book, *Teaching Character Education through Literature: Awakening the moral imagination in secondary classrooms*, constitute a significant contribution to that revival, as she explores the importance of ethical questions in the teaching of any major novel. So far as I know, hers is the first book in which a small number of major works are ethically addressed *in depth*, teaching students the intricacies entailed in any effort to "become more adept at moral reflection." By selecting key passages and episodes, many of them potentially confusing to careless readers, she offers a way to engage students in lively, thoughtful discussion about the meaning of their encounters with characters like Elizabeth Bennet, Jay Gatsby, Janie Crawford, and Sydney Carton.

Reading her manuscript I found myself regretting, again and again, that in my book on the subject I gave so little attention to the *pedagogical* questions that Bohlin embraces. Concentrating on theoretical matters, I gave far too little help of the kind this book provides.

As I think now about how I would address students younger than those I have taught in universities and colleges, I suddenly remember an experience when my son was in fourth grade. His class had been assigned Twain's *Tom Sawyer*, and when his teacher learned that I was working on a book about fiction, she asked me if I would conduct one class with them. When I asked my son what I should really talk about, he said, "Well, Dad, just ask 'em the question you are always asking me about my reading: How do you tell the good guys from the bad guys?"

So that's what I did (I hope I expanded the question to "good guys *and gals*") and it turned out that not only did it lead to lively discussion: it heightened my excitement about my project and contributed some points to my book. Those youngsters were already implicitly dealing with ethical questions, whenever they became "hooked" by a tale: "Why was I hooked?" "Should I have allowed myself to be hooked?" "Should I really care about the fate of X, when actually I care more about Y?" And so on.

Thus it seems to me that Bohlin's engagement with her four key novels will be relevant to teachers at every level—even those teaching students too young to read the four key works she deals with. When they read their first gripping story on their own (in my memory it was *The Wizard of Oz*) they are engaging with it *ethically*, either as the author intended or in blind opposition to the intentions. One of my sharpest encounters of widespread misreading was with freshmen, just after Salinger's *Catcher in the Rye* came out. I found that a majority of the students became so sympathetic to Holden Caulfield's desires that they simply ignored Salinger's many clues about Caulfield's faults and errors—the many ways in which Holden fails to exercise what Bohlin calls "the schooling of desire." Instead of joining Salinger in his deeply sympathetic but critical exploration of Caulfield's character, they simply sided with him against the whole world. Some of them read so carelessly that I wondered whether, if I taught them *The Great Gatsby*, they would find themselves simply siding with Gatsby all the way, ignoring Fitzgerald's (and his narrator, Carraway's) innumerable clues about Gatsby's failure to "school" his desires. It was clear that they had not been taught to ask, "Is the point of view of this character, as implied by the author who has created him, really reliable, or must I do some moral reflection about it?" My praise for this book might be summarized as: "I wish my students and their high school teachers, back in the 1950s, had encountered Bohlin's book before I met them as freshmen."

Finally, I would like to stress a point that Bohlin keeps mainly implicit throughout: the teaching of *teachers* that this book can achieve. If readers take it as not only a guide to pedagogy but an invitation to all of us to become, as she puts it, "more adept at moral reflection," the whole domain of literacy criticism will be enriched.

Wayne C. Booth
University of Chicago

British Foreword

The Character Education movement began gaining momentum in the early 1990s in the United States, but this development was not matched here during the decade. The Labour Government's social cohesion agenda has driven much of the policy that has underpinned educational developments in the past five years. The Crick Report (1998) and *Preparing Young People for Adult Life* (DfEE 1999) and the revised National Curriculum, premised upon a statement of values are clear exemplifications of educational imperatives.

It is unsurprising, therefore, that there is now a growing interest in Character Education in England following the development of National Curriculum Citizenship and the publication of the recent White Paper on education. Increasingly teachers and educational policy makers have been taking an interest in aspects of character development, social literacy and emotional intelligence. While recent years have seen much published on Citizenship Education, with the notable exception of James Arthur's book, *Education With Character* (RoutledgeFalmer 2002), there has been little published to support teachers in the area of Character Education.

Although some secondary schools have adopted a cross-curricular approach to Citizenship, for the most part Citizenship Education tends to be located within existing subject areas in secondary schools, predominantly, but not exclusively in the English/Humanities cluster. Therefore, the publication of *Teaching Character Education through Literature: Awakening the moral imagination in secondary classrooms* simultaneously in the United States and the United Kingdom is timely.

In the first section, *Narrative and Moral Agency*, Karen Bohlin describes her work with students and contextualises it within the wider social framework of the United States, particularly in relation to the power and perceived effects of the Media. Media Education within the English curriculum is, of course, well developed UK schools and some of the concerns discussed by Dr Bohlin might appear 'protectionist' to English readers. However, this should not detract from the book as it serves to exemplify the 'moral panic' or 'litany of alarm' that has been part of the driving force for the renewed interest in character education and citizenship education of which the author is justly critical. Hart and Hicks' *Teaching Media in the English Curriculum* (Trentham Books 2002) and Moon's *Literary Terms: A practical Glossary* (English and Media Centre 1992) have helped to support and develop the practice of UK teachers in relation to media education.

Narrative and Moral Agency focuses on the nature of desire and moral choice and considers the ways teachers can help students to practice *ethical reflection* as they study a character's growth and development. Karen Bohlin offers an approach for those teachers who wish to explore texts in a way that moves beyond what has become traditional literary criticism and an exploration of a character's development, to developing an understanding of the power of literature in the character development of adolescent readers.

Teachers of English will find the chapters on *Literature and the Moral Imagination* and *Awakening Moral Reflection* of real value. In the second part of the book *Case Studies in Character* we are provided with case studies of the moral choices made by four protagonists in four novels, three of which are in common use in the English classroom. Overall the book is thought provoking and stimulating without being prescriptive or hectoring. As the author says:

"It does not provide a set of moral lessons to help your students become better people. Nor is it a comprehensive overview of all the topics and questions that could be explored within each of these four novels. My purpose has been simply to show how a focused approach to ethical inquiry in the literature classroom can awaken and educate students' moral imaginations."

Through the presentation of texts and case studies for ethical reflection, *Teaching Character Education through Literature: Awakening the moral imagination in secondary classrooms* helps us to answer the question of how we engage young people in their own character development.

In *To Kill a Mockingbird*, Harper Lee's Scout reminds us that to really get to understand someone we must step inside their shoes and walk around a little. The strength of this book is that it not only suggests ways in which to understand literary characters better, but also it provides a way in which our pupils might come to know themselves better. For that matter, it might also enable us, as teachers, to know ourselves a little better, too.

Professor Jon Davison
London Metropolitan University

Introduction

CONTEMPORARY CONTEXT OF CHARACTER EDUCATION

> Character has gone out of fashion; and just as surely, it will come back in fashion again. Meanwhile, a vast experience has been accumulated on the now complex art of building character—private and public. It's no longer a simple matter of home and church and school. It is sociological, psychological, and both collective and individual. Dr. Hartshorne here tells what has been done, what is being done, and can be done to build character.
>
> From the cover of Hugh Hartshorne's 1932 book, *Character in Human Relations*[1]

Character education is once again a hot topic, and the approaches advocated by different academics, educators, politicians, and policymakers are as plentiful and diverse as they are controversial.[2] Anyone considering reading this book will most probably wonder—and justifiably so—just what I propose to add to this well-worn dialogue, and what particular philosophical bent I bring to the table. Therefore, I have taken a few pages at the outset to outline the most prominent schools of thought on the subject, placing my own work in context and explaining why I believe the philosophical approach that underlies this book is the one most appropriate to the task of educating for character in secondary schools and more specifically through the teaching of literature.[3]

In the United States the character education movement began gaining momentum in the early 1990s. Five White House Congressional Congresses on Character, hundreds of thousands of federal grant monies awarded to states and school districts around the country, and five years of a National Schools of Character Awards Program are just some of the tangible landmarks in this nationwide effort.[4] In the UK, more recent government initiatives have set a new "education with character" agenda. James Arthur's (2002) book, *Education With Character*, offers both an interdisciplinary perspective and a compelling case for character education in the UK. There is enormous overlap in terms of the aims and objectives of character education in both the UK and the United States. What the two nations have in common is a shared sense of urgency, a concern to respond swiftly to the growing "litany of alarm," as James Arthur puts it:

> increased violence, evidenced by brutal hazings and school shootings, chronic depression and growing incidences of suicide, high rates of alcohol and drug abuse, as well as bullying and sexual harassment at school. These patterns of behavior have raised a groundswell of concern among parents and educators in school communities around the world.[5]

Unfortunately, many character education initiatives do not engage the desires and aspirations of young people or show them the value of the effort required to attain good character or account for the complexity of moral growth. Lacking a clear moral vision or purpose, these efforts can sometimes give rise to a character education that focuses too narrowly on stamping out problem behaviors or preparing an honest and efficient future workforce to secure a more robust economy. The reality is that many efforts to educate for character at the secondary level—heralding simplistic slogans such as "Honesty is the best policy" or "Practice random acts of kindness"—are often superficial. Others are shortsighted, reducing education in character to "fixing" young people or simply teaching them how to "get along" with others. These approaches miss the mark and fail to inspire real moral improvement in young people.

Miss-the-mark character education

Most character education curricula and programs stem from one of four distinct theoretical perspectives.[6] The first stems from the tradition of Dewey's (1944) progressivism and/or Kohlberg's (1985) moral cognitive development and has among its aims: problem-solving, democratic participation, improved moral reasoning, community building, and an ethic of caring. These approaches are articulated in more practical terms in the work of Noddings (1992 and 2002), DeVries (1998), and Schapps (1998). Second, we find those arising from the school of Raths, Harmin and Simon's (1978) *Values Clarification: valuing, social consciousness, tolerance, and self-esteem.* Values Clarification seeks to empower students in identifying and defining their own personal values regardless of their moral content.[7] The third perspective with its focus on skills-building in a range of areas from social savvy and conflict resolution, to safe sexual behavior, and drug and alcohol prevention arises from the social and emotional learning movement.[8] Fourth, we find those approaches that emphasize the tradition of virtue ethics and focus on the development of sound intellectual and moral habits (Lickona 1991; Hoff-Sommers 1984 and 1992; Wynne and Ryan 1996; Ryan and Bohlin 1999; Arthur 2003).

While all of these approaches seek to promote moral development, several miss the mark. The first three approaches, while offering many valuable insights, are inadequate to the task of teaching adolescents how to identify what a flourishing life looks like and why it is desirable. They fall short because they provide no compelling motivation for leading a good life. Without an understanding of what it may mean for a person to live in an honorable way, the moral reasoning power that one develops lacks orientation. Without an understanding of what is morally good and worthwhile, clarifying one's values is an empty exercise. Moreover, while useful, social and conflict-resolution skills learned outside a moral context can lead to merely trained behaviors that evoke neither a moral commitment nor the promise of leading a good life. Without anchoring principles about the meaning of human life and happiness, without compelling answers to the questions, "Why be good, anyway?", "Character for what?" and "Character for whom?" many of these approaches run the risk of becoming reductionistic—processes empty of content (Hunter 2000). In their effort to build a moral compass in young people they neglect to offer clear directional poles.

Secondary students in particular need an approach to character education that helps them to develop a lasting moral compass. James Garrison offers a sage assessment in his *Dewey and Eros: Wisdom and Desire in the Art of Teaching*. He argues that contemporary moral education "is restricted to precepts and rules, while values education, if it has an explicit place in school at all, probably just teaches students how to calculate utilities" (1997: 2). These approaches tend to focus on the "Right"—the right thing to do and the nature of moral obligation and duty, and tend to cast into relative shade questions about the "Good"—questions about how we internalize virtuous dispositions and grow in moral maturity (Ross 1930).[9] Garrison considers this focus on the "Right" to be inadequate, and asserts that character education needs to go further in its aims:

> A good education brings out the best in us. It holistically unifies our character in judgment, compassion, and practice. It *disciplines our desires* to serve the greatest good, that is, those persons, things, and ideals that are of most value. (1997: 2, emphasis added)

These goals are arguably best fulfilled in the fourth approach that connects moral action to human excellence and leading a good life. A focus on virtue, which we will examine in more detail later, provides the most coherent framework within which to understand the schooling of desire and how a person comes to *be* virtuous, rather than simply to *act* virtuously on occasion.

Many schools and teachers are wary of character education, and with reason, as they have seen it dressed up as a "virtue of the week" program, or incentives and bought with rewards such as free limousine rides for students who agree to abstain from drugs and alcohol at the school dance (Kohn 1997 and Bohlin 2001). Students are quick to size up the superficiality of these gimmicks and learn to play the game. When thoughtful teachers see their schools engaging in such initiatives they often retreat in frustration, hoping to avoid yet one more new fad or time-waster (especially if it's made mandatory). Others protest vociferously: "This is not my job—it's the parents', the faith community's, or someone else's job! My responsibility is to teach literature, language, and writing, not to offer 'carrots' for good behavior or to waste precious class time discussing students' values." While these concerns are legitimate on some level, secondary teachers also need to avoid the pitfall of assuming a non-interference policy.

Non-interference policy

Our temptation as educators of adolescents in an increasingly pluralistic society is to remain hands-off and assume a non-interference policy when it comes to the topic of moral choices and commitments. We are sometimes inclined to leave older students free to discover for themselves what is best and right and to avoid "indoctrinating" young people with *certain* moral values. Indoctrination is precisely what many educators fear falling into. Indoctrination is to educators today what Voldemort's name is to the characters in *Harry Potter*—the word we are most afraid to utter. Indoctrination is a fear we need to confront head-on in moral education. When educators act in fear of indoctrination, they tend to adopt the hands-off approach, but this, too, misses the mark.

In response to a recommendation that schools stay focused on academic priorities and leave moral questions to the private realm, F. Washington Jarvis, headmaster of the Roxbury Latin School in Boston, Massachusetts, writes of the danger of our being too careful or too politic in conveying a moral vision to students when the pushers of pornography, gangsta rap, and self-destructive rites of passage zealously proselytize them on a much larger, much more pervasive scale. They are unrelenting in their effort to pump their messages into the mainstream via internet, billboards, and television. Jarvis cites a school head as saying the following at a meeting for school leaders:

> I think we should stick to preparing kids for college by giving them the knowledge and skills they need to get into college. In this pluralistic age we have to be careful not to offend anyone. We should avoid these big existential questions or we'll get all tangled up in religious and poli-

tical and sociological controversies. We should be careful not to inflict our opinions on students.

Jarvis counters with the following:

> The makers of videos and porn films, the editors of teenage magazines, and the rock or rap group idols are not worried about offending anyone in our pluralistic society. They're not fretful about "inflicting their opinions" on young people. . . . Every day television and videos assure them that the answer to their deepest needs comes from sexual hedonism, from escape into drugs, or from aggressive self-assertion in violence, sexual and otherwise.
>
> Meanwhile, principals and teachers timidly stand aside, sounding either an uncertain trumpet or no trumpet at all, as young people fill the spiritual vacuum in their lives by turning to those who do offer them something. Are we then to be silent about sharing our views about the meaning of life and about the behavior which flows from those views, for fear of "inflicting our opinion"? Is it wrong for us, in this free market of ideas, to tell young people that we believe life does have meaning and purpose? Is it a crime for us to try to influence or persuade them that love is better than violence, gentleness better than force, that it is better to love someone wholly than to use his or her body selfishly? In a society in which rock stars and professional athletes purvey their existential and ethical views, shall educators keep silence?
>
> We need, as never before, teachers willing to help young people ask the questions they are yearning to articulate, teachers eager—even, dare we say it, thrilled—to help students search for light on these questions in literature, history, science, mathematics, and all realms of human aspiration. It is my experience that, even as young people may seem to reject the existential and ethical "answers" we try to offer them, they nevertheless do hear us, they nevertheless long to know what we think. The influence of institutional religion has declined precipitously; at the same time schools have retreated from dealing with students' deepest existential questions. The result is a dangerous spiritual vacuum.
>
> (1993: 65–66)

Whether we believe that character education is simply not our job or whether we believe it is a dangerous form of indoctrination, the "non-interference" policy leaves students without a road map, vulnerable to any number of competing amoral ideas about what will make them happy. Samuel Taylor Coleridge illustrates this well in a record of his conversation with John Thelwall on July 27, 1830:

Thelwall thought it very unfair to influence a child's mind by inculcating any opinions before it should have come to years of discretion, and be able to choose for itself. I showed him my garden, and told him it was my botanical garden. "How so?" said he, "it is covered with weeds." — "Oh," I replied, "that is only because it has not yet come to its age of discretion and choice. The weeds, you see, have taken the liberty to grow, and I thought it unfair of me to prejudice the soil toward the roses and strawberries."[10]

While ostensibly giving students autonomy and the freedom of self-determination, the non-interference policy is inherently flawed, failing to recognize that weeds can crowd out healthy moral growth. It overlooks the danger of freedom without limits or moral standards, and it leaves students alone to figure out some of life's most difficult questions on their own.

Using fictional life narratives

The chief concern of this book is to assist English teachers in helping their students[11] draw instructive insights from fictional life narratives about the *schooling of desire*—what happens in that internal world of moral motivation and aspiration that gives rise to a character's desires and choices. It is an attempt to provide a set of lenses and questions to help illuminate the moral meaning of a text, to penetrate the surface of appearances and to help the adolescent reader look at the schooling of desire in a fictional character's life. The aim is to help students become more adept at ethical reflection. My interest is not simply the literature itself, which Kafka so generously endows with the power to melt "the frozen sea within us."[12] My questions are designed, rather, to help teachers of literature generate the metaphorical heat to help that melting process along.

The subjects of this book are four characters from novels widely taught in the secondary English curriculum in both the UK and the United States[13] — three from traditional classics and one from an emerging modern classic: Sydney Carton from Charles Dickens' *Tale of Two Cities*, Jay Gatsby from F. Scott Fitzgerald's *The Great Gatsby*, Elizabeth Bennet from Jane Austen's *Pride and Prejudice*, and Janie Crawford from Zora Neale Hurston's *Their Eyes Were Watching God*. These novels allow readers access to the moral desires of four fictionalized characters. They invite us to examine what motivates each character and why. Such questions are worth pursuing, especially with adolescents who are in the midst of sorting out their own moral identity and aspirations.

This book cannot begin to exhaust the moral insights into human experience yielded by each of these works as whole. Their literary richness and broad appeal make them practical candidates for this book rather than exclusive texts. I selected these novels for their literary eminence, as well as for their international translation and recognition. They represent a range of literary styles, periods in history, and dramatically different protagonists. Moreover, the protagonists' struggles illustrate questions of desire and the narratives account for the relevant context of their lives and motivations. Finally, each novel has a clear narrative line; they are not stream of consciousness, surrealistic, or absurdist literature. Some limitations also need to be taken into consideration. First, drawing from literary texts naturally entails some degree of interpretation. Every reader brings something to the text. My interpretative lens may be different from that of others. The data from these novels are used to help illustrate morally pivotal points and the factors influencing the schooling of desire, not to offer a particular strand of literary criticism.

Treatments of characters in literature vary enormously, and the character case studies in Part II of this book are not meant to provide a traditional character sketch or a conventional analysis of whether the character is round or flat, static or dynamic. These case studies examine characters as moral agents in distinct contexts navigating their own life journeys. Each fictional character's moral development is disclosed by the exercise of his or her free agency—intentional choices and commitments. The questions raised in each of the case study chapters challenge students to identify and examine the factors that inform and influence moral agency. Focusing on moral agency is particularly compelling, as individuals are agents of their own character development, not merely victims of circumstance or products of their environment.

In analyzing these four protagonists' moral journeys, I focus sharply on morally pivotal points and challenge points—experiences that disclose for us the characters' immediate or refined vision of an aspirational ideal or goal.[14] Morally pivotal points are dramatic markers that help to illustrate the characters' movement in a new or slightly refined direction. The characters' thoughts, decisions, dialogues, and actions form the basis of the relevant data used to illustrate these pivotal points.

Reading even narrative literature can become a chore or, at best, a minimum requirement for some students. They skim the surface of a text looking to identify what they think will be asked for on a test or a few quotable passages to back up a thesis statement they care little about. Others dutifully try to fit their reading of a narrative into the literary analysis of symbol, irony, or mood. Few young readers of literature actually take the time to ponder what happens and why. As a consequence, many of these readers miss the opportunity to see what is shaping the moral development of the characters they read about. They need help probing for meaning. And teachers have little direction as to how to make this happen, how to expose a text in such a way as to illuminate the moral journey of a soul and the factors that influence its progress or regression.

THE STRUCTURE OF THIS BOOK

Teaching character education through literature: awakening the moral imagination in secondary classrooms aims to provide theoretical and practical insight into the ways narrative literature can reveal moral growth and decline. The book is divided into two parts. Part I: Narrative and moral agency (Chapters 1 through 3) provides the rationale for this approach to literature. Chapter 1: The schooling of desire, introduces the need to help students evaluate the host of narrative images that bombard them daily. It redefines moral education as the schooling of desire and argues that narrative literature offers one of the most compelling vehicles to understand the nature of moral development. Chapter 2: Literature and the moral imagination explores the needs and dispositions of young adult readers and introduces the functions of the moral imagination. Chapter 3: Fostering ethical reflection in our classrooms provides a method for undertaking this investigation of the way in which fictional characters come to acquire or fail to acquire strong moral character and sound judgment.

Part II: Case studies in character (Chapters 4 through 7) offers a set of four annotated narrative portraits that can be used to prepare units, lessons, and assignments for each of these novels. Teachers may use all or part of each case study depending on the time they have to dedicate to the study of each novel. They are not placed in any particular sequence, although Gatsby is deliberately put at the end because his character reveals moral regression or the negative schooling of desire. The case studies as a whole demonstrate how diverse fictional characters come to discover their goals and aspirations and direct their lives in pursuit of them. Chapter 8: Final considerations presents examples from all four novels of common factors in the schooling of desire and the outcomes or new dispositions acquired as a result of this schooling. In this chapter teachers will find ideas for comparing and contrasting the novels.

The Appendices contain useful materials to support classroom instruction. Appendix A includes a set of Definitions and distinctions clarifying relevant terms used throughout the book. Appendix B features a number of questions to extend study and discussion across the novels. Appendix C comprises some reproducible charts to support students' character analyses, and Appendix D provides an annotated hotlist of web resources to assist teachers with class preparation and assignments.

Teachers can read this book from cover to cover or use the various case studies as relevant to the curriculum they teach. They may read Chapters 1, 2, 3 and 8 and apply the principles and questions to other novels and/or non-fiction narratives.

The teaching of literature is a rich and vast field with numerous points of entry. My hope is that this book serves as one of those points of entry. It is not a set of prescriptive daily lesson plans for teaching each novel. It does not provide a set of moral lessons to help your students become better people. Nor is it a comprehensive overview of all the topics and questions that could be explored within each of these four novels. My purpose has been simply to show how a focused approach to ethical inquiry in the literature classroom can awaken and educate students' moral imaginations.

This book offers guidance to teachers and students of literature at the secondary and post-secondary level. It provides a method—a set of lenses and questions—that respects the integrity of a story, embraces the complexity of a character's moral growth, and responds to the developmental readiness of the adolescent reader. The primary aim is to draw instructive insights from fictional life narratives, insights that prompt students to consider and evaluate an individual's motivations, aspirations, and choices. Fictional characters' struggles are of interest to students as they set a course for their own life journey, make their own choices, and in doing so, give consideration to the kind of person they would like to become. This book does not promise that an ethical inquiry into literature will transform the character of the reader. It does, however, aim to predispose the reader to moral attentiveness, ethical reflection, and refined judgment. It will demonstrate how teachers can provide an encounter with literature that enables students to be more responsive to ethical themes and questions. By presenting texts and case studies for ethical reflection, this book will also help English teachers to answer the question of how we engage young people in their own character development.

My hope is that *Teaching character education through literature: awakening the moral imagination in secondary classrooms* will help teachers to recast for their students the way we think about educating for character. Instead of providing a list of precepts or a set of definitions, instead of presenting students with a benefits–consequences analysis, or invoking a sense of moral duty, I am inviting students and teachers alike to examine what we can learn from the moral development of characters in literature. I hope this book will serve a wide range of readers beyond English teachers, from avid readers of the novels to those interested in character education.

Part I

Narrative and moral agency

Chapter 1

The schooling of desire

Several years ago I led a group of secondary students from Boston on a literary and theater tour of London. Shortly before leaving, one of my tenth graders confided her anticipated fear of overexposure to cultural sites and angst that we might not be able to accommodate her wide range of shopping interests. Sarah[1] was a capable student, but completely disengaged from academics; she slid by, meeting the minimum requirements. She spoke articulately about *All My Children* and *As the World Turns*, two of her favorite afternoon soap operas, and faithfully recorded television programs she was unable to watch during the day, sacrificing sleep to watch taped episodes late into the night. Nevertheless, Sarah had fulfilled her requisite preparation for the trip. She attended weekly after-school seminars (not without complaints), raised funds, and finally led a presentation on the Tower of London. She had earned her right to go. Fair is fair.

Half way into our tour, Sarah had an epiphany of sorts on our late night visit to the Tower of London. Just inside the Traitor's Gate, we gathered to witness the centuries-old Ceremony of the Keys. As the fog and cold enveloped our intimate party, the guards marched into sight to begin their nightly ritual. A startling bugle blast and shout of command broke the silence. After a formal exchange of keys and a cry of "All's well," the ceremony drew to a close. The guards disappeared through the arch, and I escorted our still-silent group to the Underground.

Upon returning to school in Boston, Sarah elected to spearhead the school's first literary magazine and sought my support. She was not a literary scholar herself, but she came to appreciate the poets and authors we had been studying after walking in their footsteps, and she wanted to encourage creative writing among her peers. Her experience in London—from the British Museum to the Tower of London—had brought history to life for Sarah in ways that far exceeded her expectations. Soap operas had now lost their appeal. In her final year of high school, she served as editor-in-chief of the yearbook, dedicated herself to the local community through volunteer work with the elderly, and secured a part-time job to finance an educational trip to Italy.

Sarah's experience at the Tower of London signaled a pivotal point, a change of focus that she has sustained into her adult life. But her transformation did not take place overnight. Her new interests required time, attention, training, and the relinquishing of former loves and habits. Entrenched in a lifestyle that afforded her neither the time nor the inclination to take her school work more seriously, she had not questioned the value of her aspirations. It is difficult to know all of the factors—internal and external—that prepared Sarah for this change. The Ceremony of the Keys and the earlier presentation she had made on the Tower certainly prompted her to envision and articulate her new goals, but investing herself in more fulfilling activities ultimately sustained her commitment to them. Her resolve also signaled a pivotal point for me as a teacher. It renewed my confidence in the potential of rich educational experiences to re-orient our students' aspirations.

A similar change occurred in the life of a fourteen-year-old gang member from a large urban middle school. He was reading well below grade-level and his behavior stirred discontent within the school community. To improve their students' literacy skills, the school inaugurated a program that paired eighth graders with kindergarteners once a week and trained the older students to read and discuss children's literature with the younger students. After six months of regular visits to the local kindergarten, this young man acquired a whole new set of interests. His mother's observation offers the most compelling testimony to his transformation. When she came home from work every night, instead of finding her son ensconced on the couch in front of the television, she discovered him reading a story to his little sister.[2]

As teachers we are familiar with the power of pivotal moments in learning—when one student becomes enamored of Shakespeare or another begins writing original poetry for publication. These turning points excite new desires and sustain interest. Rarer, perhaps, are those opportunities to witness *morally* pivotal points in the lives of our students, those moments that lead them to pursue a more fruitful direction for their lives as a whole. These are moments when they not only see the value of using their talents more constructively, but also when they commit themselves to a noble purpose.[3] This book seeks to explore the nature of such shifts in focus. How are morally pivotal moments brought about? What are the factors that gradually prepare a person for such a change?

NARRATIVE IMAGES RUN AMOK

Like Sarah and the young teenage gang member, many of our students come to school having cut their teeth on a host of negative stimuli. According to the findings of the 1999 Kaiser Family Foundation, the average American child

a   spends more than 38 hours a week using some form of media outside of
    school;
b   has an increasingly "multimedia bedroom";
c   watches television without supervision.

But it is not television or the media itself that it is the sole source of negative stimuli in young people's lives. In fact, solid media literacy education,
such as that being carried out in the UK and different parts of the United
States, broadens students' literacy and provides them with the critical
perspective they need to evaluate the range of images that bombard them
daily.

The challenge we face as educators is mitigating the range of negative
narrative images and stimuli that feed the imaginations and aspirations of
young people. These images—from widely popularized books that idealize
the fast track to fame and fortune, from overly ambitious parents who
provoke fist fights with referees at soccer matches or from friends who
inebriate or prostitute themselves at school dances, from public figures
who cast integrity and honor aside and continue to enjoy a celebrated
life—offer compelling stories and models to young people. These narrative
images feed their imagination daily and help to shape their understanding
about what people choose and why as well as how they conduct themselves
in private and public life.

A friend of mine who teaches in a large urban high school describes some
of her students as so "plugged in" to their favorite music that they cannot
stop hearing the lyrics running through their minds while they are in class.
One of her students, in fact, was so consumed by gangsta rap that he eventually pleaded for help from his English teacher saying, "the words keep
playin' in my head and tellin' me I need to hurt someone. I can't make
'em stop."[4]

We have much to learn from the power of the various stimuli—auditory,
visual, and interpersonal—that feed our students' imaginations. Experts in
psychology, those in the marketing industry, for example, know how to
grab our attention and motivate us to imitate styles and trends in language,
and in fashion. Most importantly, they know how to make us buy. What can
they teach us about motivation? Plato's Socrates in *The Republic* offers a
pioneering analysis of human motivation, one that serves as a foundation
for modern psychology and sheds light on the power of effective marketing.
For example, Socrates describes three seats of human motivation in the
human psyche or soul: reason, spirit, and appetite.[5] Reason, he explains,
desires to understand, question, and figure things out. From reason springs
our natural curiosity for learning and discovery. We see the nascent powers
of reason at work when toddlers start to ask such questions as: Why does
it get dark at night? Why do dogs bark and cats meow? The spirited part
of the soul is the seat of our emotions and ambition; it desires love and

achievement. Our desires to play and win, to become popular, to amass a fortune, all stem from the spirited part of our soul. The spirited part craves friendship and belonging, both of which are crucial in adolescence. The third seat of motivation, our appetite, seeks satisfaction; it is the origin of our hunger, thirst, and desire for sex. Like a fussy infant, the appetite clamors to be fed. Our students are barraged daily with images—both positive and negative—that aggressively appeal to their appetites and attempt to shape their desires. How can we nurture the appetites, ambitions, and curiosity of young people well? How can we counterbalance a diet that includes too much negative stimuli?

How can we tap into these three seats of motivation with appeals that are equally attractive and engaging, with pleasures, ambitions, and reasons that inspire young people to lead lives of noble purpose. Plato argues that in a healthy soul, reason captains the team, directing and guiding the spirited part and appetites so that they are inclined to choose and embrace those desires that are best for a person. Upbringing and education help children to achieve a mature or harmonious soul, to make intelligent choices rather than choices based on whim or blind ambition. Without orientation and guidance, human desires can run amok, pursuing any stimuli that strike their fancy. When this happens our reason no longer calls the shots, it acquiesces to the demands of our blind ambitions and appetites. Simply put, this is what we call rationalization. When we rationalize something we want, our reason seconds rather than questions our desires. In other words, when we want something badly enough we can justify cheating, overspending on our parent's credit card, or even maligning someone else's good name. As evidenced by the host of scandals in the corporate and political world, as well as rising domestic violence and infidelity, many adults lead their lives by rationalizing rather than evaluating their ambitions and desires.

As they strive to form their own identity, teenagers take their cues from the various narratives surrounding them about what it means to be mature, happy, successful, and accomplished. They look at the behaviors that are celebrated and rewarded, but they also look beneath the surface. In my experience, and as Sarah's story gives testimony, most adolescents are searching for something worthwhile in which to invest themselves. In his authoritative research on identity formation, Augusto Blasi defines moral identity as "the psychological need to make one's actions consistent with one's ideals" (1993: 99).[6] As they mature, teenagers want to forge an identity of their own making, to become a particular kind of person. At the same time, it is a challenge for them to examine the range of possible ideals for their lives and determine which ones are most worth embracing.

Visual and auditory stimuli excite the senses and awaken our appetites. Literature by contrast engages the mind while entertaining the appetites and moving the spirited part of the soul.[7] I do not mean to suggest that students are mindless consumers of visual stimuli. In fact, I have seen some of the strongest indignation about gratuitous sex and violence in films come from young people, particularly those who care about the story upon which a particular film is based. David Denby, film critic and author of *Great Books*, attests to the importance of literature to help a person regain perspective and see what matters most in our image-saturated age. Prior to taking a literature course as an adult he says, "I didn't know what I knew. I had a lot of opinions but no foundation. I think this is common for people who live in the Media Age. You lose your internal compass. You're caught up in a miasma of imagery" (1996: F1).

How do we help young people stop and question what they find alluring, attractive, or desirable? How do we help them to evaluate whether or not their apparent ideals will really help them to be happier, wiser, better? How can we harness the desire they have to form their own identity and help them choose worthy ideals upon which to build their lives? Narrative literature can help. It can serve as a navigational tool, a compass to help young people evaluate more carefully the life trajectory of others. Moreover, it can provide a wider range of lasting images, narratives that allow students to linger thoughtfully and raise questions about the ethical dimensions of a character's choices and commitments. English teachers can help students to contrast various accounts of success and happiness across a wide range of medium from novels to films, to websites, to television programs. This book focuses primarily on the teaching of novels in the English classroom but it presupposes ongoing as well as lively discussion and debate about the various sources of narratives that inform our collective understanding of happiness, morality, and what it means to live well or poorly. This book aspires to help English teachers provide an encounter with novels that appeals more fully to their students' appetite, spirit, and reason and sustains their interest in the protagonists' desires and ambitions. By examining the motivations of characters who pursue paths of willful self-deception or corruption, for example, we can also help students gain as much insight from bad example as from good. In the same way that media literacy helps students to become critical consumers of the media, helping students become more adept at ethical reflection on literature helps them to become more discriminating in the face of all the other narrative images and pseudo-ideals that bombard them daily.

English teachers are well positioned to tap into the latent idealism of adolescents, to harness their moral energy, to activate their own internal compass and evaluate its role in the lives of characters in literature. By facilitating more fruitful encounters with fictional characters such as Atticus Finch, Jane Eyre, Anna Karenina, and Ivan Illych, for example, students can acquire more nuanced insights into the lives of individuals who are not without their warts, but who achieve harmony of soul and are ultimately attractive as human beings. Narrative literature also provides compelling images of individuals who are slaves to their own poor choices, self-serving goals, and obsessions. On the elementary or primary school level, J. K. Rowling brilliantly achieves this contrast among characters in her renowned *Harry Potter* series. Harry, Hermione, and Ron are far from perfect, but their aspirations stand in stark contrast to those of the malicious Malfoy and the self-indulgent and spoiled Dursley boy.

THE SCHOOLING OF DESIRE

> Without the aid of trained emotions the intellect is powerless against the animal organism. . . . As the king governs by his executive, so Reason in man must rule the mere appetites by means of the "spirited element." The head rules the belly through the chest—the seat, as Alanus tells us, of Magnanimity—Sentiment—these are the indispensable liaison officers between cerebral man and visceral man. . . .
>
> And all the time—such is the tragic-comedy of our situation—we continue to clamour for those very qualities we are rendering impossible. You can hardly open a periodical without coming across the statement that what our civilization needs is more "drive," or dynamism, or self sacrifice, or "creativity." In a sort of ghastly simplicity we remove the organ and demand the function. We make men without chests and expect of them virtue and enterprise. We laugh at honour and are shocked to find traitors in our midst. We castrate and bid the geldings to be fruitful.
>
> (C. S. Lewis, *The Abolition of Man* (1975: 36–37))

Lewis' chapter, "Men Without Chests," speaks to the importance of educating the spirited part of the soul; it also addresses one of the central purposes of this book. *Teaching Character Education through Literature: Awakening the moral imagination in secondary classrooms* is essentially about the study of desires and aspirations—primarily the desires and motivations of characters in literature. I am interested in exploring with English teachers what I call the *schooling of desire*. For me, the *schooling of desire* is about what happens somewhere between the heart and the will, every time characters make a choice, particularly choices that somehow define who they are and mark an important change of focus.

We study these characters in the contexts of novels. I have selected protagonists from novels as the focus of this book not because I think the novel is more important than poetry or short fiction, or a superior genre overall, but because novels are widely read by adolescents and are a staple of secondary English curricula. Moreover, good novelists are not only good storytellers, but also great psychological portrait painters, and their characters' lives give readers access to the private, highly-personalized world of moral motivation. They yield instructive insights about the *schooling of desire*, about what happens in that internal world of moral motivation and aspiration that gives rise to a character's moral choices.

Part I: Narrative and moral agency focuses on the nature of moral choice and desire and the ways teachers can help students practice ethical reflection as they study a character's growth and development. Part II: Case studies in character provides actual case studies of the moral choices made by four protagonists from three traditional classic novels and one modern classic: Sydney Carton from Charles Dickens' *A Tale of Two Cities*, Jay Gatsby from F. Scott Fitzgerald's *The Great Gatsby*, Elizabeth Bennet from Jane Austen's *Pride and Prejudice*, and Janie Crawford from Zora Neale Hurston's *Their Eyes Were Watching God*. These protagonists have been selected for a variety of reasons. First, they come from novels that are widely taught in secondary English curricula in both the United States and the UK; two of the books are written by pre-eminent British authors and two by American. Second, I chose to feature female protagonists crafted by female authors and male protagonists by male authors spanning four different periods in literature. Third, these characters illustrate a diversity of situations: affluence and poverty, comfort and hardship, socio-political unrest and relative stability.

To illustrate the schooling of desire, each case study in Chapters 4 through 7 focuses on the protagonists' initial goals and their progressive refinement. Each case highlights morally pivotal points in the protagonists' development, moments that signal a reconsideration or sharpening of their goals or aspirations. These aspirations are akin to the Greek notion of *telos*, an ultimate end, or moral vision that lends coherence to one's desires and commitments. A *telos* embraces an intended conception of happiness. The schooling of desire, then, begins with the Greeks' idea about human nature: that we seek happiness. Perhaps the long-standing appeal of Aristotle is that he offers a motivation for morality. Human beings, according to Aristotle, have an end or *telos* they *desire* to fulfill. Why cultivate the virtuous life? "To live well and fare well," to be happy, he contends. Living well and faring well is the substance of human flourishing, what he calls "*eudaimonia.*"[8] This is the *telos* we desire for its own sake and not for the sake of any other good such as honor, pleasure, or advantage. "It is for the sake of this that we do everything else," says Aristotle.[9]

An analysis of moral development in the protagonists of these four novels underscores the nature of desire: it is determined by what it aims at achieving, its desired goal or *telos*. The multitude of desires that motivate these characters' choices and actions exist at least loosely within the embrace of a higher order desire to flourish, or to lead a happy life. Three of the characters are able to exercise free and intelligent choice; they come to discover and choose to embrace a more worthy *telos*, whereas Gatsby makes choices based on blind *eros*. His *telos* is ill-conceived and ultimately not conducive to his flourishing. Each character's *telos* is fluid. That is, each is capable of revising or rejecting a *telos* and finally choosing a different or refined goal. Part II offers three narrative portraits of characters who, by the end of their journey, acquire greater virtue and the best possible state of their souls. Their soul-turning is complete and they are freer than they were at the beginning of the novels. The one negative case study offers an image of failed soul-turning; a character who denies reality and remains content with the shadows of his own fabricated world.

Focusing on the *schooling of desire* in relation to literature is an effort to draw a contrast with conventional accounts of moral education as something programmatic and imposed upon young people through behavior modification or "feel-good" discussions in the classroom. Neither extreme provides an adequate account of desire or moral motivation. Both suggest that character education is something we "do" to students rather than an enterprise that students (particularly secondary students) take on themselves as an important lifelong project. This book seeks to explore moral motivation—that is, how characters' moral agency is *schooled* by their circumstances, relationships, attitudes, choices, and commitments. Through an analysis of literary characters' gradual moral growth (or decline), I hope to uncover new insights about the power of desire in shaping an individual's moral vision or purpose. But first we must look at what we mean by the schooling of desire.

The schooling of desire, as we will see below, encapsulates the language of character education.

SOME POINTS ABOUT THE SCHOOLING OF DESIRE

Virtue

The schooling of desire is about the coordinated and integral education of the heart, mind, and will. C. S. Lewis, in his *Letters to Children*, describes correctly schooled desires as "loves, tastes, and habits," that enable a person to lead a good life.

> Don't the ordinary old rules about telling the truth and doing as you'd be done by tell one pretty well which kinds of fun one may have and which not? But provided the thing is in itself right, *the more one likes it* and the less one has to "try to be good," the better. A perfect man w[oul]d never act from a sense of duty; he'd always *want the right thing more* than the wrong one. Duty is only a substitute for love (of God and of other people), like a crutch, which is the substitute for a leg. Most of us need the crutch at times; but of course it's idiotic to use

the crutch when our own legs (*our own loves, tastes, habits*, etc.) can do the journey on their own! (1985: 100, emphasis added)

Lewis is not talking about the mere mechanics of doing the right thing out of training, fear of punishment, or a stoic sense of duty. Nor is he talking about feeling like leading a good life but never actually taking action. Instead he captures the heart of schooling desires: learning to "want the right thing" so that individuals can gracefully navigate "the journey [of life] on their own." In a word, these mature loves, tastes, and habits—desires well-schooled—make up what we call *virtue*.

One of the main outcomes of the schooling of desire is virtuous dispositions. Virtue is the internal disposition to see and choose well among competing claims or appeals. Virtue is deeper than intellectual knowledge, heartfelt desire, or social activism. It is a disposition of heart and mind that enables a person to wholeheartedly embrace and enjoy what is both right and good. We are all familiar with the stereotypical moral theorist who can glibly cite Kant, Confucius, or the Bible (chapter and verse), but is unable to console a forlorn child who is starved for affection or to run an errand for a neighborhood shut-in. We may also be acquainted with the bleeding heart moralist, who sees injustice and victimization at every turn, but is too paralyzed by disappointment to take constructive action. Then there are those individuals who dutifully fulfill their obligations, such as those students of ours who satisfy their required service hours at the hospital or food pantry, yet who fail to reflect on, care about, or commit themselves to genuine service outside of these "required hours."

Appendix A provides a set of definitions and distinctions that lend greater clarity to what we mean by virtue.

Being versus having: the best possible state of soul

The schooling of desire is also about learning to "want the right things." This is achieved by acquiring virtuous dispositions or strong moral character, what Socrates refers to as the "best possible state" of soul. For Plato's Socrates, living well means emphasizing the importance of *being* over *having*. As author and educator, James Stenson, often puts it when speaking to parents, "Character is what you have left over after you go broke." Thus, we see Socrates challenging the Athenians in Plato's *Apology* to think about what they really desire:

> Good Sir, you are an Athenian, a citizen of the greatest city with the greatest reputation for both wisdom and power; are you not ashamed of your eagerness to possess as much wealth, reputation and honors as possible, while you do not care for nor give thought to wisdom or truth, or the best possible state of your soul? (29e)

> For I go around doing nothing but persuading both young and old among you not to care for your body or your wealth in preference to or as strongly as for the best possible state of your soul. (30b)

Socrates' message to the Athenians has an uncanny timeliness. While I am not so sure we would hear the "gadfly" any better than the Athenians did, I can imagine Socrates strolling around midtown Manhattan or central London exhorting everyone from tourists to stockbrokers and street vendors to film producers to stop and think about what they hope to attain. He points to the dangers of unchecked ambition and the indiscriminate pursuit of money, making it clear that our internal health of soul is more important than honors or material gain.

Money, power, and reputation are not in themselves the problem; it is being dominated by a desire for them that keeps us from achieving the "best possible state of soul." In their best-selling book on the importance of teaching financial literacy, *Rich Dad, Poor Dad*, the authors' voice of practical wisdom, "Rich Dad," explains why people become enslaved to money:

> Instead of telling the truth about how they feel, they react to their feeling, fail to think. They feel the fear, they go to work, hoping that money will soothe the fear, but it doesn't. That old fear haunts them, and they go back to work hoping again that money will calm their fears, and again it doesn't. Money has them in the trap of working, earning money, hoping the fear will go away. But every day they get up, and that old fear wakes up with them. For millions of people, that old fear keeps them awake all night, causing a night of turmoil and worry. So they get up and go to work hoping that a paycheck will kill that fear gnawing at their soul. Money is running their lives and they refuse to tell the truth about that. (1998: 42–43)

To achieve the best possible state of soul, we need to recognize the truth about our desires. Plato offers a dramatic illustration of desire run amok in his "Myth of Er." He describes the tyranny of a soul that gives indiscriminate equality to its desires—that is, allowing appetites and passions free rein to pursue whatever they please. In the end, however, without the guidance of reason "the tyrannical soul will also be least likely to do what it wants and . . . [will be] full of disorder and regret" (*Republic* 577e). When we are led by blind ambition or passion, we retain the freedom to choose, but we lose our capacity to choose well. Our judgment is blurred. We deceive ourselves (wittingly or unwittingly) into believing that we have chosen well when we have simply rationalized a bad decision. In short, when our vision is clouded by misguided ideals, the capacity to invest ourselves in a worthy purpose is effectively thwarted.

Fictional characters' ability to recognize and choose what is best for their lives overall is largely dependent on the goals they desire and embrace. Like ordinary human beings, they are fallible and thus can be mistaken at times about what is good for them and fail to achieve the "best possible state of soul." Anna Karenina, a woman of extraordinary intelligence and grace, gradually becomes a shrew, full of self-loathing and regret, because of her fateful choices. Dorian Gray, a remarkably attractive young man who aspires to the enjoyment of eternal youth and beauty, becomes a monster as a result of his dominant passion.

Intelligent self-direction

Without the ability to evaluate and refine their *telos*, their conception of what it means to live excellently as human beings, these characters either become morally dwarfed, mindlessly drawn by whatever captures their fancy, or worse, morally degraded, deliberately pursuing ignoble paths.

As the case studies in this book will demonstrate, acquiring virtue and achieving the best possible state of soul go hand in hand with developing a greater sense of freedom. Whereas Anna Karenina and Dorian Gray gradually lose their freedom through their enslavement to less than worthy *tele*, literary characters whose desires are successfully schooled have an increased capacity for intelligent self-direction. In short, the successful schooling of desire pulls people out of the quagmire of blinding desires, rationalization, or willful self-deception. It inoculates them against becoming unreflective, passive consumers of misguided ideas about human happiness. The schooling of desire contributes to both their moral maturity and their freedom.

In his famous allegory of the cave, Plato offers a compelling image of how intelligent self-direction can be sustained or thwarted. The cave is essentially an allegory about how a soul's desires can be schooled to pursue a more refined *telos*: the truth. It is a story of liberation. The image that Socrates offers is of imprisoned persons chained deep within a cave, forced to face a wall upon which shadows cast from objects passing in front of a fire behind them serve as the only reality they know. To see the actual objects being carried by unknown passersby and projected by the firelight as shadows onto the wall, they need to be released from their chains, and prompted to arise and turn to face the light of the fire. To see further, to understand who these passersby are, where they come from, and what they carry, they must begin the arduous ascent from the cave and venture toward the light of the sun and to the unfamiliar real world outside. Because their eyes are not accustomed to the light, each turn and movement toward the light naturally causes pain. Moreover, the steep climb demands rigorous effort. It is more comfortable to turn away, to avoid the rigors of the ascent and the blinding light of the sun, and to stay comfortably immersed in the darkness of the cave facing the familiar shadows on the wall. Yet, as Plato's Socrates observes, to avoid the ascent is to live in ignorance of the truth, satisfied with only the shadowy images of reality.

Intelligent self-direction requires the soul's movement from the visible realm—what the prisoners can physically see and recognize immediately (the shadows)—to the intelligible realm (outside of the cave)—where they can come to understand reality as it is. Plato's emphasis on "the craft concerned with . . . this turning around, and with how the soul can be most easily and effectively be made to do it" suggests that learning requires more than an intellectual grasp of the truth. It requires the schooling of desire, a determined commitment to redirect the whole soul away from one *telos* and toward another—despite the obstacles. Socrates describes this soul-turning as central to education:

> It isn't the craft of putting sight into the soul. Education takes for granted that sight is there but that it isn't turned the right way or looking where it ought to look, and it tries to redirect it appropriately. (*Republic* VII, 518d)

Leaving students to their own devices is not only impractical, it can be unfair. To return to the anecdote with which I opened this chapter, if I had excluded Sarah from the trip to London because her interests and aspirations were not up to par, she might have taken much longer to find her way out of her own familiar cave. If she had not developed an interest and appreciation for literature and culture, she would not have sustained the sacrifices necessary to launch and develop a literary magazine. If she had not reflected on the way she had been using her time, talents, and energies prior to the London trip, her experiences there would have served as merely one more fleeting source of enjoyment. If Sarah did not have the courage to acknowledge her desire to change, she might never have received the support she needed to turn that aspiration into a reality.

FACTORS IN THE SCHOOLING OF DESIRE

Moral vision or purpose is brought about by four factors in the schooling of desire, which is in itself complex. In the real world it is nearly impossible to secure all the relevant "data" about a person's choices and motivations, or the factors that have influenced their lives. Characters in literature provide us with a window to the soul, through which we can examine the internal and external factors involved in becoming or failing to become the kind of person we admire or respect. Whether examining the moral growth of Brontë's Jane Eyre or Golding's Ralph and Jack in *The Lord of the Flies*, literature can help students to attend to the persons, experiences, and dispositions that contribute to each character's moral development.

English teachers are well poised to help adolescents reflect on moral maturity without descending to moralizing. They can focus their attention on the factors central to the schooling of desire of characters in the novels they read. The four common factors in the schooling of desire are

1   relationships;
2   learning from pain and acquiring new pleasures;
3   thoughtful reflection;
4   courage to face the truth (about reality, oneself, and others).

These four factors taken collectively account for the hard-to-define influences that incite and sustain the schooling of desire in a character. Separately, they may or may not be significant in a person's life, but together they prompt a character to see and respond to the refined *telos* disclosed at each morally pivotal point in his or her life. Desire is schooled not simply by a character's seeing his or her *telos* but by those factors that collectively help to awaken both a revised moral vision and a determined desire to pursue that vision. Taken together, these four factors serve as a catalyst for moral growth, leading characters to cultivate virtue and their "best possible state of soul." Their absence leads to the negative schooling of desire or moral decline. An analysis of morally pivotal points in the lives of characters in literature can bring moral discourse and insight in the literature classroom to a new level.

Challenging students to examine how these factors work to bring about moral growth or how their absence contributes to moral regression in the four protagonists' lives described in the case studies gives them vicarious practice in navigating these factors in their own lives. Learning from relationships, learning to respond well to pain and to take pleasure in new things, developing the capacity for reflection and the courage to face the truth—are all crucial to moral maturity, to acquiring a clearer vision of one's best possible *telos*. Using these factors as a lens to approach the study of these characters gives students the opportunity to "eavesdrop on a soul," as children's author Katherine Patterson observes so tellingly in her book, *A Sense of Wonder* (1995: 69).

The character case studies provide a set of journeys. Our road map is their experiences—the terrain they cross, the course they set, the paths they take, and, most importantly, the destinations they reach. Our goal is not to learn so much by imitation as by ethical reflection. Our goal is to learn from their mistakes as well as their successes, and to evaluate the merits and limitations of their desired destinations. Let us look at these four factors in more detail.

Relationships

People are shaped by other people. The lasting influences on our lives are not a set of precepts, laws, and formulas, but relationships with people—for better or worse. Relationships inspire attraction to or aversion from a particular *telos*. Family, friends, and acquaintances also challenge a person's *telos* by pointing out insufficiencies or inconsistencies in a character's ideals or actions.

The relationships most influential in the schooling of desire are what Aristotle calls friendships of virtue—relationships in which one seeks to love more than to be loved and to bring about the best in another (*Nicomachean Ethics* VIII).[10] For example, the respective friendships of Elizabeth, Janie, and Carton provide the occasion for an exchange of love and trust, confidence, dialogue, and inquiry into the worth of their pursuits in life. In all cases, except for Gatsby's, friendship is central to the protagonist's moral growth. Jay Gatsby's lack of genuine friendships is significant to his negative schooling.

Learning from pain and acquiring new pleasures

Whether we are striving to improve our tennis game or learning to play golf, we know that the pain of losing can often spur us on to practice harder. But more often than not, the satisfaction and enjoyment of the game itself keeps us playing. Pleasure and pain figure prominently in our life and learning, and they are equally significant to the schooling of desire. Plato's Socrates insists that we are obliged to bring children up "both to delight in and be pained by the things that we ought"[11] because a healthy attraction and aversion are essential to acquiring a proper moral orientation.

Like each obstacle in the ascent from the cave, each morally pivotal point in the protagonists' journey evinces some pain, but it also brings new pleasures—acquiring a taste for something they had not previously known. For example, Carton takes enjoyment in his frequent visits to the Manette family. Janie delights in the affection she initially receives from her second husband, but eventually comes to endure enormous pain and realizes that greater pleasures of love remain yet to be discovered. After her initial disappointment with her friend's decision, Elizabeth enjoys observing Charlotte in her new marriage and collecting as much data as she can on her marital happiness.

In some respects pain serves as a catalyst for reflection, an indication that something is wrong, similar to the way that physical pain alerts us to an illness. In other respects, pain evokes the virtue of fortitude and moves the protagonist to pursue his or her *telos* despite the arduous effort required to attain it. Sydney Carton tries to anesthetize the pain of his loneliness with alcohol. He eventually learns, however, that the best pleasures are those that give rise to the deepest sense of satisfaction. Both Carton and Janie's relationships are fraught with pain, but they learn that genuine love is no less genuine because it is accompanied by suffering. For Elizabeth Bennet, stinging humiliations help her to acquire a clearer understanding of the truth about others. As Plato illustrates in his allegory of the cave and Aristotle observes in *The Politics*, "learning is accompanied by pain" (VIII.5, 1339a29). None of the characters (and again, Gatsby proves the point in the negative) escapes some form of disappointment, rejection, psychological or physical suffering. Encouraging students to track the influence of pleasure and pain in a character's development helps them to see that individuals do not usually endure pain in a vacuum; a desire to pursue their new *telos* sustains them. And as they commit themselves to a more worthy *telos*, these characters also enjoy new pleasures.

Reflection

The various relationships these characters develop as well as their experiences of both pain and pleasure all provide data for reflection on their best possible *telos*. In her book *The Morality of Happiness*, Julia Annas reminds us that virtuous dispositions come as a result of "deliberations and decisions, not other factors that can be developed in a mindless way" (Annas 1993: 51). Gatsby's unreflective character precludes him from seeing the enormous limitations of his dream. Thoughtful reflection is a central factor in the schooling of desire insofar as it helps to lead an individual from an imperfect conception of a *telos* to a clearer understanding of what that *telos* ought to be. The habit of reflection on experience enables the protagonists to investigate, question, and reorient themselves at each morally pivotal point. Janie's intense retrospection about each of her husbands enables her to gain a much more profound understanding of love and marriage. Elizabeth habitually observes and evaluates the character of others. Carton's reflections on the miserable state of his own life and missed opportunities—inspired by his relationship with the Manette family—eventually help him to see that his life is not without purpose.

It is essential that students recognize characters' moments of reflection or lack of reflection. By paying attention to characters' reflections, students can draw informed conclusions about the degree to which reflection enables characters to evaluate and revise their *tele* and direct their lives intelligently rather than impulsively. Students can also draw insights from characters' reflections about how characters make sense of pleasure, pain, and relationships.

Courage

Just because a person recognizes a goal as noble does not mean he or she is committed to doing what it takes to pursue it. Students, for example, are keen to rail against prejudice when they read Martin Luther King's *Letter from a Birmingham City Jail* and *The Autobiography of Malcolm X*, or to become indignant in the face of discrimination. Yet day-to-day in their own lunch rooms, students find themselves segregated by race, popularity, and gender. In his Russian epic, *The Brothers Karamazov*, Dostoevsky's Zosima the Elder makes this observation to Fyodor Pavlovich:

> A man who lies to himself, and believes his own lies becomes unable to recognize truth, either in himself or in anyone else, and he ends up losing respect for himself and for others. When he has no respect for anyone, he can no longer love, and, in order to divert himself, having no love in him, he yields to his impulses, indulges in the lowest forms of pleasure, and behaves in the end like an animal. And it all comes from lying—lying to others and to yourself. (44)

Literature is replete with illustrations of individuals who flee from the truth and create a persona that mocks or denies reality. What does it mean for a character to courageously accept the truth—about oneself or reality? It requires a willingness to recognize and accept reality as it is disclosed. For Twain's Huck Finn this means acting in consequence with his newfound respect for his friend Jim as a person rather than a slave. For Dickens' Pip in *Great Expectations* this means finally recognizing his own vanity and selfishness in his treatment of Joe Gargery. Helping students attend to the ways in which literary characters face and accept the truth or flee from it helps them to trace the influence of courage in each character's schooling of desire.

Relationships, pleasure and pain, reflection, and the courage to face the truth are central among the internal and external factors that enable a protagonist to discern his or her *telos* to pursue the "best possible state of soul."

The schooling of desire as it plays itself out in literary characters' lives helps teachers and students to see moral choices as not stemming primarily from a set of specific rules, skills, or moral knowledge *per se*, but rather from the particular story of one's life and the vision that animates it. The four factors that help to bring about the schooling of desire suggest that the internal and external influences on a character's life are similar to those in our students' lives. My point is simply that we can add existential depth, compelling insight, and meaningful discourse to our students' study of literature, if we take the narrative of moral development (and moral regression) seriously. The four protagonists featured in this book have unique moral starting points, backgrounds, and educational experiences that give shape to their trajectory; the *kind of person* each one becomes is highly personalized. The same is true for our students. We need to embrace the uniqueness of each person's unfolding life while at the same time holding up images and examples of different kinds of life stories from which they can draw both inspiration and insight.

Chapter 2 will now focus on students and take up the question: what is the moral imagination and what capacities can we foster in students by exercising their moral imagination?

Literature and the moral imagination

In the novel *The Things They Carried*, Tim O'Brien's fictional account of his experiences in Vietnam, the narrator, a soldier himself, reflects on one of the memories he carries with him from childhood. He recalls how his best friend Linda had fallen ill with a brain tumor when she was ten. After undergoing chemotherapy she lost her hair and wore a red beret to school every day to hide her baldness. O'Brien's reflections on how he and his classmates treated Linda in the fourth grade awaken insights about his dispositions as an adult.

> Over the next few weeks Linda wore her new red cap to school every day. She never took it off, not even in the classroom, and so it was inevitable that she took some teasing about it. Most of it came from a kid named Nick Veenhof. Out on the playground, during recess, Nick would creep up behind her and make a grab for the cap, almost yanking it off, then scampering away. It went on like that for weeks: the girls giggling, the guys egging him on. Naturally I wanted to do something about it, but it just wasn't possible. I had my reputation to think about. I had my pride. And there was also the problem of Nick Veenhof. So I stood off to the side, just as a spectator, wishing I could do things I couldn't do. I watched Linda clamp down the cap with the palm of her hand, holding it there, smiling over in Nick's direction as if none of it really mattered.
>
> For me, though, it did matter. It still does. I should've stepped in; fourth grade is no excuse. Besides, it doesn't get easier with time, and twelve years later, when Vietnam presented much harder choices, some practice at being brave might've helped a little. (1990: 262–263)

Teaching Character Education through Literature: Awakening the moral imagination in secondary classrooms does not seek to prove a direct correlation between reading particular books and changes in character, but it does seek to give students "some practice at being brave." When we practice something such as the piano, or tennis, or the violin, we can develop skills that become second nature; we can learn from our mistakes. When we practice being courageous or kind or helpful, we can evaluate the cause and effect of our choices, and receive guidance from parents, coaches, and mentors. Guided practice, then, provides a safe arena for learning. When practicing a sport, an instrument, or a virtue, mistakes are valuable; slips in judgment give rise to new wisdom; bad habits can be corrected and good habits cultivated.

Literature teachers are not unlike coaches or music instructors. Whether teaching a sport or a musical instrument, playing—practice, practice, practice—is what makes a person better. A good tennis coach seeks to instill habits, skills, and competencies in his budding athletes. He gives them practice honing their backhand, forehand, and serves. A music instructor helps her student develop a facility for playing an instrument well and creating the best musical sound.

Similarly, literature teachers can give students the practice they need to become connoisseurs of vicarious experience, sensitive readers able to make distinctions among choices and *tele* that lead fictional characters toward flourishing and those that lead them to a less than fully human life. The narratives that students read ought to provide rich content with which to practice attending to the various ways in which characters respond to challenges of stress or to challenges of leisure, when characters have the freedom to do as they please.

The study of literature provides students with an occasion for focused moral reflection and dialogue, an occasion to examine what informs the moral compass guiding fictional lives. Adolescents need a constructive context within which to talk about the lives of others—how they sorted out conflicting desires and learned (or failed to learn) to make their actions consistent with their ideals. Characters in stories are distant enough not to pose a threat to adolescents' ambitions or self-image. Literature gives students privileged insight into the moral journey of a life. Excellent narrative literature invites students to experience vicariously the desires, conflicts, trials, and triumphs of characters. In sum, excellent fiction writers reveal the moral contours of a life.

While literature teachers cannot control the choices students make outside the classroom, we can help them to become more adept at ethical reflection and hope the practice they acquire doing this will indeed carry over into their own lives. Simply put, if we take how and what students read seriously, we can strengthen their moral imagination and prepare them on some level for the challenges that life will ultimately present them. Reading rich and evocative narratives gives students practice at evaluating the worthiness of competing goals or *tele*.

THE NEED FOR STORIES

Michael Milburn argues in *The English Journal* that what adolescents "need from reading at this point in their lives is not great art so much as great stories" (2001: 93). Sometimes, as English teachers we get so bogged down in preparing students for standardized tests, acquainting them with literary criticism, and focusing on writing and language development that we can lose sight of adolescents' need for stories. Stories give them practice in sorting out conflicting desires and aspirations.

In his book, *Becoming a Reader: The Experience of Fiction from Childhood to Adulthood*, Appleyard links the experience of adolescence with the genre of tragedy precisely because adolescents, like tragic heroes, are full of desires:

> yearning to discover an authentic individuality, conceiving great ideals, agonizing over relationships to others, burdened by a sense of fate beyond their control, wondering whether the life choices they make will be the right ones, aware of the seemingly inescapable ambivalence of their feelings. (1991: 110)

Fictional characters' struggles are of interest to students as they set a course for their own life journey, make their own choices, and in doing so, give consideration to the kind of person they would like to become. Characters in literature often reveal their struggle with conflicting desires. George Eliot's *Daniel Deronda*, for example, has difficulty reconciling his affection for a married woman he once hoped to make his own lifelong love and for a young Jewish woman who wins his heart as well. The young Huck Finn is conflicted as to whether or not he should obey the law and turn Jim, a runaway slave, over to the bounty hunters, or to let his friend escape to safety. As students follow these characters' stories and trace the factors that school their desires, they can come to appreciate a *telos* worthy of commitment versus one that misleads or deceives an individual to pursue a path toward moral regression.

Appleyard also points out three main elements that determine adolescents' appreciation and level of engagement with a novel. First and most important is their ability to identify with characters as models of how one can live and set goals. Second is their ability to see the novel as a realistic account of life, complete with suffering, setbacks, and moral complexity. Third, and related to the first two, is the degree to which the novel makes them think about their own lives and ideals. Narrative literature gives students both exposure to a variety of lives and the choices that give those lives shape, and practice envisioning and setting their own life goals and worthy *tele*.

The point of this chapter is not to suggest that students need to read in a whole new way. Rather, I am suggesting that adolescent readers are disposed to read with interest in the schooling of desire. As they identify with the characters, trace those factors that give a realistic account of how their desires are schooled, and begin reflecting on their own lives in contrast, students have the opportunity to safely evaluate the choices and mistakes of others as well as their own. They have the opportunity to practice reflecting on the worthiness of life goals. And finally they acquire a repertoire of images and exemplars, memorable characters whose stories reveal a moral trajectory that students can learn from, as they pursue and embrace their own vision of happiness.

MORAL IMAGINATION

The imagination is an internal sense, and like the externally analogous sense of sight, it is exercised by responding to the data presented to it from outside. In his "Defense of Poetry," Percy Bysshe Shelley writes:

> A man, to be greatly good, must imagine intensely and comprehensively; he must put himself into the place of another and many others; the pains and pleasures of his species must become his own. The great instrument of moral good is the imagination.

Naturally, the imagination can also serve as the great instrument of the moral *bad*. Nevertheless, as a "great instrument of moral good" literature teachers need to help students strengthen their moral imagination. Moral greatness requires the ability to "imagine intensely and comprehensively" because our vision of the possible worthwhile goals open to us is limited by our knowledge and experience. A person with no exposure to exemplary moral lives in either fact or fiction suffers from a serious handicap in attempting to lead a good life. Sociology has demonstrated this truth time and again; the experience of a child born into extreme poverty and neglect seriously limits his or her ability to develop virtuous dispositions. On the other hand, there is good evidence that a mentor, a grandparent, an older sibling, or even a profound school experience can in fact serve as a powerful catalyst in turning a young person's vision and priorities around.

The four factors introduced in Chapter 1: relationships, the experience of pleasure and pain, reflection, and courage collectively serve as points of ignition that not only catalyze the schooling of desire in the protagonist but also serve to fire the moral imagination of the reader. Readers are more likely to identify with these factors than with the more abstract elements of fiction: conflict, mood, tone, and symbolism, for example. That is, students' moral imagination is awakened more by a grief-stricken parent who learns of her son's untimely death than by the description of a small town store front. While the latter may be lovely and paint a picture in the mind's eye, it does not provoke sympathy or prompt ethical reflection.

The moral imagination is the place where reason and heart desire, envision, evaluate, and choose a worthy *telos*. As such, the moral imagination is the seat of practice for adolescent readers. In the same way coaches teach students to practice improving their form, literature can give students practice exercising their moral imagination. We can strengthen students' moral imaginations by teaching them to look at characters' lives as a whole, evaluating their goals and how they achieve them, and coming to envision, desire, and choose more worthy goals for their own lives. The schooling of desire in our students' own lives, then, depends in part on the development of a well-exercised moral imagination.

Wayne Booth (1988: 293) describes imagination as a storehouse with an intelligent self-censoring capacity. The imagination is

> *capable of employing* a collection of images that I have re-created in my experience of narratives, and if I think of my character as in part made of the images my mind "contains" . . . then it should be possible to find ways of talking sense about why we might welcome some images and show others the door.

This capacity to choose what we integrate into our personal repertoire of images and ideas is both a central function of the *moral* imagination and a central feature of one's own personal character formation. The moral imagination then is not only a storehouse but also an intelligent guide. William Kilpatrick (1994: 23) points out the early relationship between the imagination and character formation in younger children:

> Imagination is one of those keys to virtue. It is not enough to *know* what's right. It is also necessary to *desire* to do what's right. Desire in turn is directed to a large extent by imagination. In theory, reason should guide our moral choices, but in practice, it's imagination much more than reason that calls the shots.

We tap into our students' moral imagination when we encourage them to trace those factors central to the schooling of desire. By highlighting morally pivotal points and challenges we provide guided practice in ethical reflection. In short, examining the schooling of desire of protagonists can help to foster students' facility in discerning what it looks like to live well or poorly. The moral imagination has a number of capacities. What follows is a sampling of those capacities that literature teachers can help students to develop within the study of narrative literature:

1   moral vision;
2   moral rehearsal;
3   moral identity; and
4   moral judgment.

Acquiring moral vision

> My task which I am trying to achieve is, by the power of the written word, to make you hear, to make you feel—it is, before all, to make you *see*. That—and no more, and it is everything. If I succeed, you shall find there, according to your deserts, encouragement, consolation, fear, charm, all you demand—and, perhaps, also that glimpse of truth for which you have forgotten to ask.
>
> (Joseph Conrad, quoted in "The Nature and Aim of Fiction,"
> Flannery O'Connor, 1962: 80)

Seeing and the "ability to see"[1] has been a leitmotif throughout the history of literature, perhaps most notably incarnated by Sophocles' famous blind but wise seer, Tiresias, a central character throughout the *Oedipus* trilogy. While physically blind, Tiresias, who possesses insight into the truth, reminds us that vision is not merely a physical capacity. He serves as a dramatic foil to both King Oedipus and Creon who have intelligence, power, prestige, and physical sight but who walk blindly to their tragic fates. The "ability to see," then, accounts for the capacity to discern and to recognize the realities that ought to be taken seriously in life. Seeing is about penetrating the surface of ordinary experience and appearances to contemplate their meaning. David Denby, film critic and author of *Great Books*, explains that literature helps us to see that actions have lifelong consequences. After reading *Oedipus* again at the age of 48, he muses,

> When you're younger. . . you think that an image is remediable—if your image doesn't work out, you can retract it. But it's not really like that. You make choices that affect your whole life that you can't take back. I think young people—well a lot of people—are afraid of this fact.
> (1996: F8)

This maturity of perspective Denby speaks of can only be acquired with the practice of learning to see. I sometimes begin my classes with a discussion of a painting. The subjects usually resonate in some way with the theme of my lecture, but more importantly, they invite my students to hone their powers of observation, attend to detail, and develop their capacity to *see*. The simple rural classroom scene in Winslow Homer's *Country School* (1871), for example, provokes numerous questions about what has just happened in this one-room schoolhouse. Similarly Rembrandt's *Return of the Prodigal Son* (1662), completed in the twilight of his career, raises questions about the dispositions of both the younger and elder brothers and sheds new light on Luke's narrative (Luke 15: 11–32). Both paintings invite reflection on motivation. Why did Homer choose to capture this particular moment in the school day? Why is the little boy rubbing his eyes? Why is the school teacher's fist clenched? Why did Rembrandt choose to depict this dramatic juncture in the narrative? Why is the elder son standing on a platform? What are the artists asking us to see? Both images depict a narrative, a story that has been brought to life by the artist and begs further interpretation.

Narratives, likewise, are artistic renderings. They tap the moral imagination by inviting readers to enjoy the story—in the same way we delight in the beauty of a painting—and to acquire a more penetrating vision by attending to the details as the drama unfolds. Stories give the moral imagination practice in learning to see because, as psychologist and scholar Paul Vitz reminds us, "Narratives allow us to stop talking about the moral life and to point to it instead. . . . In stories, literally (as in movies), or at least in the mind's eye, moral action *can be seen*" (1990: 718, emphasis added).

Rehearsing the possibilities: preparation for life's challenges

While narrative literature has enormous potential to help readers see the moral life more fully, it can also help them see things differently. Literature provides a rich context within which students can reflect and then mentally rehearse how they might act in similar circumstances. Children's author Lois Lowry explained in an interview that the books she read in childhood helped her to mourn the loss of her son who died in a military accident.

> Part of the way I dealt with the loss of my child was the books I'd read from a very young age. . . . Reading such things is a rehearsal, in a way. Without realizing it, we rehearse what we would do. And then, if we are called upon to face it, we do what we had rehearsed.
> (*Boston Globe*, p. B7, 4/28/2003)

Along the same lines, Stephen Fesmire in his book, *John Dewey and Moral Imagination* (2003), cites Dewey's theory of "deliberation as dramatic rehearsal" in which he metaphorically likens moral deliberation to an art.

The moral imagination is the place where this "dramatic rehearsal" can take place. Students acquire practice rehearsing how they might respond to the same difficulties or good fortune they witness in the characters' lives. Characters in literature provide us with examples of the various ways human beings deal with stress and leisure. In fact, part of the schooling of desire and acquiring moral maturity lies in learning to meet gracefully and admirably two tests that we all face daily. My colleague Steven Tigner (1995) characterized these in his very fine essay, "Signs of the Soul": the stress test and the leisure test of character.

Whether it is the pressure to fudge the data on a lab report to retain a certain grade point average or to steal money to help pay the bills, our students are met with their own "stress tests" of character. Ordinary life also presents challenges to character when we enjoy the freedom to do as we please, to take what we please, to make as many personal phone calls as we please, or to gossip as we please. Who we are is equally disclosed by the choices we make when we have the leisure to do whatever we want. The ability to choose well in the face of stress or leisure stems in large part from the ability to see the various objects of our choice for what they are.

When mapping out morally pivotal points in the lives of fictional characters, we are helping students to rehearse their own plans and possibilities. They can rehearse how they will respond to stress and leisure, build relationships, and deal with pleasure and pain. They can reflect on the experiences of the characters and rehearse how they might choose differently. They can rehearse the ways in which they might call on their courage to face the challenges of a particular situation. In short, when students develop the capacity to vicariously rehearse experiences within their moral imagination, they are better prepared to make good choices when they find themselves in similar circumstances.

Dumbledore, the wise old headmaster of Hogwarts, offers this sage advice to Harry Potter in *Harry Potter and the Chamber of Secrets*: "It is our choices, Harry, that show what we truly are, far more than our abilities" (Book 2: 333). Literature provides a rich context within which students can practice reflecting on the power of choices and commitments. They gain valuable perspective and vicarious experience that can help provide insights applicable to their own lives. As one English teacher explains, literature

> ". . . helps students to interpret and understand their lives as they are and will be." . . . By learning to analyze literature, "students can learn to analyze their own lives. . . . They are able to live a life, but also able to stand back and look at it."
>
> (Applebee *et al.* 2000: 416)

The company we keep: vicarious relationships as a path to identity

In his book, *The Call of Stories*, Robert Coles, psychiatrist and renowned authority on moral development in children, cites numerous conversations he has had with young people. The following illustrates the realization a young Caucasian student has while reading Ralph Ellison's *Invisible Man*.

> I had trouble at first getting into the novel, but I did, and once I was with Ellison, I stayed with him; I mean, I "connected" with the invisible man. I think, after a while, I began to see people the way he did: I watched people and tried to figure them out. I didn't want to be an outsider, but I was—the way black people are for us, for lots of us. The more I looked at people through my outsider's eyes, the more I felt alone and ignored; it was no fun—and it made me understand not only my own social problems, my trouble getting along with people, but how black people must feel in this world, especially when they come to a place like this. (69)

This student did not just mentally rehearse a similar experience; he allowed himself to live another life, to practice what it would be like to have someone else's goals and challenges, to befriend a character. This activity of his moral imagination is the ability to envision possibilities through the vicarious friendships a reader develops with the characters.

Recently, I had breakfast with a group of female graduate students from various universities in Boston and listened intently as they discussed their childhood passion for *Anne of Green Gables* and argued over their favorite book in the series. One young woman was a student of opera at the Conservatory, another from Taiwan was pursuing an MBA, and the third was a divinity student at Harvard. They talked about Anne as a mutual friend, joking about her idiosyncrasies, recounting her adventures, and admiring her strengths. Despite their diverse cultural backgrounds and professional interests, these readers felt an enormous familiarity with the young female heroine.

Wayne Booth describes how his own passion for philosophy was awakened by his acquaintance with Stephen, the protagonist in James Joyce's *Ulysses*. As he aspired to emulate the musings of this new literary friend, Booth recalls that he felt "a sense of envy and awe—not of Joyce but of Stephen. If only my own stream of consciousness could flow at that high philosophical level, what a bright young man I would be!" (1988: 274).

Another of Coles' students makes the following observation about her growing relationship with the Bennet sisters:

> I wonder which one of those Bennet sisters I resemble. Jane, maybe. I'm not as proud as Elizabeth. She was as proud as Darcy, and as prejudiced. I hope I'm not one of those selfish Bennet people, or like that aunt of Darcy's. When you read a novel, even if it's one you don't like so much—or you have a hard time getting into it, and staying into it— you can't help trying to figure out which character resembles you; or

I guess it should be the other way around: which character do you resemble most? (1989: 44–45)[2]

A third young respondent tells Coles of her desire to be like Phoebe Caulfield. "When I read *Catcher in the Rye*, I kept thinking of myself as Phoebe Caulfield, even though I knew I wasn't smart like her. It's just that I loved Holden, and he loved her in his way (he truly respected her); and I wanted his respect" (45).

I still cherish the handwritten copy I keep of one of my student's short essays on character. I was teaching eighth grade English, and we had just completed the first several chapters of Dickens' *Great Expectations*. We were studying character development, and as a new teacher, I dutifully introduced my class of 25 fourteen-year-olds to the ways they could describe a literary character as static or dynamic. I then asked them to write an in-class essay about their favorite character to date and to categorize the character accordingly. After reading one empty paragraph after another and vowing never to give the assignment again, I came across this student's response:

> My favorite character in *Great Expectations* was Herbert Pocket. Herbert was a true friend to Pip, which in fact made him a true gentleman. Herbert's staticity [*sic*] showed that his true friendship and warmth towards Pip never changed. Herbert illuminated the "goodness" in Pip. Like Joe and Magwitch, Herbert was a link, a part of Pip that was missing. When Pip and Herbert were together Pip never felt pressured. Herbert understood Pip's ambitions and "expectations." While Herbert gave advice, he never stood in Pip's way. Herbert as a character exemplified steadfastness, loyalty, friendship and warmth. Herbert was someone to hold onto when times got tough. Pip and Herbert stuck together even in the "debts of despair" (pun intended!). . . .
>
> There have been pairs of characters throughout history (Holmes and Watson, the Wright Brothers, even the cartoon characters Batman and Robin—the dynamic duo) that have acted together and helped each other. Pip and his true friend Herbert remain in that society as permanent members.
>
> Herbert Pocket will always be a part of and a true friend of Pip.

What is interesting about this quirky but delightful piece is not simply that Herbert, an amusing character given scant attention in the novel, finally enjoys an affectionate tribute. It is not the literary insight of this young student. What is striking about this piece is its unsolicited foray into the meaning of friendship. Notice the way she dutifully tips her hat to the teacher by mentioning Herbert's "staticity" from the outset. But what she reveals is much more interesting than Herbert's lack of change. What she brings to the fore are the qualities of character that make Herbert a good friend and why this level of friendship is so enviable and attractive. Most importantly, it reveals how powerfully the character of Herbert (and Pip) tapped into her moral imagination and evoked such a compelling response.

Cultivating judgment: learning to evaluate among competing *tele*

A third function of the moral imagination is its capacity to help us cultivate good judgment. If the moral imagination heightens our capacity to see, how is it nurtured to help us see well? How does it learn to distinguish virtue from vice? How do we learn to evaluate and decide among the broad array of possibilities the imagination presents to us? Readers need to be able to evaluate and step away from a narrative and decide: What makes a person a hero or a villain? What makes an action right or wrong?

It is especially important for readers to learn to distinguish between genuine and sham virtue. While at first glance, Gatsby appears virtuous, Carton looks slovenly and dissolute. We come to discover something quite different about both characters as the novels progress. MacIntyre aptly states that "Morality is never the mere inhibition and regulation of the passions; but the outward appearance of morality may always disguise uneducated passions" (1984: 241). Teachers of literature have an enormous opportunity to help students distinguish apparent virtue from genuine virtue, to see beneath the surface. Literature is one medium in which we can uncover what is disguised—the education of the passions, the nature of motivations, in a phrase, the schooling of desire.

Students need to be encouraged to question the values, assumptions, and choices presented to them in a narrative. This ability to probe, to argue, to remain somewhat skeptical keeps them from remaining wholly naïve or blindly absorbed by a story. Booth argues that "they need to learn how to think about, and possibly reject, values of the story world they first 'took in'" (1998: 49). He addresses this point in further detail in *The Company We Keep*, explaining that

> a much more important moral effect of every encounter with a story, good or bad, is the practice it gives in how to read moral qualities from potentially misleading signs. That training can be harmful, if our line-by-line progress through a work suggests that the good guys and bad guys can be readily discriminated by surface signs of dress, physical charm, or taste in wines; indeed even the most admired fictions can sometimes make moral inference seem too easy. But our best narrative friends introduce us to the practice of subtle, sensitive moral inference, the kind that most moral choices in daily life require of us. (1988: 287)

Without this capacity to make moral inference, discriminate between valuable and harmful goals or *tele*, we open the door to Nietzsche's ideal of morality as self-creation without limits. The limitless possibilities, unbound by standards of truth and falsehood, right and wrong, or good and evil, give rise to frightening possibilities. Alfred Hitchcock's *Rope* (1948, Universal Studios) offers a poignant illustration of how a student's fascination with the Nietzschean Superman who is "beyond good and evil" gives indiscriminate rein to his moral imagination to the point of finding exhilaration in plotting and executing the murder of a classmate. The satisfaction and pleasure the student takes in this act is even more chilling when the truth is ultimately disclosed, and he cannot understand why his teacher, who introduced him to Nietzsche in the first place, is not proud of his feat. This example captures the kind of moral license we see young people reveling in when they engage in egregious hazing practices that threaten the lives and psychological health of their peers.

Good judgment, the moral perspective students need to discern what is worthy among competing *tele*, cultivated through careful reading and reflection, helps to counter the danger of developing a moral imagination that loses sight of reality.

PITFALLS TO AVOID

In his provocative book, *The Courage to Teach*, Parker Palmer touches on this essential point. He advises educators not to allow students to become complacent in their own narrative world: "when my little story, or yours, is our only point of reference, we easily become lost in narcissism." The stories we need to pay attention to first, he advises, are

> stories that are universal in scope and archetypal in depth, that frame our personal tales and help us to understand what they mean. We must help our students learn to listen to the big stories with the same respect we accord individuals when they tell us tales of their lives. (1998: 76)[3]

The case studies in Part II introduce students to the "big stories." Palmer reminds us that the quality of the literature we teach matters. Just as a tennis coach cannot instruct his team with deflated balls and a violin instructor cannot train someone to play well if the instrument is missing strings, literature teachers cannot help students to exercise their moral imagination if the literature they read does not have moral depth, height, and dimensionality. I am not suggesting that we teach literature that has an explicitly moral message; I am suggesting that we can only apply this kind of character study to novels that feature characters with psychological depth and aspirations, characters who make commitments to pursue their goals.

Why do so many students find themselves bored in English class? We have engaging literature built into the academic curriculum. Are we teaching it well? One of the problems is that too many teaching guides and resources on teaching literature lack imagination. Replete with reading comprehension questions that do not challenge students to do more than recall basic facts about plot, character, and setting, these guides reduce literature study to something stale and static. Or when they do make a leap to higher-level questioning, they focus too narrowly on the analysis of some literary device and lose sight of the story as a whole. When the study of literature is dominated by exercises such as these, students inevitably become distracted and bored. What follows are some of the pitfalls to avoid.

Superficiality

One common pitfall for teachers of literature is treating narratives superficially. When we reduce tennis to learning to serve effectively we lose the big picture of the game. When a music instructor neglects to take her students beyond scales and simple medleys, she offers only a superficial introduction to the violin. Students of literature need more than plot-level questions that demand no more than mere fact-finding or simplistic and pat conclusions about a narrative. By reducing *To Kill a Mockingbird* to a lesson on racism in the south or *Romeo and Juliet* to a set of plot summary questions, we miss the opportunity to excite students' moral imagination and their interest in all of the factors that influence characters' growth and change. When we are held hostage by teaching resources that skim the surface of a text, we miss important opportunities to awaken and engage the moral imagination.

Moralizing

Another way we can stay on the surface but think we are entering more deeply into a work is by moralizing. The coach who talks about the virtues of tennis but fails to work his team hard and the violin instructor who discusses music theory with her pupil but neglects her skill development deprive their students. Similarly, when we reduce literature study too quickly to the "moral of the story," we sacrifice the complexity and richness of a narrative and run the risk of turning English class into Sunday School. By turning Atticus Finch into an exalted hero without acknowledging his weaknesses or lamenting the unrequited love of Romeo and Juliet without questioning its authenticity, we deprive students of an important opportunity to acquire a more penetrating vision of moral experience or to develop a more refined sense of judgment. In the effort to arrive at the one right answer to the moral questions, this approach to literature can turn students off and eclipse their interest in character motivation and desire. They believe the teacher has decided these already.

Seduction of sociological tract fiction

A third pitfall is to assuage adolescents' interest in moral questions by feeding them sociological tract fiction. A number of well-intentioned authors strive to appeal to young people by "meeting them where they are at." I have no objections to contemporary literature or to non-canonical young adult literature. In fact, I think we can and should supplement the required traditional works with more contemporary narratives. I object to poorly written novels marketed specifically to adolescents as contemporary, realistic, relevant, and easy to read. The purveyors of this new, widely popularized genre of teen literature are not unlike the *Merchants of Cool*, they tend to sensationalize the challenges adolescents face in dealing with drug addiction, eating disorders, divorce, sexual experimentation, and the like. Sociological tract fiction is written not so much to tell a story as to address these problems. These stories are written by adults about what they perceive to be the reality and desires of adolescents. They tend to be one-dimensional, descriptive but not penetrating, issue-focused but not sensitive to the complexities of personal identity, character, and aspirations. In short, they lack psychological depth. The characters are frequently caught in a problem or series of problems, and in the absence of a moral vision to guide them, they muddle along through the school of trial and error. While some argue that there is a place for this kind of reading—perhaps as an initial hook for non-readers—these stories do not provide the kind of imaginative richness that heightens a reader's moral vision of him or herself and the world.

Fostering ethical reflection in the English classroom raises many complex questions for teachers. How do we examine literature as character building without reducing it to a cheap and easy list of moral lessons? How can we engage students in ethical reflection that does not descend to a highly subjective reader-response approach to literature or a therapy session in the classroom? How can students and teachers map out the moral trajectory of a literary character's life?

Chapter 3 provides some answers to these questions, introduces the case study format and provides additional ideas to help teachers tap into students' moral imagination and give them some practice in acquiring moral vision, rehearsing, identifying and befriending characters, and cultivating good judgment.

Chapter 3

Fostering ethical reflection in our classrooms

MORAL LIFE AS A STORY

For the past eight summers I have led Teachers Academies with secondary school teachers from all subject areas—from music to physics to history.[1] During these Academies we work together for five days studying and discussing the "big stories" to which Palmer refers (1998: 76).

At the end of our Academies, teachers often comment on the texts that gave them new resolve to deal more directly and, in some cases, more gracefully, with the range of challenges they face in their work or in their families. One of the books, *The Things They Carried*, provided the catalysts for at least one participant's important insights. Tim O'Brien opens his Vietnam War Story by listing and categorizing what the soldiers carry with them—from love letters and dog tags, to C-rations, ammunition, and a dead man's thumb.

After discussing O'Brien's novel the teachers begin a parallel inquiry into the significance of what they carry and what their students carry—both externally and internally—and how it reflects in some way who they are.

This conversation prompted one teacher to relate a story about what she had been carrying for years.

She recounted a tragic accident she was involved in on a Christmas Eve over ten years ago. She and her husband were driving along in a snowstorm, when a two-year-old boy darted into the street right in front of their car. They braked immediately, but it was too late. The little boy was struck dead. His mother, who was watching from the kitchen window, rushed outside, scooped up her son, and called an ambulance. Waiting for the ambulance, she turned to the distraught couple and invited them into her home. Every Christmas since the tragedy, this mother invites the couple to her son's memorial service. Still deeply troubled and unable to discuss the tragedy, the woman driving the car had never related the circumstances of the event to anyone.

She chose to tell this incident at the end of the Academy because it was something she had been "carrying" like a lead weight in her haversack.

Up until that moment she had been the victim, carrying a tremendous burden. She was now able to see and relish the enormous debt of gratitude she owed the mother of this little boy.

This woman was not ready to disclose the tragedy life had dealt her up until this point. It was in our exploration of literature and specifically our discussion of Tim O'Brien's story, that she was finally able to shed this enormous burden. Up until this point she had seen herself as a victim and taken this woman's forgiveness for granted. After reflecting on her experience again in light of our discussion, she developed the moral fuel and courage she needed to face reality squarely. This teacher's experience once again underscores the unique power of literature to offer moral insight and even catalyze a significant change in a person's life.

While philosophers, psychologists, and sociologists provide us with theories about the moral life, narratives provide us with concrete illustrations and vicarious experiences of moral growth and development, as well as moral decline. Narrative provides the best context for examining desire and moral philosophy helps to explain how narrative really does serve as a roadmap.[2]

Alasdair MacIntyre, author of the groundbreaking treatise on moral philosophy, *After Virtue*, argues that the moral life is essentially like a story, a drama unfolding toward a particular vision or *telos*. And each person's desires are ultimately guided and propelled by some "conceptions of a possible shared future, a future in which certain possibilities beckon us forward and others repel us, some seem already foreclosed and others perhaps inevitable" (215).

The parable of the Good Samaritan, for example, helps to shape one such conception for the fifteen-year-old student who tells her life-changing story in the essay excerpted below. A semifinalist in a "Laws of Life," international essay competition sponsored by the John Templeton Foundation, this student writes about her volunteer experience in a hospital nursery during her stay in Peru one summer. When she realized that some infants were without parents, she made additional late night trips to the nursery.

> I remember walking towards the nursery one night. I could see, in the hallway, one crib, alone and ostracized from the others. I approached the crib, and inside, there lay a baby, crying helplessly, obviously in need of love and comfort. She was slightly bigger than my forearm and her strangely developed face suggested pre-maturity. "She was born three months early and her mother hasn't come back for her," I was told. I witnessed nurses scurrying around, inside the nursery, feeding and changing the babies of mothers who care, but ignoring the tiny person struggling for attention from inside the crib. "They have to take care of the others first, then, if there is time, she will be fed," someone explained to me. I could not imagine standing by watching as

this perfect little creature, unable to move her head, struggled to find a comfortable position and, at times, desperately gasped for a breath due to her underdeveloped respiratory system. I immediately lifted her into my arms and held her close. The improvement within those few seconds seemed miraculous, almost unbelievable. The baby stopped crying. Her hands remained in tightly clenched fists, but I could tell she was relieved. From that moment on, I knew what I had to do. It was my chance to be the person I never thought I could be, the Good Samaritan. Every night, times varying after midnight, I found my way through the laboring mothers to that baby in the hallway. I spent hours just rocking her and at times, even singing to her. I began to notice gradual improvements. She seemed to let go of all her worries and anxieties the moment I picked her up each night. By the end of my stay, even her tight, frustrated fists would spread open into wide, reaching hands.

The Good Samaritan represents one of those individuals in our collective imagination who inspires our response to the question, "How should I live?" As the four factors in the schooling of desire—relationships, pleasure and pain, reflection, and courage—have enormous resonance with our students' own experience, so does the structure of narratives. The "image of some future . . . *telos*" that MacIntyre speaks of is precisely what moves or fails to move a person to choose certain paths or forego others, as our four protagonists show us. Similarly, we are protagonists in our own life narrative. As MacIntyre explains,

> Unpredictability and teleology . . . coexist as part of our lives; like characters in a fictional narrative we do not know what will happen next, but nonetheless our lives have a certain form which projects itself towards our future. (216)

Teaching novels is an inescapable part of our work with students; why not take advantage of this intersection between literature and life to help students become more adept at ethical reflection? Inherent to narrative are questions related to the nature of moral choices and commitments. MacIntyre's "central thesis" is that, through one's history and experiences, a person becomes "a teller of stories that aspire to truth." These stories are not, as Macbeth proclaims in despair, "a tale told by an idiot signifying nothing." Rather, he argues, "the key question for men is not about their own authorship; I can only answer the question 'what am I to do?' if I can answer the question 'of what story or stories do I find myself a part?'" (216).[3] In other words, our own life journey requires a search for narrative meaning. We all seek to discover the history and *telos* that gives us a sense of origin as well as a sense of purpose and direction to our lives. Reading narrative literature provides an important point of comparison and entry into the stories of others. By witnessing their journey, we learn to appreciate the narrative quality of all human life. By attending to each protagonist's evolving *telos*, we learn to question the North Star guiding our own lives. In his book, *Moral Imagination*, Mark Johnson draws the following analogy and offers an apt illustration of MacIntyre's point:

> Every one of us is actively plotting our lives, both consciously and unconsciously, by attempting to construct ourselves as significant characters within what we regard as meaningful life stories. (1993: 165)

> Narrative can illuminate *purposes*, plans, and *goals*, which are the forms by which our lives have some *direction, motivation, and significance* for us. (171, emphasis added)

As English teachers, we have the opportunity to help students to trace and ponder the "direction, motivation, and significance" of literary characters' choices, and hopefully to become more capable of evaluating the significance of their own choices. In his book, *Sources of the Self*, Charles Taylor (1989) highlights the importance of narrative to our sense of identity and purpose.[4]

> We know where we are through a mixture of recognition of landmarks before us and a sense of how we have traveled to get here. . . . Thus making sense of my present action . . . requires a narrative understanding of my life, a sense of what I have become which can only be given in a story. And as I project my life forward and endorse the existing direction or give it a new one, I project a future story, not just a state of the momentary future but a bent for my whole life to come. (48)

Adolescents, in the midst of constructing meaningful life stories for their own lives, are well disposed to identifying such "landmarks" in literary characters' lives and exploring the factors that help each protagonist attain them. By asking them to attend to each character's evolving *telos* they learn to detect the "bent for [his or her] whole life to come" (48).

What these authors suggest is that we can only understand a person's life if we have some context for making sense of the question, "Where is this person headed and why?" This is precisely the question at the heart of growing up, perhaps even at the heart of discovering what it really means to be human. As Martha Nussbaum writes, the central Aristotelian question "how should one live?" is implicit in literary narratives and reminds readers interested in an ethical reflection to ask, "What sorts of human beings are presenting themselves to us?" (1990: 26, 32). Keeping these questions before us helps us to make sense both of literature and of life.

Fostering ethical reflection in the English classroom, then, raises many complex questions. How do teachers pursue literature as character building without reducing it to a cheap and easy list of moral lessons? How can they engage students in moral reflection that does not descend to a highly subjective reader-response approach to literature or a therapy session in the classroom? How can students and teachers map out the moral vector of a literary character's life? What constitutes a morally pivotal point in a character's life? What factors contribute to bringing such points about? In short, how can the teacher and reader explore moral motivation—that is, how a character's moral agency is informed by circumstances, relationships, choices, and personal dispositions? To address these questions I offer a pedagogical framework that fosters both rigorous textual analysis and ethical reflection.

Characters in literature provide us with a window to the soul through which we can examine the internal and external factors involved in becoming or failing to become the kind of person we admire or respect. Thus, a writer of fiction can provide us with insights about fictional characters' choices and commitments—their consistency or idiosyncrasies, their merits and limitations. As English teachers we can help students become more adept at evaluating the choices that individuals make in the context of other genres: short story, biography, autobiography, and memoir, for example. More importantly, we also teach them to become more critical consumers of the various media images and messages they receive daily. By teaching students to see beyond the superficial, to notice and take stock of all that informs characters' choices and commitments—how they deal with relationships, pleasure and pain, and how they reflect upon and face the various challenges that they meet—we help to refine their powers of discrimination and judgment. By prompting students to pay attention to how fictional characters respond to the truth, we help them to acquire greater respect for integrity, contempt for hypocrisy, and sensitivity to what accounts for moral growth or moral decline.

MAPPING MORALLY PIVOTAL POINTS

Each character's moral trajectory is dramatically mapped out by highlighting aspirational ideals or *tele*—what it is that a character desires at a given point in his or her life and why.[5] These *tele* are brought into sharp relief at *morally pivotal points*. By asking students to pay attention to how these morally pivotal points are brought about, they can begin to track the factors that help or hinder moral growth over time. The case studies that follow in Part II, then, are designed to focus students' attention on identifying and evaluating

a the evolving aspirations (*tele*) of the characters;
b the internal and external factors that help to shape or inform these *tele*; and
c the changes in moral dispositions required to achieve them.

Morally pivotal points are transformational episodes, events, experiences, or encounters that compel individuals to reassess or refine their life goal(s) or path(s). In one of his recent "On Language" columns in *The New York Times Magazine*, master wordsmith William Safire defines a "pivot" as "an axis on which something turns," explaining that pivotal is "a good word to suggest decision-making power" (2003: 12). This emphasis on decision-making captures precisely the sense in which I am using the term. Unlike a significant advance in one's career (such as Carton's success in the Old Bailey courthouse), or an epiphany (like Elizabeth's realization that her father has been remiss in carrying out his family duties), an event, experience, or encounter is *morally* pivotal only if it inspires commitment to or aversion from a particular goal or path. At each morally pivotal point, the protagonists acquire a new or refined vision of what John Dewey calls their "ends in view" (1933: 125), and this refined vision of their *telos* gives new direction to their choices and actions.

In Dante's *Purgatorio*, the second book of his *Divine Comedy*, the pilgrim souls learn to progress toward heaven through what Dante the poet repeatedly refers to as a "*conversio*," a turning around or pivoting, which gives them an ability to see more clearly where they are headed and why. Each *conversio* on their journey through Purgatory gives them new momentum and purpose despite the pains of purification they must endure. Similarly, morally pivotal points signal moments when the protagonist has acquired a more focused vision of his or her goal.

To help map out the moral trajectory of the protagonists in these four novels, I have placed *morally pivotal points* and *challenge points* in sharp relief. To facilitate comparisons and contrasts among them, I consistently focus on three dramatic moments: two *morally pivotal points* and one *challenge point* within each character case study. Mapping *morally pivotal points* and *challenge points* provides a useful framework for character analysis but not an archetype for all ethical reflection on literature. Novels with unconventional narrative structure, such as stream of consciousness, for example, may not be suited for this kind of character mapping at all. Character studies undertaken with other novels may yield several morally pivotal points. Others, because of the slow, gradual nature of moral change, may illustrate few to none. Dostoevsky's *Crime and Punishment* and Tolstoy's *Death of Ivan Illych*, for example, reveal a gradual process of moral growth that culminates in a dramatic moral revelation for each of the protagonists.

Through my analysis of the novels, I have found that as each character's schooling evolves from one morally pivotal point to the next, a pattern of moral progress (or regression) emerges. In broad terms, moral progress evoked by the schooling of desire can be described as a gradual movement from a lower, less rational state where a character is dominated or blinded by competing or misguided desires, to a nobler, more compelling and co-ordinated action-guiding desire for a worthy *telos*. Elizabeth Bennet initially trusts her own judgment but is blind to her prejudice; Sydney Carton has a deep knowledge of virtue but lacks the will to live it; Janie Crawford is morally good from the outset, but lacks mature understanding to choose well. The schooling of desire illustrates the integration of character and competence in each of these cases.

The successful schooling of desire follows a similar pattern and involves certain internal and external factors (relationships, pleasure and pain, reflection and courage), while failed schooling follows from the absence of these factors. A general framework emerges, therefore, for studying moral development not only in these four cases, but also in other works of literature and in real life.

A FRAMEWORK FOR MORAL ANALYSIS

Each character begins with his or her own moral starting points: a set of personal dispositions and habits. A change is signaled at the first *morally pivotal point*, which marks the beginning of the schooling of desire. Some experience of dissonance awakens the characters and prompts them to assess their *telos*, to ask themselves, "Where am I headed and why?" They are challenged to see things differently. Their vision of what is worthwhile is called into question, or confronted — even if incompletely. This *morally pivotal point* is perhaps best characterized as a shake-up, a moment of realization; they see something differently for the first time — Elizabeth realizes she has misread Charlotte's views on marriage and Darcy's over-tures; Carton sees in Darnay everything he could have been and admires; Janie realizes that her ideal of love cannot be found in just any marriage — but they are not yet able to commit themselves to pursuing their refined aspirations.

The second *morally pivotal point* gives rise to both a leap in self-knowledge and a heightened desire to pursue a revised *telos*. The pro-tagonists achieve greater clarity of understanding; their mind and heart are more sharply aligned. Armed with a clearer conception of what will genuinely contribute to their happiness, the characters have the opportunity to act with greater integrity, embracing these newly "seen" ends and following the trajectory of intelligent self-direction. While the first morally pivotal point helps to raise questions about the worthiness of their *telos*, the second helps them to re-channel their desires energetically toward a refined *telos*.

The third point is a *challenge point* more than a pivotal point. The character's "turn" of moral direction is challenged. The *challenge point* dramatically signals the need for the protagonist to make a deliberate choice in the face of conflict. The character does not pivot, does not change his or her *telos*. Nevertheless, that *telos* is challenged and the character is required to make a choice that will influence his or her life as a whole, setting the course for subsequent flourishing or degradation. The *challenge point* indicates the nature of virtues as "modes of choice," those habits and dispositions that enable a person to choose well.[6] At the challenge point, those protagonists whose desires have been correctly schooled are able to choose the best means to reach their goal. And those whose desires are incorrectly schooled, such as Gatsby, blindly pursue a path to self-destruction.

The morally pivotal points and challenge point for Sydney Carton from *A Tale of Two Cities* are laid out in the table below. Appendix C provides reproducible blank tables that students can complete with examples from the text as they read.

Sydney Carton

	The schooling of desire leads to a character's refined understanding and pursuit of an ideal that is both worthwhile and compelling		
Mapping pivotal points	**Definition**	**Example/illustration**	**Telos/object of desire**
Moral starting points Habits, dispositions, and context	What we know about the character's habitual behavior, attitudes, dispositions as well as initial aspirations and goals (*tele*).	Indifferent, slovenly, drunkard, savvy, competent lawyer "careless and slovenly if not debauched"; "almost insolent".	To remain an effective lawyer but to also remain committed to anesthetize his misery with alcohol.
1st morally pivotal point	Shake-up, realization that character is not pursuing the best possible *telos*.	Carton meets with Darnay. Ashamed, self-hate, envious of Darnay, desirous of virtue but unable to put it into practice.	To surround himself with individuals he admires.
2nd morally pivotal point	Leap in self knowledge, clearer perspective on a worthy path.	Carton chooses to disclose his unhappiness to Lucie and offer his gratitude for her friendship with a promise.	To offer himself in friendship and service.
Challenge point	Meets a challenge that imposes stress or pressure; *telos* becomes clear but it is difficult to pursue. The character chooses a course of action and exercises practical wisdom in achieving that goal.	Carton chooses to go to Paris and save Darnay despite the risk to his own life. He employs all of his intelligence, skill, and virtue to complete his mission.	To fulfill his promise of friendship—and to be the kind of person he always aspired to be but always felt unable to be.
Change: new dispositions			Peace, self-possession, and self-dominion, liberation from bad habits; satisfaction.

Case studies in character

INTRODUCTION TO THE CASE STUDIES

The primary purpose of Part II: Case studies in character is to provide an annotated passage study and questions for reflection designed to elicit moral insights yielded by the protagonist's development and the novel as a whole. I have selected passages from the novel, excerpts that highlight the evolving moral development of the protagonist. Moreover, each case study raises both explicit and implicit questions relevant to students' own character development: What can we learn from the characters' conflicts and challenges? What conclusions can we draw from the novel about how pride, naïveté, self-hate, and blind ambition, for example, influence our own judgment and character?

STRUCTURE OF THE CASE STUDIES

The four case studies proceed in the following manner. Each is introduced with a brief commentary on the book's literary significance and context. The *Tapping the moral imagination* section highlights the resonances between the protagonist's experience and our students', encouraging them to look at the novel not just as another burdensome homework assignment, but as a means of gaining insight into their own lives and the issues that concern them most deeply. Approaching the novels in this way primes students to engage in an aesthetic and morally sensitive reading.[1]

The case study itself, *Fostering ethical reflection*, places morally pivotal points and challenge points in sharp relief. The bulleted questions for reflection inserted at key dramatic junctures are addressed to the students and support focused engagement with the novel. They may be used as prompts for readers' journals, classroom discussion and small group presentations, or to create writing assignments for students. These questions and the passages are, of course, not exhaustive, and they vary in depth and analytical complexity. As a teacher, you can tailor these studies to the needs and skill level of students, choosing the most appropriate questions, crafting new ones, and supplementing the analysis with other related passages. Each case study concludes with *Summary reflections* on the character's journey and a set of *Extension questions* for follow-up discussion, writing, or research assignments.

I envision numerous uses for these case studies. If you are a literature teacher teaching any of these novels for the first time, the cases will acquaint you with the protagonist's development and provide a framework for thinking and teaching about a character's moral growth (or decline). If you are a veteran teacher looking for new insights and approaches to a novel, you can test these passages and questions for reflection with students and see what they yield. If you are using other novels with your students, you will find a framework that you can adapt to those works. If you are a student of English education or a teacher educator, you can use these case studies as a springboard for the creation of lessons and units. In short, these case studies will prompt you and your students to bring additional passages and questions to the study of each character's moral development.

As the context of each character's life is central to understanding and evaluating the choices he or she makes, the case studies draw heavily from the novels to help illustrate how each individual's moral drama unfolds. Each case study provides a narrative context for guiding students' exploration of the evolving *telos* or multiple *tele* of each protagonist. This context provides rich evidence the reader can use to evaluate the characters' choices.

Each character possesses his or her own unique temperament and dispositions. Gatsby is highly imaginative and erotic, whereas Carton is seemingly indifferent and cynical. Janie is naïve and romantic, and Elizabeth is self-assured yet judgmental. While these characterizations may be a bit oversimplified, it bears noting that each protagonist has also developed (or failed to develop) certain virtues; they are at different stages in their schooling of desire when we meet them in the novel. These moral starting points are important to take into account, because the characters are not empty slates when we first encounter them in the novel.

Like real people whom we encounter for the first time in the middle of their lives, they have already developed good and bad habits, nurtured or suppressed certain dispositions and character traits, and formed more or less conscious goals and visions for their lives. This moral "baggage" profoundly shapes the characters' reactions and choices. The traits acquired "before" the novel, however, are as mysterious in their origin as those we observe in real life individuals. We can guess about the formation of these traits based on clues, but cannot actually trace their development in detail. In fact, what we are looking at in the context of these case studies are examples of mature virtues or bad habits. What evolves in these studies is the development of practical wisdom. The characters' virtues or lack thereof help or hinder this development.[2] One would imagine, however, that those previously-acquired habits developed in much the same way as those that we can examine in the novel. Therefore we have to take these dispositions as a given, considering their influence on the characters' abilities to make moral progress but focusing primarily on the changes that actually unfold throughout the novel.

The successful schooling of desire ultimately leads to a character's determined pursuit of an ideal that is both worthwhile and compelling. The questions and activities throughout these case studies help students discover that the schooling of desire is not achieved through a detached intellectual grasp of an ideal or goal that fails to inspire commitment. In the successful schooling of desire, the characters' *tele* not only become clearer at each morally pivotal point, but each turn provides them with new impetus to lead a more flourishing life. Elizabeth Bennet's case study shows how stubborn prejudice can be corrected to embrace a truer understanding of oneself and others. The next case study, Janie Crawford, demonstrates how a naïve desire for marriage can mature into a profound understanding of love. Sydney Carton's story exemplifies how conflicted desires—recognizing what is right but being incapable of choosing it—can be harmonized and ultimately liberate him from the baser habits that enslave him. Finally, Jay Gatsby's case study illustrates, by contrast, what happens when desires are incorrectly schooled and blind *eros* impels a soul.

Naturally, all of the characters in a novel are affected or influenced on some level by the other characters that animate the fictional world in which they live. In other words, other characters—both minor and major—often experience morally pivotal points and challenge points. Some characters provide a dramatic foil to the protagonist or help to highlight important relationships among and between characters. By focusing on the protagonists in each of these novels, I do not mean to downplay the moral growth and change of the other characters. Nor do I mean to diminish their influence on the protagonist's development. In this book I have chosen to focus primarily on the characters named, although as a teacher you may wish to draw out more fully the moral growth of other characters in these novels.

The case studies are not substitutes for the rich and varied ways to bring Austen's *Pride and Prejudice*, Hurston's *Their Eyes Were Watching God*, Dickens' *A Tale of Two Cities*, and Fitzgerald's *The Great Gatsby* to life. Rather, they serve as points of entry in your efforts to guide students' ethical reflection. They should not exclude important considerations about authorial and historic context, or the range of conflicts, themes, and questions raised by the work as a whole. These case studies can be used as a resource to prepare lectures and to engage students in any number of exercises: discussion, debate, dramatic interpretation, formal literary analysis, and creative or expository writing. In short, they are a means to help students to become more adept at ethical reflection, while at the same time achieving the teaching and learning goals articulated in the broader English curriculum.

All too often the teaching of English remains at the level of formal analysis of plot, symbol, mood, and irony, excluding existential questions. Many times the discussion of literature is either devoid of any serious reflection, or at the other extreme, too quickly or too superficially reduced to simple moral lessons and shibboleths that ignore the complexity of a narrative.[3] The case studies that follow in Chapters 4 through 7 explore the ways we can prompt genuine conversation about four novels and the protagonists that animate them. Examining morally pivotal points in the lives of fictional characters helps us to remind students of the importance of subjecting life's experiences, both great and small, to ethical reflection. This kind of analysis yields rich data that give students an opportunity to reflect on the moral dimensions of experience, on morally pivotal points in individual lives. What factors help to bring these moments about? How does the schooling of desire reveal moral progress? What is ultimately achieved in an individual's soul by successfully schooling desire? By exploring these questions in the context of literature study, we are inviting students to engage in a parallel inquiry about their own lives.

Chapter 4

Elizabeth Bennet—humbled heroine

Widely taught in both American and British secondary schools, Jane Austen's *Pride and Prejudice* brilliantly depicts the subtleties of class conflict, economic standing, personal character, and reputation as they pertain to romance, courtship, marriage, family, social justice, and personal happiness. Jane Austen provides a masterful and amusing commentary on nineteenth-century social mores and conventions, a commentary that has remarkable resonance to this day.

Whether you are teaching *Pride and Prejudice*[1] for the first or the thirty-first time, you can still plumb the depths of the novel's moral insights. Replete with timeless psychological portraits of character, *Pride and Prejudice* features countless narrative reflections—both lighthearted and scathing—on relationships and human nature.

TAPPING THE MORAL IMAGINATION

I taught *Pride and Prejudice* for the first time as a sheer act of will. My introduction to Jane Austen at school was less than tepid. We were assigned to read *Pride and Prejudice* and be prepared for a five-question quiz on the reading. After the quiz, my English teacher stood firmly at the lectern and delivered a forty-minute presentation on the Romantic period and Austen's life. We had a brief discussion about the story on Tuesday, and by Wednesday we had moved on to our next work. I never did read beyond the first chapter of *Pride and Prejudice*. Uninspired as I was then by the dialogue I now relish, I had picked up a *Cliff Notes* summary and prayed I would pass the quiz. Years later when I found myself in front of a classroom teaching British literature to tenth graders, I experienced a rush of guilt mixed with resentment when I saw *Pride and Prejudice* on the required reading list. There were no fond memories of my first encounter with Darcy and Elizabeth. There were no powerful class discussions I could call to mind and recreate for my students.

And for every Jane Austen lover out there who was eager to assist me (you know who you are—the first time you picked up *Sense and Sensibility* or

Emma you savored every witty exchange with delight and have now committed lengthy scenes to memory), there was always a nay-sayer: one who balked that *Pride and Prejudice* is a "girls' book," or another who complained that it's stuffy, dated, and all about manners and morals. I knew I would have some hurdles to overcome.

I was determined this time around to enjoy *Pride and Prejudice* and not let my students leave tenth grade English jaded by their first brush with Austen. I set out to read the novel with an open mind and discover ways my students could do the same.

My most amusing recollection of teaching *Pride and Prejudice* is watching two fifteen-year-old girls re-enact Darcy's first proposal to Elizabeth at Hunsford Living. The student playing Darcy gave such an extraordinary performance that the rest of the class clamored to act out the remainder of the novel! In the end we found a stage adaptation, which gave rise to a wonderful spring performance of *Pride and Prejudice* for the wider school community.

This kind of enthusiasm can spill over into any classroom. One of the great appeals of *Pride and Prejudice* for young people is its uncanny relevance to their lives. First impressions, battles of pride, the power of prejudice, pervasive gossip, and tensions between the genuine and the dis-ingenuous in both friendship and romance are all quite real to them. Secondary school is full of rites of passage in which first impressions are essential. Image, style, and the "stuff" one owns—CDs, cars, clothing—can all be seen as crucial indicators of one's identity, popularity, or even success. Prejudice surfaces in any number of ways among and between cliques, ethnic groups, student leaders, and gangs. Pride is more difficult to identify and even harder to categorize. Adolescents are familiar with the healthy pride that accompanies work well done or a sense of belonging to a cultural or faith community, but they are perhaps even more familiar with the pride of the cocky young person who struts into a classroom, onto a playing field, or into a party flaunting his bravado and thriving on immature rivalries. And young people also have sensitive radar to detect the hypocritical antics and mind-numbing platitudes of their teacher-sycophants.

In short, students have met Mr. Collins in their own schools. They have befriended and been deceived by the Mr. Wickhams and sought solace in the Charlotte Lucases of the world. And even if they haven't known a Darcy or an Elizabeth, they have known plenty of individuals, including themselves, who have either misjudged or been misjudged. They watch Lydias and Marys and hope that they do not fall into either extreme. They know teachers and parents just like the Gardiners and the Bennets, and they are skillful at mocking the Lady Catherines of the world.

When teaching the novel, therefore, you can tap into students' experiences to help them draw parallels between Jane Austen's world and their own. While students may be quick to recognize similarities between the characters they read about and the people they know, they may be less adept at *understanding* these characters—that is, understanding what informs and inspires their moral agency.

FOSTERING ETHICAL REFLECTION: ELIZABETH BENNET

As a warm-up for the character analysis that follows (or as an exercise to complete midway through the novel), lead a discussion with students about the power of appearance, socio-economic background, and speech on public perception. For example, ask students to identify what detracts from a news anchor's effectiveness on television, and what makes another effective and compelling. Image consultants say that 55 percent of a first impression is based on appearance and behavior. At least ten value judgments are made—consciously or unconsciously—within the first seven seconds of meeting or viewing someone—about class, education, and even trustworthiness. Only 7 percent of the impression made is based on the actual content of what the person says (Nanfeldt 1996). While the accuracy of these claims may be debatable, they suggest something that seems intuitively true. Consider again the news anchor. Ask students if they have ever been distracted by one anchor's garish tie or another's dramatic make-up. An exercise like this can help students to see just how superficial and media-saturated we can be and set the stage for a discussion about some of the critical differences between viewing and reading.

Austen's writing certainly predates our era of 24-hour news programs, sitcoms, talk shows, and soap operas. Nevertheless, you can discuss with students how she, as a writer, helps to shape our impressions of the characters we meet. As they read, ask students to record the specific details that qualify each character's introduction: his or her demeanor, annual income, property value, type of chaise, manner of speech, and idiosyncrasies. You can get enormous mileage out of a discussion of Austen's rhetorical play with first impressions, appearances, and indicators of social class. *Pride and Prejudice* is rich with provocative first impressions; consider, for example, Darcy's infamous snub of Elizabeth at the Meryton ball early in the novel:

> She [Elizabeth] is tolerable; but not handsome enough to tempt *me*; and I am in no humour at present to give consequence to young ladies who are slighted by other men. (7)

Students will find a number of contemporary parallels to this dramatic moment, but more importantly, Darcy's attitude gives students an opportunity to draw inferences about his character. This sort of exercise will prime students for the analysis of character development in the novel by inviting them to consider the personal qualities of each character they meet just as they naturally do when introduced to someone new in real life. Having entered the world of the novel as a critical observer of character, students will be prepared to deal with the kinds of questions raised in this case study.

Looking at the novel as a whole, remind students that many rhetorical conventions help to advance the plot in Austen's *Pride and Prejudice*, among them coincidence, chance meetings, and letters. As they read, ask them to consider how these factors also help to reveal character. The bulleted questions for reflection inserted throughout the case study provide an opportunity for students to track the experiences, events, and relationships that seem to have the greatest impact on Elizabeth. All of these questions are designed to emphasize the four factors central to the schooling of desire, and in this specific case, Elizabeth Bennet's moral development.

Volume I, Chapters I–VIII

Elizabeth Bennet, the second eldest of five daughters, exemplifies the ideals of Jane Austen's world in Georgian England. Elizabeth stands outside convention in that she believes she is not dependent on marriage to find happiness or to derive her sense of self. In contrast to her four sisters and other women of her time who see marriage as a means for security and economic stability, Elizabeth's spirited independence puts her in a category of her own. Elizabeth's mother, however, has a very pragmatic agenda for her daughters' happiness. She knows that unless one of them marries Mr. Collins, the estranged cousin of Mr. Bennet and closest male heir, the family estate will be entailed to Collins upon her husband's death, leaving Mrs. Bennet and her daughters destitute.

Mr. Collins, then, quickly becomes one of the chiefly eligible suitors for the Bennet daughters, but other gentlemen candidates—Mr. Bingley, Mr. Darcy, and Mr. Wickham, for example—also make their way into the lives of the Bennet family. They come under careful scrutiny from both Jane Austen and her protagonist, Elizabeth Bennet. Regarded by her father as the brightest and most sensible of her sisters, Elizabeth is confident that she is not only a perceptive judge of character but also a good judge of men and their intentions.

At a Meryton ball, Elizabeth quickly sizes up Mr. Darcy, the visitor from Derbyshire, as a man whose pride and haughtiness are unforgivable. An aristocrat, Mr. Darcy is temporarily settled at Netherfield estate with his good friend Mr. Bingley and Bingley's sister, Caroline. After much speculation about the new residents of Netherfield, Elizabeth's dearest friend, Charlotte Lucas, defends Darcy for his aloofness at social gatherings:

> His pride does not offend *me* so much as pride often does, because there is an excuse for it. One cannot wonder that so very fine a young man, with family, fortune, everything in his favour, should think so highly of himself. If I may so express it, he has a *right* to be proud. (13)

Charlotte also observes that Elizabeth's older sister and confidante, Jane, is too "guarded" and "uniform" in her cheerfulness and manner toward Bingley. She suggests that it would be wise if Jane were to offer a little more "encouragement" (15). "Bingley likes your sister undoubtedly; but he may never do more than like her, if she does not help him on" (15). Charlotte reminds Elizabeth that Bingley "does not know Jane's disposition" as well as she does, urging Elizabeth to help Jane be more forthcoming (15).

Elizabeth holds strong convictions about love and marriage and challenges Charlotte's "design" for Jane. "Your plan is a good one . . . where nothing is in question but the desire of being well married; and if I were determined to get a rich husband, or any husband, I dare say, I should adopt it. But these are not Jane's feelings; she is not acting by design" (15). Elizabeth's assessment of her sister's situation seems entirely reasonable. Only she is perhaps too confident in her assessment of Jane's feelings: "[Jane] cannot be certain of the degree of her own regard or of its reasonableness. She has known him only a fortnight. . . . This is not quite enough to make her understand his character" (15).

The above conversation serves as a wonderful introduction to students' becoming acquainted with Elizabeth and Charlotte. We secure two very different views of Darcy and of Jane from Elizabeth and Charlotte. Encourage students to take note of Elizabeth's perceptions and to contrast them with those of other characters. Based on their brief introduction to Elizabeth and Charlotte, ask the students to consider which of the two characters they trust more at this point in the novel. The following set of questions will help to frame your reflection and discussion.

- In her conversation with Charlotte, Elizabeth reveals her settled opinions about both Darcy and Jane. Charlotte's perceptions are quite different. Compare and contrast their perceptions with each other's and with your own. What are your first impressions of Elizabeth and Charlotte?
- How do Elizabeth and Charlotte's personalities emerge in this conversation? Can you imagine each character's tone and manner of speaking? How does Austen produce this effect?
- Jane Austen, unlike Dickens and Hurston, is sparse on physical description. We never learn about eye color, physique, or sensory details. How do you see this as strengthening or limiting her characterization?

- Describe Elizabeth and Charlotte's friendship.
- Do you agree with Elizabeth's reservations about Charlotte's "design" for Jane? What is the basis for Elizabeth's assessment of Jane's feelings? What are the advantages and disadvantages of knowing our friends and siblings so well that we believe we can answer for them on certain topics?

Volume I, Chapters IX–XI

Elizabeth persists in her negative opinion of Darcy. At the next ball, when Darcy fixes his gaze on Elizabeth, she draws her own preliminary conclusions.

> She hardly knew how to suppose that she could be the object of admiration to so great a man; and yet that he should look at her because he disliked her was still more strange. She could only imagine however, at last, that she drew his notice because there was something about her more wrong and reprehensible, according to his ideas of right, than any other person present. . . . She liked him too little to care for his approbation. (38)

Elizabeth presumes to understand Darcy's intentions when he invites her to dance a reel, and replies to his invitation sarcastically: "You wanted me, I know, to say 'Yes' that you might have the pleasure of despising my taste; but I always delight in overthrowing those kinds of schemes, and cheating a person of their premeditated contempt" (38). Convinced that she understands Darcy's character, Elizabeth continues to engage him sardonically.

> I hope I never ridicule what is wise or good [Elizabeth remarks]. Follies and nonsense, whims and inconsistencies *do* divert me. . . . But these, I suppose, are precisely what you are without.
>
> [I]t has been the study of my life to avoid those weaknesses which often expose a strong understanding to ridicule [Darcy replies].
>
> Such as vanity and pride.
>
> Yes, vanity is a weakness, indeed. But pride—where there is a real superiority of mind, pride will always be under good regulation.
>
> Elizabeth turned away to hide a smile. . . .
>
> I am perfectly convinced . . . that Mr. Darcy has no defect. He owns it himself without disguise. . . .
>
> I have made no such pretension. I have faults enough, but they are not, I hope, of understanding. . . . My feelings are not puffed about with every

attempt to move them. My temper would perhaps be called resentful. — My good opinion once lost is lost for ever.

That is a failing indeed . . .

There is, I believe, in every disposition a tendency to some particular evil, a natural defect, which not even the best education can overcome.

And *your* defect is a propensity to hate everybody.

And yours . . . is *wilfully to misunderstand them.* (43)

The dialogue between Elizabeth and Darcy throughout the novel offers rich data for character analysis. Ask students to characterize this conversation: Is it merely flirtatious banter or is something else going on here? The following set of questions draws students' attention to the text and asks them to evaluate both the content and manner with which Elizabeth and Darcy address each other. They help students to see that Elizabeth is far from open to discovering anything new about Darcy. Her perceptions are firmly fixed; she is prejudiced and doesn't realize it.

- On what grounds does Elizabeth draw her conclusions about Darcy? Does her assessment of Darcy seem accurate thus far? Why or why not?
- Discuss the implications of Darcy's final accusation. Were you shocked by Darcy's assessment, or do you agree with him?
- Darcy raises a provocative observation in this exchange with Elizabeth: "There is, I believe, in every disposition a tendency to some particular evil, a natural defect, which not even the best education can overcome." Is this a pessimistic or realistic statement? Is this something a *proud* person would think?

Volume I, Chapters XII–XVIII

Elizabeth is undaunted; she believes her understanding and judgment to be quite sophisticated. Upon meeting Mr. Wickham, she quickly formulates an opinion of this new member of the militia. Confident in her assessment of Mr. Wickham's character, Elizabeth regards him "as far beyond" all of the other officers "in person, countenance, air, and walk" (57). Upon further acquaintance, Elizabeth offers her opinion of Darcy to Mr. Wickham. "Every body is disgusted with his pride. You will not find him more favourably spoken of by any one" (59). Mr. Wickham reveals the history of his relationship with Darcy. "His behaviour toward myself has been scandalous; but I verily believe I could forgive him anything and everything rather than his disappointing the hopes and disgracing the memory of his father" (59). Elizabeth listens with great sympathy to Wickham "whose very countenance may vouch for your being amiable" (61). In short, what Wickham reveals is that Darcy shortchanged him on the inheritance that Darcy's late father had promised Wickham on his deathbed. There is no doubt in Elizabeth's mind that Wickham's story is true, as she later exclaims to Jane, "there was truth in his looks" (65).

Elizabeth's confidence in her own judgment is further revealed at the Bingley Ball when she tells Darcy that she "never allows herself to be blinded by prejudice." Here she attempts to "illustrate [Darcy's] character" explaining that "she hears such puzzling accounts." Darcy asks that she "not sketch my character" under the circumstances. When Caroline Bingley tries to defend Darcy from the accusations of Wickham, Elizabeth hastily dismisses her for her "own willful ignorance of Darcy."

The following set of questions helps students to see the potential danger of Elizabeth's tendency to project lack of knowledge or "willful misunderstanding" onto others while failing to recognize it in herself, and they prepare them to see the significance of the forthcoming morally pivotal point.

- What is the basis for Elizabeth's judgment of Wickham's character? Why is she inclined to accept Wickham's account of Darcy so uncritically? Does she have good reason for dismissing Caroline's defense of Darcy?
- How might Elizabeth's ignorance of Darcy's character influence others?
- What does all of the storytelling and banter about other people's reputations remind you of? Does this have modern-day parallels?

Volume I, Chapters XIX–XXIII: first morally pivotal point

The first morally pivotal point or moment of reassessment for Elizabeth is dramatically illustrated by her response to Charlotte's acceptance of Mr. Collins' marriage proposal. For the first time, Elizabeth realizes that she can be mistaken, even about a dear friend she regards as sensible. Mr. Collins first proposes to his cousin, Elizabeth, in hopes of healing the family breach and securing the Longbourn estate for the Bennet family. Elizabeth is amused by Collins' absurd and pompous overtures. She declines his proposal despite his determined attempt to win her. "You could not make *me* happy, and I am convinced I am the last woman in the world who would make *you* so" (82). From this point on, Elizabeth is attentive to the importance of her own commitment and convictions—to avoid a compromise in marriage, to assess the character of men carefully, and to seek happiness and mutual respect and esteem, or not to marry at all. And she projects a similar commitment onto Charlotte as well.

Shortly after his proposal to Elizabeth, however, Collins manages to secure the hand of Charlotte Lucas. Elizabeth is stunned by the news of Charlotte's engagement. That Mr. Collins could think himself in love with

Charlotte did not surprise Elizabeth, "but that Charlotte could encourage him, seemed almost as far from possibility as that she [Elizabeth] could encourage him herself" (96). Charlotte, like Elizabeth, sees that Mr. Collins is "neither sensible nor agreeable" (93). Nevertheless, "Without thinking highly either of men or of matrimony," in her mind, "[marriage] was the only honourable provision for well-educated young women of small fortune" (94). Thus Charlotte "felt all the good luck of it." Yet, being a good friend of Elizabeth, she knew Elizabeth would "wonder, and probably would blame her" (94). Charlotte accepts Collins purely out of the need for financial security. Charlotte is a realist, but Elizabeth is indignant at her action.

Charlotte is the first to challenge Elizabeth's righteousness: "Do you think it incredible that Mr. Collins should be able to procure any woman's good opinion because he was not so happy as to succeed with you?" (96). She attempts to help Elizabeth understand that she is "not romantic"; her primary interest is to secure "a comfortable home." In terms of prospects for happiness, she tells Elizabeth frankly, "I am convinced that my chance of happiness with him is as fair as most people can boast upon entering the marriage state" (96).

This moment is pivotal for Elizabeth because, for the first time, someone she respects and admires calls her better judgment into question. Troubled by her friend's decision, Elizabeth is not quickly "reconciled to the idea of so unsuitable a match" (96). It is as much Elizabeth's revulsion toward Mr. Collins as Charlotte's conventional and short-sighted vision of marriage that confirms Elizabeth's desire for a higher order love. Seeing a friend whom she has judged to be intelligent and refined settle for less than happiness in marriage causes her to reassess her own views. She is not only motivated to consider her own options for happiness in marriage more carefully, but also to revise her estimation of Charlotte.

> She had always felt that Charlotte's opinion of matrimony was not exactly like her own, but she could not have supposed it possible that when called into action, *she would have sacrificed every better feeling to worldly advantage. Charlotte the wife of Mr. Collins, was a most humiliating picture!*—And to the pang of a friend disgracing herself and sunk in her esteem, was added the distressing conviction that it was impossible for that friend to be tolerably happy in the lot she had chosen. (96–97, emphasis added)

As a consequence,

> Elizabeth felt persuaded that no real confidence could ever subsist between them again. Her disappointment in Charlotte made her turn

with fonder regard to her sister, of whose rectitude and delicacy she was sure her opinion could never be shaken. (98)

- What does Elizabeth's response to Collins reveal about her character?
- Reread Elizabeth's response to Charlotte. Why is she so shocked? What affects Elizabeth more: the fact that Charlotte agreed to marry Collins or that she was mistaken about Charlotte's aspirations? Explain.
- Compare and contrast Charlotte and Elizabeth's attitudes toward marriage. Does Charlotte's decision to marry for "a comfortable home" compromise her beliefs about marriage and happiness? Why or why not?

1　Discuss what Elizabeth might now be feeling about herself as a judge of character. Does she reassess her ability?
2　How would you describe Elizabeth's self-knowledge at this point in the narrative?
3　How, potentially, could this moment reshape Elizabeth and Charlotte's friendship?

Volume II, Chapters I–IX

Elizabeth is prompted from this point on to attend carefully to Charlotte's happiness as her marriage with Mr. Collins unfolds. Elizabeth does not abandon faith in Charlotte altogether; she graciously accepts an invitation to visit her at Hunsford living, her new home. The visit provides Elizabeth with more data for reflection. While at first Elizabeth "looked with wonder at her friend that she could have so cheerful an air with such a companion [Mr. Collins]," she observes the adroitness with which Charlotte handles Mr. Collins' ostentatious manner: "When Mr. Collins said anything of which his wife might reasonably be ashamed, . . . Charlotte wisely did not hear" (120). When Mr. Collins expresses his pleasure at working in the garden, Elizabeth notes with admiration "the command of countenance with which Charlotte talked of the healthfulness of the exercise," understanding it to be a clever means by which Charlotte procured time for herself alone in the house (120). As for the house itself, "everything was fitted up and arranged with a neatness and consistency of which Elizabeth gave Charlotte all the credit" (121). She comes to see that Charlotte is not doomed to misery, but managing quite well.

> Elizabeth in the solitude of her chamber had to meditate upon Charlotte's degree of contentment, to understand her address in guiding, and composure in bearing with her husband, and to acknowledge that it was all done very well. (122)

Elizabeth's harsh judgment of Charlotte is soon ameliorated, even giving way to admiration at her realistic and sagacious way of mitigating the annoyances that could accompany living with Mr. Collins. When Elizabeth wonders why "the room in which the ladies sat was backwards," and why Charlotte did not prefer the larger dining parlor for common use, she learns that Charlotte "had an excellent reason for what she did." It provided a natural way to keep some distance from her husband, "for Mr. Collins would undoubtedly have been much less in his own apartment, had they sat in one equally lively." Elizabeth "gave Charlotte credit for the arrangement" (129).

Elizabeth's confidence in Charlotte is renewed, although she remains firm in her desire to avoid a similar marriage for financial convenience. While her judgment of Charlotte has been mildly revised, Elizabeth does not relinquish her stubbornness on at least one point. She will not heed her friend's suggestion that Darcy is interested in her. Charlotte is the first to suggest, after Darcy visits Elizabeth at Hunsford, that he "must be in love" with her friend, explaining that "he would never have called on us in this familiar way" (138). Later, she again suggests that Darcy's overtures are genuine, "but Elizabeth always laughed at the idea; and Mrs. Collins did not think it right to press the subject" (139).

While Elizabeth demonstrates a new determination to observe and understand her friend Charlotte, she is still unchanged in many ways. The following questions help to draw into focus the more subtle changes gradually being brought about in Elizabeth.

- Evaluate Elizabeth's reflections about Charlotte after visiting her at Hunsford. In what ways has Elizabeth changed? In what ways is she unchanged?
- Has Elizabeth made concessions that she was unable to make earlier? How so?

Volume II, Chapters X–XI

Soon enough, however, Elizabeth's judgment is proven wrong a second time. Charlotte has been accurate in her assessment of Darcy's attention and interest. Elizabeth has not. Mr. Darcy visits Elizabeth at Hunsford and professes his love to her. "In vain have I struggled. It will not do. My feelings will not be repressed. You must allow me to tell you how ardently I admire and love you" (145). Elizabeth is astonished.

Satisfied with her own assessment of Darcy's character and intentions thus far, Elizabeth receives his proposal with indignation. When he reveals his apprehension and anxiety about making his feelings known—reservations that stem from the "inferiority" of Elizabeth's class and connections— Elizabeth is bitterly angered and hurt. She replies,

> It is natural that obligation should be felt, and if I could *feel* gratitude, I would now thank you. But I cannot—I have never desired your good opinion, and you have certainly bestowed it most unwillingly. . . . I might as well inquire . . . why with so evident a design of offending and insulting me you chose to tell me that you liked me against your will, against your reason, and even against your character? (145–146)

She lashes back at Darcy telling him that she has "every reason in the world to think ill" of him. She blames him for separating Jane and Bingley—ruining her sister's happiness. Then she levels her severest criticism. She accuses Darcy of having "reduced [Mr. Wickham] to his present state of poverty . . . [by withholding] the advantages . . . designed for him . . . [and having] deprived [him of] the best years of his life" (147).

Darcy attempts to point to Elizabeth's pride: "These offences might have been overlooked, had not your pride been hurt by my honest confession of the scruples that had long prevented my forming any serious design" (147). Elizabeth, insulted by Darcy's references to her "relations whose condition in life is so decidedly beneath my own," retains her contempt for Darcy.

> From the very beginning, from the first moment, I may almost say, of my acquaintance with you, your manners impressing me with the fullest belief of your arrogance, your conceit and your selfish disdain of the feelings of others, were such as to form that ground-work of disapprobation on which succeeding events have built so immoveable a dislike; and I had not known you a month before I felt that you were the last man in the world whom I could ever be prevailed on to marry. (148)

Despite the bitter insults inveighed against him, Darcy graciously takes his leave, and Elizabeth withdraws into thought.

> The tumult of her mind was now painfully great. She knew not how to support herself, and from actual weakness sat down and cried for half an hour. Her astonishment, as she reflected on what had passed, was increased by every review of it. . . . [I]t was gratifying to have inspired unconsciously so strong an affection. But his pride, his abominable pride. (148–149)

Elizabeth has gathered all of the evidence against Darcy. She cannot fathom happiness with someone who is so ill-deserving of her respect and esteem. She remains focused on her pristine vision of marriage. Charlotte's concession in marrying Collins and Darcy's insulting proposal heighten her conviction that she must carefully assess her prospects for marriage. She believes thus far that she has exercised sound judgment in rejecting both offers.

The following questions help students to see that what really causes Elizabeth to pivot is the insight that she has been seriously mistaken on two counts: about Charlotte's aspirations for happiness and Darcy's intentions. Again, Elizabeth is far from transformed; however, she does realize that her perceptions are fallible. Students will identify with Elizabeth's humiliation and shock at Darcy's proposal. Ask them to pay attention to the ways it affects Elizabeth and the choices and commitments she makes as a result.

- Darcy and Elizabeth level strong words at one another. Analyze their exchange. Is Elizabeth's anger justifiable? Why or why not?
- Describe the motivations behind Darcy's proposal, as you've come to understand them thus far. Describe the motivations behind Elizabeth's harsh response.
- What additional insights do we gain into the characters of Elizabeth and Darcy from this falling out? How does their manner and use of language in conversation with each other reveal character?
- What might Elizabeth be feeling about the mounting evidence against her judgment?
- What evidence might there be to suggest that Elizabeth is beginning to learn about herself? About the verity of her beliefs? Is she regressing or making moral progress? Explain.
- What do you suspect will happen next?

Volume II, Chapters XII–XVIII: second morally pivotal point

Up until this point Elizabeth's judgment of Darcy has been fixed. However, Elizabeth changes her perspective when Darcy discloses the truth—a detailed response to her accusations—in a lengthy letter he writes after their last encounter.

Darcy meets Elizabeth the day after his proposal: "I have been walking in the grove for some time in the hope of meeting you. Will you do me the honour of reading this letter?" Elizabeth turns to the letter with curiosity after having reflected at length over the previous day's proposal. Darcy explains that he writes "without any intention of paining you"; he asks her only to read it out of "justice." Darcy gives his reasons for separating Bingley and Jane. Among other things, he says, he watched Jane to see if he could detect her feelings for Bingley. He found, however, that "[h]er look and manners were open and cheerful and engaging as ever, but without any symptom of peculiar regard" (151).

But it was not only Jane's lack of encouragement and "want of connection" that moved him to separate Bingley from Jane. It was "the total want of propriety" of her mother, her three younger sisters, and even her father. Darcy concludes by asking for pardon: "It pains me to offend you," and, "If I have wounded your sister's feelings it was unknowingly done" (152–153).

Referring to "the more weighty accusation" that he has been the source of ruin to Mr. Wickham, Darcy responds by offering a complete account of their relationship and Mr. Wickham's particular history. Elizabeth learns about the failed commitments of Mr. Wickham, whom she was convinced was so forthright and "amiable." Darcy's father, Wickham's godfather, arranged for him to pursue a profession in the church. While Wickham was careful to guard his "vicious propensities" and "want of principles" from Darcy's father, they did not escape young Darcy's notice. After Mr. Darcy died, Wickham asked Darcy if instead of the church living and one thousand pound legacy, he could receive three thousand pounds and the opportunity to study law. Darcy agreed to the offer but soon learned that Wickham's intent to study law was "a mere pretense, and being now free from all restraint, his life was a life of idleness and dissipation" (154). For three years Darcy did not hear from Wickham until he wrote in dire need explaining that he found law "unprofitable study" and that he would like to be ordained. Wickham's duplicity was revealed when, in another attempt to secure a generous income, he falsely professed his love to Darcy's fifteen-year-old sister, Georgiana, and took her away to elope with him. Darcy was able to intervene in a timely fashion and stop the marriage.

The letter transfixes Elizabeth. "Her feelings as she read were scarcely to be defined" (156). She was so convinced of her own judgment that only "[w]ith amazement did she first understand that he believed any apology to be in his power; . . . that he could have no explanation to give, which a just sense of shame would not conceal" (156). Elizabeth acknowledges her biased judgment for the first time. She read the letter "[w]ith a strong sense of prejudice against every thing he might say" (156). Upon first reading his account of separating Bingley from Jane, Elizabeth still maintains that "[i]t was all pride and insolence."

And as she reads Darcy's compelling account of Mr. Wickham, "[a]stonishment, apprehension, and even horror, oppressed her. She wished to discredit it entirely." Nevertheless, she rereads the letter carefully, examining "the meaning of every sentence." She compares Wickham's accounts with Darcy's: "it was impossible not to feel that there was gross duplicity on one side or the other" (157). Thinking of Wickham she recalls that "his countenance, voice, and manner, had established him at once in the possession of every virtue" (157). As she tries to recall some instance of integrity to redeem him from the newly disclosed picture of his character, she could not: "She could see him instantly before her in every charm of air and address; but she could remember no more substantial good than the general approbation of the neighbourhood and the regard which his social powers had regained him in the mess" (158).

Remembering her conversations with Mr. Wickham, she is *"now* struck with the impropriety of such communications to a stranger, and wondered it had escaped her before" (158). She recalls that Wickham "had no scruples in sinking Mr. Darcy's character. . . . How differently did everything appear now in which he was concerned!" (158). Every testimony about Darcy's character, in contrast, was positive—that he was "esteemed and valued" by those who knew him well and that there was nothing "unprincipled or unjust" about him, nothing "immoral or irreligious" despite his aloof and proud manner (159).

Elizabeth sees the error of her judgment.

> How despicably have I acted! . . . I, who have prided myself on my discernment!—I, who have valued myself on my abilities! who have often disdained the generous candour of my sister, and gratified my vanity in useless or blameable distrust.—*How humiliating is this discovery!—Yet, how just a humiliation!*—Had I been in love, I could not have been more wretchedly blind. But vanity, not love, has been my folly. Pleased with the preference of one, and offended by the neglect of the other, on the very beginning of our acquaintance, *I have courted prepossession and ignorance, and driven reason away, where either were concerned. Till this moment I never knew myself.* (159, emphasis added)

Upon careful reading and rereading of Darcy's letter, Elizabeth's understanding is again refined; she realizes that her judgment has been terribly mistaken. Elizabeth comes to see that it is not simply a single-minded pursuit of one's own happiness that matters, but also openness, attentiveness to the real truth about persons beyond their external trappings. Elizabeth realizes that she has not been as accurate or as just a judge as she regarded herself to be. Moreover, as a consequence of learning the truth about Darcy, she acquires more penetrating insight into her self, her family and Mr. Wickham. Finally, she has acquired a heightened sensitivity to attend to the truth of the matter.

Elizabeth's reflections remind her of Charlotte's observation about the danger of Jane's uniform cheerfulness, and her sage advice that Jane show just a little more "encouragement" to Bingley—advice that Elizabeth dismissed at the time. She could not "deny the justice of his [Darcy's] description of Jane" in the letter. Elizabeth also sees the inappropriateness of her family's behavior. "The justice of the charge [against her family] . . . could not have made a stronger impression on his mind than on hers" (160). She is drained upon consideration of it all.

> After wandering along the lane for two hours, giving way to every variety of thought, reconsidering events, determining probabilities, and

reconciling herself as well as she could, to a change so sudden and so important, fatigue, and a recollection of her long absence, made her at length return home. (160)

The letter—her first confrontation with the truth about her family's impropriety, about her own erroneous judgment, and about Darcy—duly humbles Elizabeth. This self-knowledge and clarification of the facts enable her to attend more carefully to the substance of people's characters—who they are as opposed to what they appear to be. Elizabeth now sees more keenly the danger in Lydia and Kitty's entertaining members of the militia, especially because their immaturity and vanity cloud better judgment. When Lydia is invited to Brighton where the militia will be stationed for the summer, Elizabeth presses her father to reconsider allowing Lydia to go. She is keenly aware of the danger her sister's behavior can induce. "If you were aware," she tells her father, of the "unguarded and imprudent manner . . . our respectability in the world, must be affected . . . [Lydia's] character will be fixed [as a] most determined flirt." As Elizabeth begins to see, however, Mr. Bennet is only interested in "peace at Longbourn" (176).

The following questions help students to see the limitations of Elizabeth's perceptions to date: she has been influenced by her father's praise of her and by her own willful prejudices toward others. Upon reflection, Elizabeth comes to see her own blindness as well as her father's. Challenge students to explore the factors—relationships, her own reflections, what she begins to take pleasure in and what she finds painful, and the courage she has to face the truth—that are collectively at work prompting a "turn" or change of perspective. Students should be able to discuss what that change of perspective is and the choices Elizabeth makes as a result.

- Up until this point in the novel, Elizabeth has seemed self-possessed and confident in her perceptions. What does she finally realize about herself? Trace evidence of her change in her forthcoming choices and actions.
- Darcy's letter gives rise to a host of realizations for Elizabeth. Would Elizabeth have been so profoundly affected had Darcy related such a persuasive account in a conversation? Why or why not? What advantage is it to Elizabeth to receive the letter? What advantage is it to Darcy to write it?
- Some people hear about the truth and still retain their biases, which Elizabeth does for quite some time. How does each realization inform Elizabeth's attitudes, choices, and actions?
- Why is Elizabeth's insight into her father's negligence particularly poignant? What does she mean by, "Till this moment I never knew myself" (159)?

- Based on examples from the novel, what virtues do you think are necessary to the exercise of sound judgment? What keeps people from developing good judgment?
- What is humility? How is humility important for understanding other people, events, and oneself?
- How is it that Elizabeth's admission of her erroneous judgment with regard to Darcy enables her to judge other matters—like her father's character—more accurately? Note how her judgment improves throughout the rest of the novel.

Volume II, Chapter XIX–Volume III, Chapter XIII

After reflecting on Darcy's letter, Elizabeth also judges her parents' marriage with a newfound clarity. She recognizes that for her father, "respect, esteem, and confidence [toward Mrs. Bennet] had vanished forever; and all his views of domestic happiness were overthrown." Up until this point Elizabeth

> had never been blind to the impropriety of her father's behaviour as a husband. She had always seen it with pain; but respecting his abilities, and grateful for his affectionate treatment of herself, she endeavoured to forget what she could not overlook, and to banish from her thoughts that continual breach of conjugal obligation and decorum which, in exposing his wife to the contempt of her own children, was so highly reprehensible. But *she had never felt so strongly as now*, the disadvantages which must attend the children of so unsuitable a marriage, nor ever been *so fully aware of the evils arising from so ill-judged a direction of talents*; talents which rightly used, might at least have preserved the respectability of his daughters, even if incapable of enlarging the mind of his wife. (180–181, emphasis added)

Elizabeth sees Wickham in a new light and upon meeting him again, she is more guarded but truthful: "Mr. Darcy improves on acquaintance," she tells him, and clarifies that "from *knowing* him better, his disposition was better understood" (179; emphasis added). Elizabeth's picture of Mr. Darcy is rounded out by testimony from credible sources. When her aunt and uncle Gardiner take her to visit Pemberley (with assurances that the master of the estate, Mr. Darcy himself, is away), Elizabeth receives a thorough account of Darcy's character from the housekeeper, Mrs. Reynolds. She tells them that she has

> never had a cross word from him in my life, and I have known him ever since he was four years old. . . . He is the best landlord, and the best master. . . . There is not one of his tenants or servants but what will give him a good name. (188)

Elizabeth also learns from Mrs. Reynolds that Darcy is an exceptionally good brother to his younger sister Georgiana. Elizabeth muses, "What praise is more valuable than the praise of an intelligent servant? As a brother, a landlord, a master, she considered how many people's happiness were in his guardianship!" (189). As she revises her judgment of Darcy's character, he arrives at Pemberley unexpectedly and meets Elizabeth and the Gardiners. Elizabeth is embarrassed and ashamed at being found at his home. Nevertheless, upon introducing him to her aunt and uncle,

> she could hardly suppress a smile at his being now seeking the acquaintance of some of those very people, against whom his pride had revolted, in his offer to herself. . . . [Nevertheless] [i]t was consoling that he should know she had some relations for whom there was no need to blush. She listened most attentively to all that passed between them, and gloried in every expression, every sentence of her uncle [a man of trade], which marked his intelligence, his taste or his good manners. (193)

Elizabeth is so taken by Darcy's cordiality and genuine interest in her and her family that she cannot stop thinking about her visit to Pemberley, "and wonder, of Mr. Darcy's civility, and above all, of his wishing her to be acquainted with his sister" (196). Elizabeth is keenly aware of how her feelings and understanding of Darcy have undergone correction and change. She reflects on this self-consciously.

> But above all, above respect and esteem, there was a motive within her of goodwill which could not be overlooked. It was gratitude.— Gratitude not merely for having once loved her, but for loving her still well enough to forgive all the petulance and acrimony of her manner in rejecting him, and the unjust accusations accompanying her rejection. . . . Such a change in a man of so much pride, excited not only astonishment but gratitude. (201)

Darcy brings his sister and Bingley to meet Elizabeth at the Gardiners' modest home in Lambton. On his second visit, he finds Elizabeth distressed by news she has received in a letter from Jane. She explains that her younger sister Lydia has fled Brighton with Mr. Wickham, expecting to elope with him in Scotland. Elizabeth exclaims, "She has no money, no connections, nothing that can tempt him to—she is lost for ever" (209). In the end, however, she is deeply humiliated that she has disclosed such a family scandal to Darcy.

> Her power was sinking; every thing *must* sink under such a proof of family weakness, such an assurance of the deepest disgrace. . . . Never had she so honestly felt that she could have loved him, as now, when all love must be vain. (210)

This scene provides a rich context for examining Elizabeth's vulnerability. Up until this point in the novel, she has been self-possessed, above her sisters and her peers in intelligence, judgment, maturity. At the moment she discloses this deep family embarrassment to Darcy she is so weak, she nearly faints. Ask students to reflect on whether or not they see Elizabeth becoming weaker or stronger. Earlier we witnessed her upset at realizing what an egregious misjudgment she had made of Darcy. Now she feels guilty and helpless at the thought of her foolish younger sister falling prey to Mr. Wickham.

- Why is Elizabeth so upset at this point in the novel?
- How does Elizabeth's vulnerability help or hinder her relationship with Darcy? Her self-knowledge? Her growth? Discuss.

The humiliation of the Wickham–Lydia scandal also yields greater understanding. Elizabeth now sees the frivolity of Lydia's character and the fault of her upbringing.

> [S]he has never been taught to think on serious subjects; and for the last half year, nay for a twelvemonth, she has been given up to nothing but amusement and vanity. She has been allowed to dispose of her time in the most idle and frivolous manner, and to adopt any opinions that came in her way. Since the ——shire were first quartered in Meryton, nothing but love, flirtation, and officers, have been in her head. . . . And we all know that Wickham has every charm of person and address that can captivate a woman. (214–215)

Mr. Bennet rushes to London to search for the young couple but is unsuccessful. Elizabeth learns from her uncle Gardiner that the couple have been found and that he will see to their marriage if Mr. Bennet approves the financial terms of the agreement and grants him permission to act in his name. It is not until much later that Elizabeth learns it is Darcy who searches out and finds the couple, pays off Wickham's debts, and insists that they marry. He wished it to remain a secret but Mrs. Gardiner eventually reveals the whole truth of his dealings to Elizabeth. She is shocked and moved to profound gratitude.

Elizabeth's desires undergo a secondary schooling during her visit to Pemberley. She not only learns more about Darcy, but she also finds herself taken with the grandeur and beauty of his estate: "at that moment she felt to be mistress of Pemberley might be something!" (185). Give students the opportunity to discuss Elizabeth's "mixed motivation," and ask them to evaluate the sincerity of her newfound interest in Darcy. The following questions help the students to explore the various factors that continue to school Elizabeth's desire.

- Why is Elizabeth's conversation with Mrs. Reynolds and Darcy's meeting with the Gardiners so important? In what ways do these encounters provide Elizabeth with more reliable data for reflection than her previous sources?
- What sources do people tend to rely on when assessing a person's character? Why? In what sources does Elizabeth now choose to put more trust? Is it important or even just to assess someone's character? Why or why not?
- Elizabeth reflects on Darcy's responsibility for the first time, "As a brother, a landlord, a master, she considered how many people's happiness were in his guardianship!" How might this realization give us more insight into what Elizabeth means when she thinks to herself, *"to be mistress of Pemberley might be something!"*?
- Why does Elizabeth feel gratitude toward Darcy? Note the frequency of references to gratitude from this point forward in the novel. What is the significance of gratitude to Elizabeth's moral development? How does it affect her ability to love or the quality of her love?
- Has Darcy changed at all?
- Why does Elizabeth believe that "all love must be vain" now?

Volume III, Chapter XIV: challenge point

Elizabeth's self-knowledge and understanding of Darcy have increased significantly. Her desire to seek what is best for her own happiness has been refined to embrace a fuller appreciation of the truth and reality. Charlotte's marriage provides an important reality check for Elizabeth, and Darcy's letter, combined with her visit to Pemberley, bring her face to face with the truth. Elizabeth is disposed now to face new challenges and to base her decisions not solely on opinion or appearances, but on knowledge and credible sources of information. Her desires have been aligned with her corrected judgment. In facing her own bias and prejudice, she has acquired the capacity to discern more carefully what and who will make her truly happy.

Elizabeth is delighted to see Bingley renew his attention to her sister Jane and ask for her hand in marriage. She realizes that Darcy has encouraged him to reconsider the attachment after having previously advised him against the match. In the meantime, Darcy's aunt, the august Lady Catherine de Bourgh and mistress of Rosings estate, pays Elizabeth a visit. Elizabeth's refined sense of judgment and mature understanding come into play in her conversation with Lady Catherine. She will not be coerced or daunted by reputation and class, despite the humiliation to which Lady Catherine subjects her.

As she walks with Lady Catherine, Elizabeth reflects again on her misjudgment of Darcy, "How could I ever think her like her nephew?" (269). Lady Catherine gets right to the point:

> [Y]ou ought to know, that I am not to be trifled with. But however insincere *you* may choose to be, you shall not find *me* so. My character has ever been celebrated for its sincerity and frankness. . . . A report of a most alarming nature reached me two days ago. I was told that not only your sister was on the point of being most advantageously married, but that *you*, Miss Elizabeth Bennet, would, in all likelihood, be soon afterwards united to my nephew, . . . Mr. Darcy. Though I *know* it must be a scandalous falsehood, though I would not injure him so much as to suppose the truth of it possible, I instantly resolved on setting off for this place that I might make my sentiments known to you. (270)

Elizabeth is nonplussed by Lady Catherine's domineering manner. She responds with her characteristic sardonic wit:

> If you believed it impossible to be true . . . I wonder you took the trouble of coming so far. What could your ladyship propose by it?

> At once to insist upon having such a report universally contradicted. . . . And can you . . . declare that there is no *foundation* for it?

> I do not pretend to possess equal frankness with your ladyship. *You* may ask questions, which *I* shall not choose to answer.

> This is not to be borne. Miss Bennet, I insist on being satisfied. Has he, my nephew, made you an offer of marriage?

> Your ladyship has declared it to be impossible.

> It ought to be so. . . . But *your* arts and allurements may, in a moment of infatuation, have made him forget what he owes himself and to all his family. You may have drawn him in.

> If I have, I shall be the last person to confess it. . . .

> I am almost the nearest relation he has in the world, and am entitled to know all his dearest concerns.

> But you are not entitled to know *mine*; nor will such behaviour as this ever induce me to be explicit.

Lady Catherine goes on to argue that this match is impermissible because Darcy has been engaged to her daughter—an arrangement she and his mother made when the two were in their cradles. . . . [A]nd now, at the moment when the wishes of both sisters would be accomplished, in their marriage, to be prevented by a young woman of inferior birth, of no importance in the world, and wholly unallied to the family! (270–271)

Elizabeth responds coolly; Lady Catherine becomes increasingly emotional.

If Mr. Darcy is neither by honour nor inclination confined to his cousin, why is he not to make another choice? And if I am that choice, why may not I accept him?

Because honour, decorum, prudence, nay, interest, forbid it. . . . You will be censured, slighted, and despised by everyone connected with him. Your alliance will be a disgrace; your name will never even be mentioned by any of us.

These are heavy misfortunes. . . . But the wife of Mr. Darcy must have such extraordinary sources of happiness necessarily attached to her situation that she could, upon the whole, have no cause to repine.

Obstinate, headstrong girl! I am ashamed of you! . . . I have not been used to submit to any person's whims. I have not been in the habit of brooking disappointment.

That will make your ladyship's situation more pitiable; but it will have no effect on *me*. (271–272)

Austen is a master of dialogue and wit. This exchange provides students with a wonderful opportunity to examine how Austen creates humor. Invite students to perform this encounter between Lady Catherine and Elizabeth before discussing what it reveals about Elizabeth's growth.

- Elizabeth has always possessed a confident spiritedness. How is her boldness different now? What evidence is there of a change?
- In what ways are Elizabeth and Lady Catherine alike? In what ways do they differ?
- Compare and contrast Darcy's family and Elizabeth's family.
- How are Mrs. Bennet and Lady Catherine alike?

Volume III, Chapters XIV–XV

Elizabeth's happiness and sense of self are independent of Lady Catherine's opinion of her. She has a newfound sense of assertiveness. Nevertheless, Lady Catherine persists.

If you were sensible of your own good, you would not wish to quit the sphere, in which you have been brought up.

In marrying your nephew, I should not consider myself as quitting that sphere. He is a gentleman; I am a gentleman's daughter; so far we are equal. (272)

Lady Catherine objects again to Elizabeth's mother and to her aunt and uncle's low connections. Elizabeth responds confidently, "if your nephew does not object to them, they can be nothing to *you*." (272)

Elizabeth finally concedes that she is not, in fact, engaged to Darcy. Nevertheless, when Lady Catherine asks her to promise that she will not "enter into such an engagement," Elizabeth says, "I will make no promise of the kind." Lady Catherine is once again "shocked and astonished" and claims she will not leave until she secures the requisite promise from Elizabeth. Here Elizabeth makes a definitive choice. She not only rejects Lady Catherine's command but also accepts the potential censure that Lady Catherine insists will most assuredly fall upon her.

And I certainly *never* shall give it [her promise]. I am not to be intimidated into anything so wholly unreasonable. . . . You have widely mistaken my character if you think I can be worked on by such persuasions as these. (273)

Lady Catherine raises the scandal of Lydia and Wickham, and then protests, "Are the shades of Pemberley to be thus polluted?" Elizabeth responds curtly.

You can *now* have nothing further to say. . . .You have insulted me in every possible method. . . .

You are then resolved to have him?

Elizabeth makes her decision clear.

I have said no such thing. I am only resolved to act in that manner which will, in my own opinion, constitute my happiness without reference to *you*, or to any person so wholly unconnected with me.

. . . You are determined to ruin him in the opinion of all his friends, and make him the contempt of the world.

. . . And with regard to the resentment of his family, or the indignation of the world, if the former *were* excited by his marrying me, it would not give me one moment's concern—and the world in general would have too much sense to join in the scorn. (273–274)

Elizabeth reflects upon her encounter with Lady Catherine, assuming the conversation will be recounted to Darcy. She has taken a risk, boldly pursuing her now-refined *telos* without regard for what other people will think. She concludes decidedly, "If he is satisfied with only regretting me, when he might have obtained my affections and hand, I shall soon cease to regret him at all" (276).

- In what ways are Darcy and Elizabeth equal? In what ways are they unequal?
- Is Elizabeth more willing to take risks now more than she was before? Why or why not? What is the source of her courage?
- Cite evidence of motivation—all of the external and internal factors influencing and impelling Elizabeth to make the choices she makes.
- In what ways has Elizabeth's conversation with Lady Catherine changed Elizabeth's attitude toward Darcy? Has it changed her attitude toward marriage in general?

Volume III, Chapters XV–XVI

Mr. Bennet, on receiving a letter from Mr. Collins cautioning him about a marriage that may not be "properly sanctioned" by Lady Catherine, is both amused and surprised. He wonders at the absurdity of Elizabeth and Darcy being engaged, and Elizabeth suffers at his reaction:

Elizabeth had never been more at a loss to make her feelings appear what they were not. It was necessary to laugh when she would rather have cried. Her father had most cruelly mortified her by what he said of Darcy's indifference, and she could do nothing but wonder at such a want of penetration, or fear that perhaps, instead of his seeing too *little*, she might have fancied too *much*. (278)

To Elizabeth's surprise the next day Darcy accompanies Bingley on his visit to see Jane. At the first opportunity to speak with Darcy alone, when the whole company goes for a walk, Elizabeth confesses her family's deepest gratitude for Darcy's help in resolving Lydia and Wickham's situation. Darcy assures her that as much as he respects her family, he thought only of her. And he adds, "If your feelings are still what they were last April, tell me so at once. *My* affections and wishes are unchanged" (280). Elizabeth struggles to help Darcy understand that her sentiments had undergone *so material a change*, since the period to which he alluded, as to make her receive with *gratitude and pleasure* his present assurances. . . .

She soon learned that they were indebted for their present good understanding to the efforts of his aunt [Lady Catherine], who *did* call on him in her return through London, and there, relate . . . the substance of her conversation with Elizabeth. . . . But, unluckily for her ladyship, its effect had been exactly contrariwise. (280, emphasis added)

Darcy tells Elizabeth that his aunt's report gave him hope because he knew Elizabeth well enough "to be certain that, had you been absolutely, irrevocably decided against me" she would have made it known to Lady Catherine. Darcy recalls that Elizabeth's earlier judgments of him were "ill-founded, formed on mistaken premises," but admits that "my behaviour to you at the time had merited the severest reproof" (280–281).

Elizabeth draws their self-accusations to a close, "The conduct of neither, if strictly examined will be irreproachable; but since then, we have both, I hope, improved in civility." Darcy is not so easily distracted from the theme. He recalls Elizabeth's reproof: "had you behaved in a more gentleman-like manner," and explains that the words "tortured" him but, more importantly, sparked an important growth in self-knowledge for which he is grateful (281).

Darcy recounts his upbringing and marks out his relationship with Elizabeth as the single most powerful influence awakening him to his own selfishness and arrogance.

I have been a selfish being all my life, in practice, though not in principle. As a child I was taught what was *right*, but I was not taught to correct my temper. I was given good principles, but left to follow them in pride and conceit. Unfortunately an only son (for many years an only *child*) I was spoiled by my parents, who though good themselves (my father, particularly, all that was benevolent and amiable), allowed, encouraged, almost taught me to be selfish and overbearing, to care for none beyond my own family circle, to think meanly of all the rest of the world, to *wish* at least, to think meanly of their sense of worth compared with my own. Such I was, from eight to eight and twenty; and such I might still have been but for you, dearest, loveliest Elizabeth! What do I not owe you! You taught me a lesson, hard indeed at first, but most advantageous. By you, I was properly humbled. I came to you without doubt of my reception. You showed me how insufficient were all my pretensions *to please a woman worthy of being pleased*. (282, emphasis added)

- How does Elizabeth's reaction to her father's "want of penetration" reveal her growth and change?
- What is disclosed throughout the novel about the influence of family and upbringing on an individual's moral development and character?
- What account can you provide for the character differences between Lydia and Elizabeth despite their similar upbringing?
- How do Elizabeth's relationships with characters other than Darcy help to shape her aspirations? Why is Darcy's influence particularly powerful?
- What does Darcy mean when he tells Elizabeth, "You showed me how insufficient were all my pretensions to please a woman worthy of being pleased"? Discuss Darcy's moral growth in the novel.
- Look back at Elizabeth's *morally pivotal points* and *challenge point*. What new pleasures does Elizabeth enjoy after each? What kind of pain does she endure? How do pleasure and pain help to school her desires?

Volume III, Chapters XVII–XIX

Elizabeth's growth in self-knowledge is drawn into focus again when she speaks to her father after Darcy has asked permission for her hand. She realizes that her own misjudgments have informed her father's opinion of Darcy.

> How earnestly did she then wish her former opinions had been more reasonable, her expressions more moderate! It would have spared her from the explanations and professions which it was exceedingly awkward to give [her father]; but they were now necessary, and she assured him, with some confusion, of her attachment to Mr. Darcy. (288)

Mr. Bennet expresses his own concern for her happiness. "He is rich, to be sure, and you may have more fine clothes and fine carriages than Jane. But will they make you happy?" (288). Elizabeth asks if he has any other objection beside her "indifference" and her father responds, "None at all." Elizabeth confesses her love for Darcy and defends his character against the caricature she popularized of the haughty man. "He is perfectly amiable. You do not know what he really is" (288).

Mr. Bennet gives Elizabeth his consent with the following advice:

> I know your disposition, Lizzy. I know that you could be neither happy nor respectable, unless you truly esteemed your husband, unless you looked up to him as a superior. Your lively talents would place you in the greatest danger in an unequal marriage. You could scarcely escape

discredit and misery. My child, let me not have the grief of seeing *you* unable to respect your partner in life. You know not what you are about. (288–289)

Elizabeth offers her assurances, explaining

the gradual change which her estimation of him had undergone, relating her absolute certainty that his affection was not the work of a day, but had stood the test of many months suspense, and numerating with energy all his good qualities, she did conquer her father's incredulity, and reconcile him to the match. (289)

After making the truth of Darcy's character known and her sincere regard for him, "Elizabeth's mind was now relieved from a very heavy weight; and after half an hour's quiet reflection in her own room, she was able to join the others with tolerable composure" (289).

When Darcy and Elizabeth marry, Elizabeth weaves an extraordinary web of relationships transcending class distinctions and resentments. After the newly married couple settle in Pemberley, for example, Mr. Bennet frequents their home "especially when he was least expected" (295). Jane and Bingley move to a neighboring county and "Kitty to her every material advantage, spent the chief of her time with her two elder sisters. In society so superior to what she had generally known, her improvement was great" (295). "As for Wickham and Lydia, their characters suffered no revolution from the marriage of her sisters . . ." (296).

Darcy's sister Georgiana and Elizabeth get along marvelously.

[T]he attachment of the sisters was exactly what Darcy had hoped to see. They were able to love each other, even as well as they intended. Georgiana had the highest opinion in the world of Elizabeth; though at first she often listened with an astonishment bordering on alarm at her lively, sportive manner of talking to her brother. . . . By Elizabeth's instructions she began to comprehend that a woman may take liberties with her husband, which a brother will not always allow in a sister more than ten years younger than himself. (297)

Moreover, Lady Catherine is eventually welcomed to Pemberley.

[B]y Elizabeth's persuasion, he [Darcy] was prevailed to overlook the offence and seek a reconciliation. . . . [Eventually] she condescended to wait on them at Pemberley, in spite of the pollution which its woods had received, not merely from the presence of such a mistress, but the visits of her uncle and aunt from the city. (297)

Finally, "With the Gardiners they were always on the most intimate terms. Darcy, as well as Elizabeth, really loved them; and they were both ever sensible of the warmest gratitude towards the persons who, by bringing her into Derbyshire, had been the means of uniting them" (297–298).

The following questions help students to focus on the changes in Elizabeth that follow from her challenge point.

- How do Elizabeth's choices during and after her encounter with Lady Catherine reveal a change in character?
- Elizabeth was always favored by her father. How can you explain Mr. Bennet's range of views on marriage? He seems to have one view regarding his own marriage, another for Lydia, Kitty, and Mary, and another for Jane and Elizabeth.
- What do you think of Darcy's change? Did you suspect it, or were you as surprised as Elizabeth was? Do you think he has any reason to be grateful to Elizabeth?
- To what extent is Darcy's change and growth dependent on Elizabeth's, and vice versa?
- As the novel comes to a close Austen calls our attention to the inter-connected relationships within which Elizabeth is an animating force. What does Austen seem to suggest about the connection between an individual's moral growth and the wider community?

SUMMARY REFLECTIONS

Elizabeth's moral progress as the ability to reverse her judgments

Educated, articulate, and the most apparently virtuous among the four characters, Elizabeth Bennet cares deeply about, and regards herself as an apt judge of, character and intelligence. From the outset of her moral journey, she possesses a reasonable knowledge of and desire for happiness, as well as a sophisticated conception of love. In Elizabeth's mind, marriage should be based on love, affection, and mutual respect, not convenience or pleasure. Despite her clear sense of commitment and noble purpose, Elizabeth's quick judgment, clouded by pride, limits her ability to pursue her ideal. She tends to deflect her own flaws onto others, especially Darcy, who while perhaps equally as proud as Elizabeth, also undergoes a change, one that parallels Elizabeth's own in some respects.[2]

What Elizabeth painfully and surprisingly comes to see is that she has not been as perceptive as she thought; she has, in fact, misjudged people on several counts. Despite her virtue, Elizabeth still has room to progress. With each morally pivotal point and stinging humiliation she not only gains understanding but also the capacity to reverse her judgments. Perhaps the successful schooling of Elizabeth's desire is the result of her highly reflective disposition—which enables her to acquire greater knowledge of herself and others–combined with her already well-formed habit of shaping her actions in accordance with her ideals.

The first *morally pivotal point* shakes Elizabeth out of her complacence. She learns of Charlotte's willingness to marry Collins, "a most humiliating picture," and a situation in which she believed it "impossible . . . to be tolerably happy" (97). Elizabeth is not only distressed by Charlotte's choice, but also by the fact that she had misread her friend's feelings and intentions. Elizabeth realizes that her assessment of Charlotte's ideal of marriage has been inaccurate. Indignant Elizabeth "felt persuaded that no real confidence could ever subsist between them again" (98). Her quick judgment and prejudice against the match is proven unreliable, however, when Elizabeth comes to spend time with Charlotte in her new home and chooses to renew their friendship. She realizes that Charlotte is quite clever and making her marriage work. While Elizabeth would have never made the choice Charlotte makes, she is able to come to admire Charlotte's realism.

This first *morally pivotal point* prompts Elizabeth to assess happiness in marriage and her own options for the future more carefully. Charlotte's acceptance of Mr. Collins' hand and Darcy's surprising proposal challenge her preconceptions about individuals, their desires, and their reasons for marrying. In Charlotte and Collins, she sees clearly what she does not want—a marriage of utility or convenience. In Darcy's proposal she also sees what she wants to avoid—a marriage based on one person's condescension. With this proposal, her aversion to Mr. Darcy increases. Despite insights into the imperfections of her judgment, Elizabeth persists in quickly assessing people's character. She strikes up a familiar relationship with Mr. Wickham and maintains a strained, formal relationship with Mr. Darcy, convinced that she understands both men quite well. At the second *morally pivotal point* Elizabeth realizes that she has misjudged both Darcy and Wickham. She sees for the first time that happiness is not dependent solely on her own judgment, but on an understanding of and openness to the truth about others. Her growth in self-knowledge is accompanied by a growth in humility and a keener understanding of others, including her parents, her sisters, and Mr. Darcy. Subsequently, her desires are rechanneled. She sees and is disposed to learning more about Darcy's honorable character.

At the *challenge point*, Elizabeth is resolved to act in the interest of her refined conception of happiness. From Charlotte she has learned a kind of open-mindedness through newfound respect for her friend's decision even though it contradicted what Elizabeth believed to be best and right. From Darcy she has discovered that her judgment of people can be enormously inaccurate. Her ability to reverse judgment helps Elizabeth to reorient her desire and embrace individuals for who they are. Before reading Darcy's clarifying letter and coming to recognize Darcy's virtues through the testimony of his servant and his magnanimity in resolving the situation with Wickham and Lydia, the stubborn Elizabeth Bennet would have obliged Lady Catherine and definitively refused Darcy's second proposal. Now that her judgment has been refined, she avails herself to Darcy with the hope that he will ask for her hand again. A more humble and open-minded Elizabeth risks loving Darcy without knowing whether another proposal of marriage will ever be offered again. Elizabeth fulfills her ideal. She not only marries for love, she marries her equal—in intelligence and character. While her *telos* never really changes, her ability to reverse judgment and see her *telos* more clearly does. She comes to appreciate people with their limitations, and she opens like a fan accepting and welcoming everyone into her new home at Pemberley from Lydia to Lady Catherine.

EXTENSION QUESTIONS

1   Look back at the morally pivotal moments for Elizabeth. At each moment in Elizabeth's moral growth where is Darcy in his? Can you identify morally pivotal points and/or a challenge point for Darcy? How do their journeys toward self-knowledge and virtue intertwine with one another? What do your observations suggest about why Austen titled her book, *Pride and Prejudice*?

2   Overall, which of the characters in the novel have the most reliable judgment? Explain.

3   Revisit Darcy's remark to Elizabeth when they first converse, "There is, I believe, in every disposition a tendency to some particular evil, a natural defect, which not even the best education can overcome." To what extent do the main characters in *Pride and Prejudice* prove or disprove this statement?

4   In many respects *Pride and Prejudice* is a novel about learning from one's mistakes. In Elizabeth's case, her mistakes are brought to light within the context of disappointing, humiliating, and even painful experiences. In what ways can pain or shame serve as an impetus for moral growth? What insights can you glean from Elizabeth Bennet about the educational power of humiliation?

5   What do we learn from Elizabeth (or any other character) about the value of reflection and good judgment? What do we learn from Elizabeth and Darcy about how self-knowledge is acquired? What can we learn from Elizabeth about what it means to think through the implications of our choices, attitudes, and actions?

6   Read Plato's Allegory of the Cave in Book VII of *The Republic* with students. Examine Socrates' notion of education as soul-turning. Pay close attention to the details in the allegory describing the ascent from

the cave—what it involves and the internal and external factors that assist one in making the ascent. In the allegory the prisoners are urged to ascend from the realm of shadows to the realm of things as they are. We can draw a parallel between the appearance of truth—the shadows on the wall—and the first impressions, biases, prejudices, and blinding pride at work in Jane Austen's novel. In what ways can Elizabeth's experience at each dramatic juncture in the novel be likened to the cave dwellers' imprisonment and ascent? Link key passages from Plato's allegory with Austen's depiction of Elizabeth's change.

7   Character and economics. Jane Austen takes the economics of marriage and social life quite seriously. Compare and contrast the "worth" of at least two characters from the novel. Austen provides the detail regarding property, annual income, and type of chaise owned, but you will need to do a little research to determine the class and exact worth of this collateral during Austen's time. Draw some conclusions about how you see Austen making connections between character and class or character and worth in *Pride and Prejudice.*

8   Develop an essay that explores one of the following motifs in the novel: marriage, family, or social class relations. Divide and categorize the different types of marriages, families, or classes described in *Pride and Prejudice.* For example, echoing Aristotle's three types of friendship, we find marriages of pleasure, marriages of utility or convenience, and marriages based on love and mutual respect.

CONCLUSION

What we find in the study of Elizabeth Bennet's moral development is a character education that is achieved not only by careful reflection on the truth as it is gradually revealed, but also by her relationship with Darcy, who is her peer and in some respects more virtuous than she. Elizabeth sheds her prejudices as she comes closer and closer to understanding who people are and why they do what they do, and it is her relationship with Darcy that helps to move this discovery along. Her character education is accompanied by both embarrassment and joy. Elizabeth's pains and joys prompt reflection and help to school her desires in such a way that she learns to seek a truer love and deeper friendships. Moreover, despite her disdain for her father's abnegation of parental responsibility and her sisters' blind impulsiveness, she also gains a wider sympathy and tolerance for each of them. Most importantly, Elizabeth is actually flourishing at the end of the novel; she is no longer duped by petty gossip or quick to dismiss certain individuals for their demeanor, choices, or reputation. Elizabeth Bennet's story teaches us that character education guided by a steady pursuit of the truth and by losing the fear of facing such truth can lead to greater moral maturity and happiness.

There is enormous opportunity in literature classrooms to help students shed their prejudices, to amend their first impressions, and to evaluate their preconceived notions about individuals and events. Adolescence is a wonderful time to widen one's perspective on people and to gain clearer insight into the truth of particular situations—be they larger social conflicts or family and peer-related difficulties. Through reflection, investigation, listening, and seeking to understand, our students can develop a wider sense of appreciation for individuals and the complexity of life. Literature provides a rich array of individuals and stories that help to disclose this kind of character development.

Janie Crawford—trial and transcendence

Rich in poetic language and sensuous imagery *Their Eyes Were Watching God*[1] is primarily a novel about a woman who discovers her voice and identity over a fourteen-year period. The emerging identity of Janie Crawford is dramatically revealed through her relationships and experiences as a mulatto woman in the newly liberated South. Perhaps more than anything, *Their Eyes* is a story of self-discovery and resilience. Janie is afflicted by enormous suffering, injustice, and humiliation, yet she emerges self-possessed, serene, and at peace with life.

TAPPING THE MORAL IMAGINATION

I read Hurston's *Their Eyes Were Watching God* for the first time when I was teaching a Women in Literature course to a group of high school students participating in a summer leadership program. I had not included Hurston on my list of options for outside reading and was met by a fervent protest from my class. "Where is Zora Neale Hurston's *Their Eyes Are* [*sic*] *Watching God*?" "Talk about powerful women in literature. . . . It's one of the best books I've ever read!" Then they launched into conversation with each other about their favorite scenes, what they thought of the significance of her hair, what they loved about Tea Cake, the drama of the storm. When I read the novel for the first time, I was struck by the depth of Janie's character and her extraordinary capacity for reflection. Some have argued that *Their Eyes* is a woman's book. This point I leave up to you to decide and perhaps to let your students debate. It is a marvelous story of desire, love thwarted, love denied, love gained, and love lost. The male characters are powerful as well and merit our careful scrutiny. It is not only through their choices and actions that Hurston's characters come to life; their voices and language assume powerful shape and help to disclose their depth or one--dimensionality.

To begin engaging students in the moral themes of Hurston's novel, ask them to consider how much disappointment they believe one person can bear before it breaks them. Numerous examples of tragic fate and suffering fill history and literature: some classics include: *Oedipus Rex*, *The Book of Job*, *A Day in the Life of Ivan Denisovich*, and Elie Wiesel's *Night*. Ask students to identify contemporary examples of suffering, experience by victims of war and terrorism, families who have lost homes or loved ones to arson, school communities that have been riddled with senseless violence. What account can they provide for the resilience of those who have endured trauma, abuse, and injustice yet do not remain bitter? What account can be provided for those who do become bitter or cynical? Ask students to identify those factors that enable a person to not only to endure physical or psychological pain but to emerge stronger as a result. For insights from contemporary works, consider Mitch Albom's *Tuesdays With Morrie*, Margaret Edson's play, *Wit*, or Viktor Frankl's *Man's Search for Meaning*. Ask students to brainstorm a list of the dispositions of mind and character that allow a person to move forward purposefully after tragedy.

FOSTERING ETHICAL REFLECTION: JANIE CRAWFORD

Their Eyes Were Watching God challenges readers to consider what love entails and how it influences suffering and personal resilience as well as self-development and wisdom. Encourage students to pay attention to Janie's emerging definitions of love and marriage, as well as her own definition of self as the novel unfolds. Ask them to trace Janie's reflections on the meaning of love: *Who are her sources of information? What experiences shape her understanding? How do her definitions change? Why?*

As students begin reading the novel, tell them to pay particular attention to the interests and aspirations of the young Janie Crawford, and ask them to identify the factors—relationships, events, and personal dispositions—that awaken, prompt, and sustain her moral agency. That is, what are the factors that help Janie to set new goals and ideals for herself? Prompt students to discuss the varying degrees of influence these factors have on Janie's choices and commitments throughout the novel. Encourage students to track the experiences, events, and relationships that seem to have the greatest impact on Janie.

Chapters 1–2

Born in West Florida, Janie Crawford is raised by her maternal grandmother, affectionately referred to as Nanny. When Nanny was a young woman, she was raped by her slave master and gave birth to a daughter she named Leafy, who would one day become Janie's mother. To save her newborn daughter and her own life, Nanny flees with her one-week-old infant from a Georgia plantation and escapes to safety in Florida. After the slaves are formally freed in the South, Nanny remains in Florida with a white family named Washburn. Nanny never marries. When her daughter, Leafy, is seventeen, she is raped in the woods by her schoolteacher and abandoned. Janie is born nine months later. The rape is so traumatic for Janie's mother that she becomes a drunkard and eventually disappears from the community. From that moment on, Nanny rears and protects her new granddaughter. Janie and her grandmother stay with the Washburn family for about six years, until Nanny has scrimped and saved enough money to buy a small piece of land where she can raise Janie away from white folks.

As Janie develops into a young woman of sixteen, her interest in romantic love and marriage is awakened. Lying beneath a pear tree one spring day Janie muses

> The pear tree had called her to come and gaze on a mystery. From barren brown stems to glistening leaf-buds; from the leaf-buds to snowy virginity of bloom. *It stirred her tremendously*. What? How? Why? This singing she heard that had nothing to do with her ears. The rose of the world was breathing out smell. It followed her through all her waking moments and caressed her in her sleep. It connected itself with other vaguely felt matters that had struck her outside observation and buried themselves in her flesh. *Now they emerged and quested about her consciousness.*
>
> She was stretched on her back beneath the pear tree soaking in the alto chant of the visiting bees, the gold of the sun and the panting breath of the breeze when the inaudible voice of it all came to her. She saw a dust-bearing bee sink into the sanctum of a bloom; the thousand sister calyxes arch to meet the love embrace and the ecstatic shiver from root to tiniest branch creaming in every blossom and frothing with delight. *So this was a marriage! She had been summoned to behold a revelation. . . .*
>
> *She was seeking confirmation of the voice and vision, and everywhere she found and acknowledged answers.* A personal answer for all other creatures except herself. . . . Where were the singing bees for her? . . . She searched as much of the world as she could from the top of the front steps and then went on down to the front gate and leaned over to gaze up and down the road. Looking, waiting, breathing short with impatience. Waiting for the world to be made. (pp. 10–11, emphasis added)

Imagining the love of her life to be seeking her out, Janie sees the young fellow "she had known as the shiftless Johnny Taylor," and gratefully receives his kiss (10–11). Thus, with her first kiss Janie recounts, "My conscious life commenced at Nanny's gate" (10). Janie engraves the image of the pear tree on her imagination and memory and wanders aimlessly in pursuit of her goal: a love that can provide a comparable pleasure. Nanny's conception of marriage, however, is more pragmatic than Janie's. She insists that Janie marry Logan Killicks, a local farmer, for security and protection — a definition of marriage that stands in contrast to the one Janie has defined for herself. "'Taint Logan Killicks I want you to have, baby," Nanny insists, "it's protection. . . . De nigger woman is the mule of the world so far as I can see" (14). Thus, at sixteen years old, Janie enters her first marriage with some trepidation and uncertainty: "The vision of Logan Killicks was desecrating the pear tree, but Janie didn't know how to tell Nanny that" (13). Janie marries Logan because she convinces herself that

> *she would love Logan after they were married. She could see no way for it to come about, but Nanny and the old folks had said it, so it must be so.* Husbands and wives had always loved each other, and that was what marriage meant. It was just so. *Janie felt glad of the thought, for then it wouldn't seem so destructive and mouldy. She wouldn't be lonely anymore.* (20, emphasis added)

Janie trusts her grandmother despite her reservations. A naïve romantic, she is hopeful that love will follow naturally from marriage in the same way the singing bees found delight in the bloom.

These passages provide numerous points of entry for discussion. The sensuous pear tree alone invites reflection on the evocative power of images. These first two chapters give you ample opportunity to examine with students Janie's dispositions and attitude. The questions below will help to frame your discussion of what has informed Janie's dispositions and attitudes thus far. The opening of the novel makes several references to vision and sight, to what Janie "sees." Encourage students to pay attention to the various ways Janie seeks "confirmation of the voice and vision."

- What is unique about the way Hurston sets up the narrative in this novel?
- Examine the rich imagery Hurston employs in describing the pear tree. What does the pear tree evoke in Janie? Does it go beyond what is purely sensual or sexual?
- How would you characterize the kind of attraction Janie has for Johnny? For Logan Killicks?
- Why does Janie agree to marry Logan despite the fact that her "vision" of him was "desecrating the pear tree"?
- Nanny wants to keep Janie from becoming "the mule of the world." How does she believe marriage will save her from this plight?
- What is Janie seeking in a relationship right now?
- To what extent is Janie "grown-up" when she marries; in what ways is she still a youth?

Chapters 3–4: first morally pivotal point

Janie's initial reluctance to wed Logan is borne out in a short and unhappy marriage. She does not experience the romantic love she had hoped marriage would bring. After a year Janie leaves Logan in the hope of pursuing her ideal elsewhere. The first morally pivotal point in Janie's life is her realization that "marriage did not make love. . . . [H]er first dream was dead, so she became a woman" (24).

Up until this point Janie's desire is essentially blind and naïve. In marrying Logan, however, she comes to see what she does *not* want in a spouse. Janie's new home with Logan is "a lonesome place like a stump in the middle of the woods where nobody had ever been" and "absent of flavor, too." Janie perseveres in search of flavor; she longs to taste the sweetness of the pear tree in bloom, so she "went on inside to wait for love to begin" (21). After a month and a half of marriage, Janie, long-faced and dejected, visits Nanny. When Nanny inquires about Janie's apparent discontent, Janie explains, "Cause you told me Ah mus gointer love him, and Ah don't. Maybe if someone was to tell me how, Ah could do it." When Nanny scolds her, Janie asserts, "But Nanny *Ah wants to want him sometimes.* Ah don't want him to do all the wantin'" (22, emphasis added).

Nanny quickly shatters Janie's romantic idealism, "if you don't want him, you sho oughta. . . . Dat's de very prong all us black women gits hung on. Dis love!" (22). But Janie's desire for love is impelled by her aversion to Logan. Indeed, he does "desecrate" her pear tree. Janie launches into a litany of complaints to her grandmother. He is ugly, he smells, "He don't even never mention nothin' pretty." And then she laments, "Ah wants things sweet wid marriage lak when you sit under a pear tree and think. Ah . . ." (23). She realizes that she desires more than mere protection and stability. While Janie wants to love Logan, ultimately she cannot because he repulses her.

Nanny still insists, "Wait awhile baby, your mind will change." Yet Janie has tried to trust the conventional wisdom that "husbands and wives had always loved each other." She wants to align her desire for love with a desire for Logan, but her aversion to Logan makes it impossible.

> So Janie waited a bloom time, and a green time, and an orange time. But when the pollen again gilded the sun and sifted down on the world, *she began to stand around the gate and expect things.* What things? She didn't know exactly. Her breath was gusty and short. (24, emphasis added)

The springtime again awakens her desires for love. Janie relinquishes some of her naïveté, but her desire to love someone lovable remains a fixed ideal. Janie's relationship with Logan worsens, but she finds consolation in the springtime.

"[W]hen she heard whistling coming down the road" (26), Janie rushes impulsively to the water pump and pumps noisily so that the whistling stranger would take notice of her. He does and asks for a cold drink. The "stranger," Joe Starks, introduces himself and explains that he has "been working for white folks all his life" (27). Now he was on his way to a town of all "colored folks." He tells Janie "he had always wanted to be a big voice. . . . It had always been his desire and wish to be a big voice and he had to live nearly thirty years to find a chance" (27). Janie is taken with Jody.

> They sat under the tree and talked. . . . Every day after that they managed to meet in the scrub oaks across the road and talk about when he would be a big ruler of things with her reaping the benefits. (28)

Janie is attracted but hesitant "because he did not represent sun-up and pollen and blooming trees." He did, however, speak "for a far horizon. *He spoke for change and chance.*" Upon reflection though, Janie "*hung back. The memory of Nanny was still powerful and strong*" (28). Nevertheless, Janie's desire for love makes Jody a compelling alternative to Logan. He promises marriage and gives his word that he will make Janie happy: "Janie, if you think Ah aims to tole you off and make a dog outa you, youse wrong. Ah want to make a wife outa you."

> You mean dat, Jody?
> De day you puts yo' hand in mine, Ah wouldn't let de sun go down on us single. Ah'm a man wid principles. (28)

After Jody's proposal that she escape with him the next day, "Janie debated the matter that night in bed" (28).

In what appears to be loyalty to Logan, Janie attempts to discuss her plans: "S'posin I wuz to run off and leave yuh sometime. . . . Ah might take and find somebody dat did trust me and leave yuh." Logan ends the conversation "resentful in his agony and pretended sleep. He hoped that he had hurt her as she had hurt him" (29). Not entirely resolved in her determination to leave Logan, Janie prepares breakfast for him the next morning. However, when Logan calls and insists that she help him move a pile of manure, she challenges, "Youse in yo' place and Ah'm in mine" (30). Logan commands her to obey him, and Janie's resentment is unleashed:

> Mah mama didn't tell me Ah wuz born in no hurry. So what business Ah got rushin' now? Anyhow dat aint what youse mad about. Youse mad

cause I don't fall down and wash up dese sixty acres uh ground you got. You aint done me no favor by marryin' me. . . . (30)

Logan threatens Janie, "Ah'll take holt uh dat ax and come in dere and kil yuh!. . . . Ah guess some low life nigger is grinnin in yo' face and lyin tuh yuh. God damn yo' hide" (30). The bitter exchange prompts Janie to reflect. "She turned wrongside out just standing there and feeling. When the throbbing calmed a little she gave Logan's speech a hard thought and placed it beside other things she had seen and heard" (31). Then she carries on cooking:

> she dumped the dough on the skillet and smoothed it with her hand. She wasn't even angry. Logan was accusing her of mama, her grandma, and her feelings, and she couldn't do a thing about any of it. (31)

Janie wonders, "What was she losing so much time for? A feeling of sudden newness and change came over her. Janie hurried out the front gate and turned south" (31). She sets off to escape with the stranger, Jody. And she believes that

> From now until death she was going to have flower dust and springtime sprinkled over everything. A bee for her bloom. Her old thoughts were going to come in handy now, but new words would have to be made and said to fit them. (31)

At this point in the novel invite students to reflect on the contrast between Logan and Jody as well as Janie's careful reflections on both. While Janie marries Logan at her grandmother's urging to keep herself from becoming "the mule of the world," in fact Logan buys a plow but not a mule; he turns Janie into his work animal. Jody makes a direct promise to Janie; he doesn't want to make a dog out of her, but rather a wife. Ask the students to pay attention to the change Janie undergoes in her marriage to Jody.

- What was Janie's first dream? How did it die?
- What role do disappointments and suffering play in personal maturity?
- Is this phenomenon of maturation following the loss of a dream specifically feminine? How might this experience be different for a young man?
- Compare and contrast Janie's aspirations for love and marriage with Nanny's. Why are they so different?
- What attracts Janie to Jody? What do we know about Jody and his ambitions thus far?
- Why is Janie still tentative about his proposal? How does she deal with her reservations? What finally causes her to decide to leave Logan for Jody?

Chapter 5

Janie's words and voice, however, are eventually shut out of conversation. When Jody unanimously wins the support of the crowd in the mayoral election in their new town of Eatonville, Janie is called to take the floor, "And now we'll listen to a few words of encouragement from Mrs. Mayor Starks." Jody interrupts the applause, "Thank yuh fuh yo' compliments, but mah wife don't know nothin' 'bout no speech-makin'. Ah never married her for nothin' lak dat. She's uh woman and her place is in de home" (40–41). Janie is enormously humiliated.

> Janie made her face laugh after a short pause, but *it wasn't too easy.* She had never thought of making a speech, and didn't know if she cared to make one at all. It must have been *the way Jody spoke without giving her a chance to say anything one way or another that took the bloom off of things.* (41, emphasis added)

The fracture in their relationship, however, is perceivable only to Janie.

> But anyway, she went down the road *behind him* that night *feeling cold.* He strode along invested with his new dignity, thought and planned out loud, *unconscious of her thoughts.* (41, emphasis added)

Still desirous of winning Jody's love, Janie persists in loving him and asks if he can spend more time with her in the store. But Jody insists, "Ah got too much else on mah hands as Mayor. Dis town needs some light right now." Facetiously, Janie responds, "Unh hunh, it is uh little dark right long heah" (41). Jody misses her innuendo.

While Janie's image of Jody begins to grow dim, she remains faithful to him. After the great lamplighting ceremony—the "first street lamp in a colored town" is lighted—Jody asks Janie how she enjoys "bein' Mrs. Mayor." Janie takes advantage of the invitation to be frank,

> It's all right Ah reckon, but don't you think it keeps us in a kinda strain? . . . It looks lak it keeps us in some way we ain't natural wid one 'nother. You'se always off talkin' and fixin' things, and Ah feels lak Ah'm just markin' time. Hope it soon gets over. (43)

Jody does not perceive her need. "Over, Janie? I god, Ah aint even started good. Ah told you in de very beginnin' dat Ah aimed to be a big voice. You oughta be glad, 'cause dat makes uh big woman outa you" (43). Disappointment sets in: "A feeling of coldness and fear took hold of her. She felt far away from things and lonely" (44).

Janie's acquiescence belies her increasing loneliness and frustration. As Jody grows in wealth and fame, people are "cowed" by him. Moreover, the townspeople observe that Jody is tough on Janie: "He gits on her ever now and then when she makes mistakes at the store" (46). And they notice that Janie, "sho don't talk much" (47). Jealous of other men admiring her hair, Jody forces Janie to keep it tied up in a head rag when she's in the store. "The business of the head rag irked her endlessly. But Jody was set on it. Her hair was NOT going to show in the store" (52). Janie sublimates her feelings; she habitually "took the easy way away from a fuss. She didn't change her mind but she agreed to change with her mouth" (59). In the meantime Jody continues to exaggerate her mistakes in the store and to scold her publicly. When he cannot find an order for pigs' feet, Janie suffers his wrath: "If you'd get yo' mind out de streets and keep it on yo' business maybe you could git somethin' straight sometimes" (66).

- Why does Jody believe that his "big voice" will make "uh big woman outa" Janie? How would you describe his ideal of marriage?
- What is Janie beginning to realize and *see*? In what respects is she still blind or naïve?
- To what extent do Janie's reflections inform her judgments, choices, actions, and commitments? To what extent is she motivated by other forces?
- Despite Jody's ridicule and harsh demands, Janie continues to acquiesce and support him. Why?
- What qualities of character are revealed in Janie thus far? Are they primarily strengths or weaknesses? Explain. What qualities of character do you see revealed in Jody? What are his aspirations and ambitions?
- Compare and contrast Janie's internal thoughts and feelings with her external behavior.

Chapter 6: second morally pivotal point

Jody's abuse eventually prompts Janie to see that their relationship, like her marriage to Logan, also violates her ideal of married love. After seven years of marriage, Janie abandons her romantic expectation of finding love in loving Jody. One particularly dramatic experience discloses Janie's refined understanding.

> She wasn't petal-open anymore with him. *She was twenty-four and seven years married when she knew. She found that out one day when he slapped her face in the kitchen.* . . . Janie was a good cook, and Jody had looked forward to his dinner as a refuge from other things. So when the bread didn't rise, and the fish wasn't quite done at the

bone, and the rice was scorched, he slapped Janie until she had a ringing sound in her ears and told her about her brains before he stalked back to the store.

She stood there until something fell off the shelf inside her. Then *she went inside there to see what it was.* It was her image of Jody tumbled down and shattered. But looking at it she saw that it never was the flesh and blood figure of her dreams. Just something she had grabbed up to drape her dreams over. *In a way she turned her back upon the image where it lay and looked further.* She had no more blossomy openings dusting pollen over her man, neither any glistening young fruit where the petals used to be. She found that *she had a host of thoughts that she had never expressed to him, and numerous emotions that she had never let Jody know about. Things packed up and put away in parts of her heart where he could never find them. She was saving up feelings for some man she had never seen. She had an inside and outside now and suddenly she knew how not to mix them.* (67–68, emphasis added)

Spend time with students on this central passage in the novel. Encourage students to identify other passages that highlight Janie's marked separation of her inner self and her external self, her intentional fragmentation. The following set of questions will help them to reflect on the significance of the evolving change in Janie.

- Hurston is deliberate about her use of "inside" and "outside." What does this language help us to understand about Janie? In what respects has she grown? In what respects is she still the same?
- How have Janie's aspirations changed or undergone revision?
- What is it about this particular experience that prompts Janie to a deeper reflection about her life and dreams? Why does it sometimes require pain or a crisis to awaken moral reflection?

Chapter 7

Up until this point Janie has been a dedicated wife, loving Jody and assisting him with his store. It finally occurs to her, however, that she has squandered her aspirations—and much of herself—in pursuit of an ill-formed ideal. Janie turns inward to pick up the pieces of her own life. She seeks happiness and fulfillment independent of her husband. Janie sees for the first time that it is not just the one-sided pursuit of love that brings happiness; reciprocity is also needed, a reciprocity that she cannot secure from Jody. Thus, to recover some sense of meaning in her life she relies on her own pursuit of self-knowledge.

From this moment forward Janie carefully bows to the "outside" by tolerating Jody despite his cruelty; she stays with him until his death. Nevertheless, the years of quiet endurance have taken a toll on Janie's spirit:

> The years took all the fight out of Janie's face. For a while she thought it was gone from her soul. No matter what Jody did, she said nothing. *She had learned how to talk some and leave some. She was a rut in the road. Plenty of life beneath the surface but it was kept beaten down by the wheels.* Sometimes she struck out into the future imagining her life different from what it was. But mostly she lived between her hat and her heels, with her emotional disturbances like shade patterns in the woods—come and gone with the sun. She got nothin' from Jody except what money could buy, and she was giving away what she didn't value. (72, emphasis added)

Janie survives but she does not thrive in her remaining years of marriage to Jody. She accepts the emptiness of their relationship to protect herself from becoming vulnerable to disappointment again. Yet no matter how much Janie tries to separate herself from Jody, she still sees her identity as intimately connected to his.

> "Maybe he aint nothin'," she tries to convince herself, "but he is something in my mouth. He's got to be else Ah aint got nothin' tuh live for. Ah'll lie and say he is. If Ah don't life won't be nothin' but uh store and uh house." (72)

Janie "didn't read books so she didn't know that she was the world and the heavens boiled down to a drop. Man attempting to climb to painless heights from his dung hill" (72). Regardless of her lack of formal education Janie continues to reflect on her experiences and desires. She wants to overcome her loneliness. Janie's renewed spirit of reflection and interior strength incites her courage to speak plainly with Jody. After he publicly embarrasses Janie for a mistake in the shop, "Janie took the middle of the floor to talk right into Jody's face, and that was something that hadn't been done before" (74). Jody tries to diffuse her anger, "'Taint no use in gettin' all mad Janie, 'cause you ain't no gal no mo'. Nobody heah ain't lookin' for no wife outa yuh. Old as you is." In defending her own dignity, Janie robs Jody of his own.

> "Ah reckon Ah looks mah age too. But Ah'm a woman every inch of me, and Ah know it. Dats a whole lot more than you kin say. You big-bellies round here and put out a lot of brag, but tain't nothin' to it but yo' big voice. Humph! Talkin' 'bout me lookin' old! When you pull down yo' britches, you look lak de change uh life."

. . . Then [Jody] realized all the meanings and his vanity bled like a flood. Janie had robbed him of his irresistible maleness that all men cherish, which was terrible. . . . For what can excuse a man in the eyes of other men for lack of strength? . . . There was nothing to do in life anymore. Ambition was useless. And the cruel deceit of Janie! Making all that show of humbleness and scorning him all the time! Laughing at him, and now putting the town up to do the same. Jody didn't know the words for all this, but he knew the feeling. So he struck Janie with all his might and drove her from the store. (75–76) At the beginning of the chapter, despite Janie's quiet, Hurston describes the "plenty of life beneath the surface."

- What kind of life does Janie choose to lead? Can she find happiness this way? Is it good for a person to lead a deliberately fragmented life? Why or why not?
- Why does Janie originally insist that she only has Jody to live for? Is her identity dependent on his?
- Think of examples of friendships and lasting relationships. In what ways are the identities of the individuals involved in that relationship interdependent? To what extent is each individual's identity autonomous? Explain.
- What does Janie mean when she says, "Ah'm a woman every inch of me, and Ah know it"? In what ways does this statement signal a change in Janie? What does it tell us about her emerging sense of identity?

Chapter 8

From this point on there is a physical separation between Janie and Jody. Jody moves out of their room to sleep downstairs. Janie struggles to make sense of his response in light of his ongoing treatment of her. "*Why must Jody be so mad with her for making him look so small when he did it to her all the time?* Had been doing it for years" (77, emphasis added). Humiliated and brought down by Janie's public reproach, Jody falls physically ill. Janie knows his time is short; she strives to make herself understood to Jody before he dies. This is particularly challenging because "[s]he must talk to a man who was ten immensities away" (80). Jody is resistant to Janie's entrance, but she persists.

Naw, Jody, Ah come in heah tuh talk widja and Ah'm gointuh do it too. It's for both of our sakes Ah'm talkin'. . . . Jody, maybe Ah aint been such uh good wife tuh you, but Jody—

Dat's 'cause you ain't got the right feelin' for nobody. You oughter have some sympathy 'bout yo'self. You ain't no hog.

But Jody, Ah meant tuh be awful nice.

Much as Ah do fuh yuh. Holdin' me up tuh scorn. No sympathy!

Naw, Jody, it wasn't because Ah didn't have no sympathy. Ah had uh lavish uh dat. Ah just didn't never git no chance tuh use none of it. You wouldn't let me.

Dat's right, blame everything on me. Ah wouldn't let you show no feelin'! When, Janie, dat's all Ah wanted or desired. Now you come blamin' me!

'Taint dat, Jody. Ah aint here tuh blame nobody. *Ah'm just tryin' tuh make you know what kinda person Ah is befo' it's too late . . .*

Janie! Janie! don't tell me Ah got tuh die, and Ah aint used tuh thinkin' 'bout it.

. . . Dat's just whut Ah wants tuh say, Jody. You wouldn't listen. *You done lived wid me for twenty years and you don't half know me at all.* And you could have but you was so busy worshippin' de works of yo' own hands, and cuffin' folks around in their minds till you didn't see uh whole heap uh things yuh could have.

Leave heah Janie. . . .

Ah knowed you wasn't gointuh lissen tuh me. You changes everything but nothin' don't change you—not even death. But Ah ain't goin' outa here and Ah aint gointuh hush. Naw, you gointuh listen tuh me one time befo' you die. Have yo' way all yo' life, trample and mash down and then die ruther than let yo'self heah 'bout it. Listen, Jody, you aint de Jody ah run off down de road wid. You'se what's left after he died. *Ah run off tuh keep house wid you in uh wonderful way. But you wasn't satisfied wid me de way Ah was. Naw! Mah own mind had tuh be squeezed and crowded out tuh make room for yours in me.*

Shut up! . . .

Too busy listening tuh yo' own big voice. . . . All dis bowin' down, all dis obedience under yo voice—dat aint whut Ah rushed down de road tuh find out about you. (80–82, emphasis added)

Janie has pity on Jody "for the first time in years." She considers his life pursuits: "Maybe if she had known some other way to try, she might have made his face different. . . . She thought back and forth about what had happened in the making of a voice out of a man." Janie speaks her piece, and with a few final groans Jody dies.

Then she thought about herself. Years ago, she had told her girl self to wait for her in the looking glass. . . . Perhaps she had better look. She went over to the dresser and looked hard at her skin and features. The young girl was gone, but a handsome woman had taken her place. She tore off the kerchief from her head and let down her plentiful hair. The weight, the length, the glory was there. She took careful stock of herself, then combed her hair and tied it up again. Then she starched and ironed her face, forming it into just what people wanted to see, and opened the window and cried, "Come heah people! Jody is dead. Mah husband is gone from me." (83)

- How does Janie's speaking frankly with Jody give rise to new self-realizations? How does it free her in a way?
- What does it mean to know someone? Why does Jody fail to know Janie after 20 years of marriage?
- What does Janie mean when she says she wished "she might have made his face different"? How could Jody have a "voice" and not a face?

Chapter 9

Janie is careful to maintain the proper external appearance while cultivating her interior world. She fulfills her role as the grieving wife of Mayor Joe Starks. Internally, however, she celebrates a change in her soul.

The funeral was going on *outside*. All things concerning death and burial were said and done. Finish. End. Nevermore. Darkness. Deep hole. Dissolution. Eternity. Weeping and wailing outside. *Inside the expensive black folds were resurrection and life. She did not reach outside for anything, nor did the things of the death reach inside to disturb her.* She sent her face to Jody's funeral, and herself went roll-icking with the springtime across the world. . . . Before she slept that night she burnt up every one of her head rags and went about the house the next morning with her hair in one thick braid swinging well below her waist. *That was the only change people saw in her.* (84–85, emphasis added).

Janie's first step toward independence from Jody is burning her head rags. Jody's death helps Janie take a second step toward independence—rejecting the tradition of her grandmother, which impoverished her ideal of love.

She hated her grandmother and had hidden it from herself all these years under a cloak of pity. She had been getting ready for her great journey to the horizons *in search of people*; it was important to all the world that she should find them and they find her. But she had been whipped like a cur dog, and run off down a *back road after things. It was all according to the way you see things.* Some people could look at a mud-puddle and see an ocean with ships. But Nanny belonged to that other kind that loved to deal in scraps. Nanny had taken the biggest thing God ever made, the horizon—for no matter how far a person can go the horizon is still way beyond you—and pinched it to such a little bit of a thing that she could tie it about her granddaughter's neck enough to choke her. *She hated the old woman who had twisted her so in the name of love.* (85, emphasis added)

A young, attractive widow, Janie becomes the object of attention again, but she prefers to remain independent. "Besides *she liked being lonesome for a change. This freedom feeling* was fine" (86, emphasis added). Janie enjoys a newfound peace and deflects the flattery of a host of admirers. When her friend Pheoby suggests that she consider an undertaker as a prospective husband, Janie responds, "No hurry." When Pheoby advises her to be careful about advertising her newfound freedom because "Folks will say you ain't sorry he's gone," Janie responds, "Let 'em say what they wants tuh, . . . To my thinkin' mourning oughtn't tuh last no longer'n grief" (89). Janie no longer feels compelled to "bow to the outside of things."

- How has Janie changed? In what ways is Janie still the same?
- In what ways has Janie's voice changed? What do you hear in her attitude toward her grandmother? How does this affect her attitude toward herself?
- In what ways has her *vision* changed? What does she see differently now?
- Janie takes on new themes for reflection. Why is it so important that she resists her grandmother's views?
- What does Janie's attitude about the conventions of mourning disclose about her emerging sense of self? Does she continue to maintain an internal and external world?
- How is it that Janie likes "being lonesome for a time"? Wasn't she lonely in her marriages to Logan and to Jody? When do you enjoy or look forward to being lonesome?

Chapters 10–11

Janie grows desirous of a companion, however. She finds "herself glowing inside" when Tea Cake (Vergible Woods) nearly twelve years her junior strolls into her store one evening and invites her to a game of checkers. "Somebody wanted to play. Somebody thought it natural for her to play. That was even nice. She looked him over and got little thrills from every one of his good points." She is taken with him and laughs several times during their exchange. Janie is struck that it "[s]eemed as if she had known him all her life. Look how she had been able to talk with him right off!" (92). She is not only able to speak freely with him, but is, in fact, invited to do so.

Tea Cake follows Janie home—he is the first suitor since Jody's death able to get beyond her porch. Janie wonders what kind of person he is. She learns that he has a clean record but a dubious income. Tea Cake flatters Janie, and she delights in his company, humor, and musical talent. Nevertheless, she is cautious about this newfound attention. Janie wants to protect herself from being "squeezed and crowded out" as she was by Jody. She does not want to be misled. She struggles to keep her desires in check.

> All the next day in the house and store she thought resting thoughts about Tea Cake. She even ridiculed him in her mind and was a little ashamed of the association. But every hour or two the battle had to be fought all over again. (101)

When she holds Tea Cake up to her cherished image of the pear tree, he almost exceeds it.

> She couldn't make him look just like any other man to her. He looked like the love thoughts of women. He could be a *bee to blossom—a pear tree blossom in the spring. He seemed to be crushing scent out of the world with his footsteps. Crushing aromatic herbs with every step he took. Spices hung about him. He was a glance from God.* (101–102, emphasis added)

When he disappears for four days, Janie "plunged into the abyss and descended to the ninth darkness where light has never been" (103). Upon his return, however, Tea Cake assures Janie of his love and encourages her to "have de nerve to *say what you mean.*" Janie is honest, "*Ah wants tuh go wid you real bad*, but,—oh, Tea Cake, don't make no false pretense wid me!" She does not want to make the same mistake she made with Jody. Tea Cake gives his word. "Janie, Ah hope God may kill me if Ah'm lying" (104).

At this point in the novel call students' attention to the degree of introspection and reflection Janie submits herself to; she holds her feelings in check and subjects them to careful consideration. Janie's musings are not highly intellectual, but they are thoughtful nonetheless. The following set of questions will elicit students' careful examination of Janie's musings and her ability to draw deep conclusions based on apparently superficial observations.

- Notice the content of Janie's reflections. While she has little formal education and calls upon romanticized and sensual images to characterize Tea Cake, "He could be a bee to blossom. . . . He seemed to be crushing scent out of the world with his footsteps," she is able to go beneath the surface and draw more profound conclusions. From where does she gain her insights?
- Why is it significant that Janie can speak openly with Tea Cake?
- Describe the struggle Janie is experiencing with her feelings for Tea Cake. Does she have reason to exercise caution? Why or why not?

- What would you advise Janie at this point in her relationship with Tea Cake?

Chapters 12–13: challenge point

Pheoby visits Janie to inform her of the talk among the townsfolk. "Fools seen you out in colors and dey thinks you ain't payin' de right amount uf respect tuh yo' dead husband" (107). Janie responds frankly, "Ah ain't grievin' so why do Ah hafta mourn? Tea Cake love me in blue, so Ah wears it. Jody ain't never in his life picked out no color for me. De world picked out black and white for mournin', Jody didn't. So Ah wasn't wearin' it for him. Ah was wearin' it for the rest of y'all" (107–108). Janie sheds the mask she has been wearing and gives her reasons for wanting to marry Tea Cake. She tells Pheoby, "*Ah wants to utilize mahself all over again*" (107). Pheoby advises her to marry someone more "endurable," reminding Janie that she will not live as comfortably with Tea Cake as she did with Jody. Pheoby echoes Janie's grandmother, which prompts Janie to assert her own desire: "Dis aint no business proposition, and no race after property and titles. *Dis is uh love game. Ah done lived Grandma's way, now Ah means to live mine*" (108, emphasis added).

Janie explains to Pheoby that she was able to climb, to enjoy some of the privileges of the white folks—this is precisely what her grandmother had wanted for her, security, protection, material comfort. However, Janie continues, it did not bring love or happiness.

> She [Nanny] didn't have the time tuh think what tuh do after you got up on de stool of do nuthin'. De object was to git dere. So I got up on de high stool lak she told me, but Pheoby, Ah done nearly languished tuh death up dere. (109)

Pheoby listens sympathetically to Janie but warns her about what happened to their friend, Annie Tyler, whose husband swept her off her feet and then took all of her money and abandoned her. With Pheoby's advice in mind, Janie heads off to marry Tea Cake in Jacksonville, Florida.

A week into her marriage with Tea Cake, Janie settles in Jacksonville. At Pheoby's urging she does keep two hundred dollars hidden from her new husband but laughs to herself and cannot wait to share this silly fear with Tea Cake. Before she can, however, she awakes one morning to discover Tea Cake gone and the two hundred dollars missing. When he does not return all day or night, Janie despairs. She recalls the story of Annie Tyler, who like herself "had waited all her life for something, and it had killed her when it found her" (114). A cloud of doubt overshadows her soul; "it was always going to be dark to Janie if Tea Cake didn't get back soon" (115). She tempers her fear of betrayal with concern for Tea Cake's safety, and she prays that God not rob her of her only real joy. Janie hopes Tea Cake proves to be worthy of her love.

> But oh God, don't let Tea Cake be off somewhere hurt and Ah not know nothing about it. And God, please suh, don't let him love nobody else but me. Maybe Ah'm is a fool, Lawd, lak dey say, but Lawd, ah been so lonesome, and Ah been waitin', Jesus. Ah done waited a long time. (115)

Tea Cake arrives home by daybreak and lifts his new bride from her descent into anxiety. He tells his tale, a fantastic escapade of masquerading as a rich man with two hundred dollars to spend. He details how, where, and why he spent the money. The next day he successfully gambles back the two hundred dollars and wins some more. Janie

> was not shocked at Tea Cake's gambling. It was part of him, so it was all right. She rather found herself angry at imaginary people who might try to criticize. . . . Tea Cake had more good nature under his toe-nails than they had in their so-called Christian hearts. She better not hear none of them backbiters talking about her husband! (120)

Eager to forgive, Janie is determined that they do everything together — "don't keer what it is" (119).

Chapters 14–17

After Janie's trust in Tea Cake has been restored, he tells her that he wants to take her to live and work in the Everglades. Janie realizes this means abandoning the comfort of her home in Eatonville and living in a shanty on the mucks. Nevertheless, as Tea Cake drifts off to sleep that night, "Janie looked down on him and felt a self-crushing love. *So her soul crawled out from its hiding place*" (122). Janie embraces her choice to accompany Tea Cake despite the risks because she sees for the first time, an ideal truly worth embracing, forging a marriage based on reciprocal love. This clearer conception of her goal liberates Janie. She is free now to integrate her internal and external self and to live in accord with her ideal. Her desire is no longer to protect her fragile "inside" life or to pursue a romantic ideal but to reveal her whole self by leading a fully integrated private and public life.

On the one hand, life on the mucks represents a step down; it marks the beginning of a life side by side with "people ugly from ignorance and broken from being poor" (125). On the other hand, it also marks the beginning of Janie's flourishing as a wife, "Janie fussed around the shack making a home while Tea Cake planted beans. After hours they fished" (124). She enjoys her work for the first time. Tea Cake buys guns and launches Janie's formal training in marksmanship. Soon Janie "got to be a better shot than Tea Cake. They'd go out late in the afternoon and come back loaded down with game" (125). Unlike her work in Jody's store, Janie's work on the mucks proves to be creative, fulfilling, and pleasurable.

> Janie stayed home and boiled big pots of blackeyed peas and rice. Sometimes baked big pans of navy beans with plenty of sugar and hunks of bacon lying on top. That was something Tea Cake loved so no matter if Janie had fixed beans two or three times during the week, they had baked beans again on Sunday. She always had some kind of dessert too, as Tea Cake said it gave a man something to taper off on. Sometimes she'd straighten out the two-room house and take the gun and have fried rabbit for supper when Tea Cake got home. She didn't leave him itching and scratching in his work clothes, either. The kettle of hot water was already waiting when he got in. (126)

Tea Cake drops in to visit Janie "at odd hours" during the day because "Ah gits lonesome out dere all day 'thout yuh," he tells her (126). Moved by this gesture, "the very next morning Janie got ready to pick beans along with Tea Cake," and Tea Cake, realizing the demands of her additional work, "would help her get supper afterward" (127). Their home becomes the center of community—visitors, storytelling, music, laughter—in all of which Janie is a key participant. Janie compares her situation to life at the store in Eatonville: "Only here [on the mucks] she could listen and laugh and even talk some herself if she wanted to" (128).

Tea Cake cares vigilantly for Janie. When they "stayed up so late at the fire dances. . . . Tea Cake wouldn't let her go with him to the field. He wanted her to get her rest" (146). Janie is no longer the object of a man's abuse and control; she is the object of her husband's undivided love.

- How has Janie's daily life changed? Despite the material limitations and discomforts, she is happy. Why?
- What new talents and abilities does Janie acquire? Why?
- Janie and Tea Cake have real intimacy, not simply a physical relationship. How is this intimacy achieved, and how does it affect Janie's sense of identity?

Chapter 18

Janie and Tea Cake's love for one another increases when tested by trials. They are met with a major challenge that comes in the form of a violent hurricane. Janie draws the courage and strength to endure the nightmare of the storm from being alongside her husband. Tea Cake worries that he has disappointed Janie and asks, "Ah reckon you wish now you had stayed in yo' big house 'way from such as dis, don't yuh?" Janie responds, "Naw. People don't die till dey time come nohow, don't keer where you at. Ah'm wid mah husband in uh storm, dat's all." Tea Cake presses her, however, "'sposing you wuz tuh die, now. You wouldn't git mad at me for draggin' yuh heah?" Janie discloses her gratitude. "If you kin see the light at daybreak, you don't keer if you die at dusk. It's so many people never seen de light at all. Ah wuz fumblin' round and God opened de door." Surprised, Tea Cake finally exclaims, "Ah never knowed you wuz so satisfied wid me lak dat" (151).

When the storm builds momentum, Tea Cake and Janie attempt to escape the mucks carrying only their money and insurance papers in a piece of oilcloth. They forge their way by foot with the rising lake behind them: "The monstropolous beast had left his bed. The two hundred miles an hour wind had loosed his chains. He seized hold of his dikes and ran forward until he met the quarters; uprooted them like grass" (153). They swim, run, rest, and then swim, run and attempt to rest again. Tea Cake shows extraordinary calm and skill in the face of it all and helps individuals in his path. "Deh snake won't bite yuh," Tea Cake shouts to a man stuck between a huge piece of sheet metal swinging precariously toward him and a rattlesnake with its head reared. The snake, Tea Cake shouted, is "skeered to go into uh coil. Skeered he'll be blowed away. Step round dat side and swim off!" (156).

Ignoring her own exhaustion Janie looks out for her husband. When Tea Cake is finally able to rest along a stretch of road, Janie spies a piece of tar paper roofing and sets out to get it as a blanket and shield for her husband. As Janie lays hold of the tar paper, "the wind lifted both of them" and Janie is thrust into "the lashing water" (157). Tea Cake awakes to Janie's call for help. As she thrashes around in the water, Tea Cake advises her to swim to the cow: "grab hold of her tail! Don't use yo' feet. Jus' yo' hands is enough." A savage dog stood atop of the cow and "raced down the back bone of the tail of the cow to the attack." Simultaneously, "Tea Cake split the water like an otter, opening his knife as he dived." Janie managed to slip back,

> just out of the reach of the dog's angry jaws. Within a moment Tea Cake rose out of the water . . . and seized the dog by the neck. . . . They fought and somehow he managed to bite Tea Cake high up on his cheek bone once. Then Tea Cake finished him and sent him to the bottom to stay there. (158)

The cow drags Janie to the fill while Tea Cake weakly strokes in. Janie tends to Tea Cake's wound and then they continue walking the rest of the day until they reach Palm Beach.

Janie's gratitude is heightened. After finally finding a place to sleep, Tea Cake "humbly" asks Janie, "reckon you never 'spected tuh come tuh dis when you took up wid me, didja?" And Janie responds,

> Once upon uh time, Ah never 'spected notin', Tea Cake, but bein' dead for standin' still and tryin' tuh laugh. But *you came along and made somethin' outa me*. So Ah'm thankful for anything we come through together. (158, emphasis added)

• Has Tea Cake really made something out of Janie? Or has Janie made something out of herself?
• Contrast Tea Cake's aspirations for Janie with Logan Killick's and Jody's.

Chapter 19

When they return to the mucks, Tea Cake helps to reconstruct the dike and houses, but after three weeks his health begins to fail. Janie nurses him as best she can. But when he gags on water and has violent nightmares, "The sickness was worse to Janie than the storm" (166). When Janie fetches a doctor and explains the incident of Tea Cake's struggle with the dog, he responds, "Janie, I'm pretty sure that was a mad dawg bit yo' husband. . . . It's mighty bad dat it's gone on so long" (168). The doctor is able to give Tea Cake some pills to keep him calm but tells Janie that he has "almost no chance to pull through and he's liable to bite somebody else, specially you. . . . It's mighty bad." Janie, however, is willing to go to any lengths to help him; "Doctah, Ah loves him fit tuh kill. Tell me anything tuh do and I'll do it." But when he advises Janie to send him to the hospital so as not to jeopardize her own life, she refuses. She prefers to care for him at home where he is more comfortable. The doctor agrees to wire Palm Beach for a serum but reminds Janie that the prognosis is not hopeful.

Tea Cake's condition worsens, and Janie's courage and loyalty grow. Something one of his friends says to Tea Cake on a visit makes him suspicious of Janie—"Mrs. Turner's brother was back on the mucks and now he had this mysterious sickness" (171). But Janie reassures him, "Tea Cake, 'taint no use in you bein' jealous uh me. In de first place Ah couldn't love nobody but yuh. And in de second place Ah jus' uh ole woman dat nobody don't want but you." Tea Cake challenges her: "wid de eye you'se young enough to suit most any man. Dat aint no lie. Ah knows plenty mo' men would take yuh and work hard fuh de privilege. Ah heard 'em talk" (171–172).

> Maybe so, Tea Cake, Ah ain't never tried tuh find out. Ah jus' know dat God snatched me out de fire through you. And Ah loves yuh and feel glad. . . .

> God made it so you spent yo' old age first wid somebody else, and
> saved up yo' young girl days to spend wid me.
> Ah feel dat way too, Tea Cake, and Ah thank yuh fuh sayin' it. . . .
> Everytime Ah see uh patch uh roses uh somethin' over sportin' they
> selves makin' out they pretty, Ah tell 'em "Ah want yuh tuh see mah
> Janie sometime." You must let de flowers see yuh sometimes, heah
> Janie? (172)

Tea Cake unwittingly makes his final profession of love. And Janie is able to
thank him before the progression of his disease renders him mad. During
their exchange Janie notices "the pistol under the pillow" (172). When Tea
Cake becomes hostile, Janie realizes her life is in danger. That evening "Tea
Cake had two bad attacks. . . . Janie saw a changing look come in his face.
Tea Cake was gone. Something else was looking out of his face" (172).
Janie tries to leave for the doctor, but Tea Cake does not trust her to go.
"He gave her a look full of blank ferocity and gurgled in his throat" (173).
When he steps outside, she deftly empties the first three of the six bullets
from the cylinder of his gun before he returns. Then she "take[s] the rifle
from [the] back of the head of his bed. She broke it and put the shell in her
apron pocket and put it in a corner in the kitchen almost behind the stove
where it was hard to see" (173). All the time she persists in her concern
that "poor sick Tea Cake do something that would run him crazy when he
found out what he had done" (174).

Janie wonders why the doctor has not arrived yet with the serum. Tea
Cake challenges her when he enters the room again. "'How come you
ruther sleep on uh pallet than tuh sleep in de bed wid me?' Janie saw that
he had the gun in his hand that was hanging to his side. 'Answer me when
Ah speak'" (174). Janie tries to encourage him to rest until the doctor
arrives. But then,

> The gun came up unsteadily but quickly and leveled at Janie's breast. . . .
> The pistol snapped once. Instinctively Janie's hand flew behind her on
> the rifle and brought it around. . . . If only the doctor would come! If
> only anyone would come! She broke the rifle deftly and shoved in the
> shell as the second click told her that Tea Cake's suffering brain was
> urging him to kill. . . . No knowledge of fear nor rifles nor anything
> else was there. He paid no more attention to the pointing gun than if
> it were Janie's dog finger. She saw him stiffen himself all over as he
> leveled and took aim. The fiend in him must kill and Janie was the
> only thing living he saw.
> The pistol and the rifle rang out almost together. The pistol just
> enough after the rifle to seem its echo. Tea Cake crumpled as his bullet
> buried itself in the joist over Janie's head. . . . She was trying to hover
> over him as he closed his teeth into the flesh of her forearm. (175)

As Janie holds her beloved Tea Cake dead by her own hand, she reflects.

> It was the meanest moment of eternity. A minute before she was just a scared human being fighting for its life. Now she was her sacrificing self with Tea Cake's head in her lap. She had wanted him to live so much and he was dead. No hour is ever eternity, but it has its right to weep. Janie held his head tightly to her breast and wept and thanked him wordlessly for *giving her the chance for loving service.* (175, emphasis added)

In one swift dramatic juncture Janie moves from nursing her husband to shooting him in self-defense to thanking him. She is not bitter or angry although her fate is bleak—"the grief of outer darkness descended" and "that same day . . . Janie was in jail" (175). She is brought to court and accused of betrayal—Tea Cake's friends on the mucks turned against her—but is acquitted because of the doctor's testimony. During the trial, however,

> *It was not death she feared. It was misunderstanding.* If they made a verdict that she didn't want Tea Cake and wanted him dead, then that was a real sin and a shame. It was worse than murder. (179, emphasis added)

Janie's primary desire now is that the truth of her love, her story, be known. After her acquittal Janie moves on to attend to her dead husband. She buries Tea Cake "with a brand new guitar" in Palm Beach because the 'Glades "were too low for him. . . . Tea Cake was the Son of the Evening Sun, and nothing was too good." Janie wears her overalls to the funeral because "she was too busy feeling grief to dress like grief" (180). Janie is independent and self-possessed; she does not feel compelled to "bow to the outside" the way she did for Jody. Her "inside" and "outside" life are finally one.

Help students to raise questions about what Hurston has accomplished at this point in the novel. In many ways the intense drama in Janie's life heightens the importance of her inner self. Despite all the turmoil and disorder in the world outside her, she has a deep internal strength and calm with which to navigate these circumstances.

- Within moments of this extraordinary trauma, Janie's reflections embrace new insights on love. What do her reflections reveal about what she has come to understand love to mean?
- Why does Janie fear misunderstanding more than death?
- What do understanding and misunderstanding have to do with her sense of identity?
- What does it mean that Janie does not need to "bow to the outside" anymore?

Chapter 20

She returns to Eatonville because "the muck meant Tea Cake and Tea Cake wasn't there. So it was just a great expanse of black mud" (182). She takes some seeds with her because they remind her of Tea Cake and "Now that she was home, she meant to plant them in remembrance" (182). It is Janie's "remembrance" of Tea Cake which now serves as both her anchor and compass. She is contented with herself and able to move on because as she explains to Pheoby:

> Ah done been to de horizon and back and now Ah kin set heah in mah house and live by comparisons. Dis house ain't so absent of things lak it used tuh be befo' Tea Cake come along. *It's full uh thoughts.* . . . (182, emphasis added)

Janie knows the neighbors will be straining to know her story, so she urges Pheoby to tell them the truth of her experience.

> Dey gointuh make 'miration 'cause mah love didn't work lak they love, if dey ever had any. Then you must tell 'em dat love ain't somethin' lak uh grindstone dat's de same thing everywhere and do de same thing tuh everything it touch. Love is lak de sea. It's uh movin' thing, but still and all, it takes its shape from de shore it meets, and it's different with every shore. (182)

Moved by Janie's story, Pheoby exclaims, "Ah done growed ten feet higher jus' listenin' tuh you, Janie. Ah ain't satisfied with mahself no mo'" (182). Pheoby promises Janie that she will not let anyone criticize her in her presence. Janie tells her not to worry, to let people console themselves with talk if they want to because

> talkin' don't amount tuh uh hill uh beans when you can't do nothin' else. And listenin' tuh dat kinda talk is jus' lak openin' yo' mouth and lettin' de moon shine down yo' throat. It's a known fact, Pheoby, you got tuh *go* there tuh *know* there. Yo' papa and yo' mama and nobody else can't tell yuh and show yuh. Two things everybody's got tuh do for theyselves. They got tuh go tuh God, and they got tuh find out about livin' fuh theyselves. (183)

When Pheoby leaves, Janie goes to her room and sits "[t]hinking" (183). Memories of Tea Cake flood her imagination and nourish her soul.

> Then Tea Cake came prancing around her where she was and the song of the sigh flew out of the window and lit the top of the pine trees. Tea

Cake, with the sun for a shawl. Of course he wasn't dead. He could never be dead until she herself had finished *feeling and thinking*. The kiss of his memory made pictures of love and light against the wall. Here was peace. She pulled in her horizon like a great fish-net. Pulled it from around the waist of the world and draped it over her shoulder. So much of life in its meshes! *She called in her soul to come and see.* (183–184, emphasis added)

Students may be surprised at the calm with which Janie assesses her life and circumstances at this point. Encourage them to compare and contrast her musings at the close of the novel with those at the beginning beneath the pear tree. In what respects has Janie continued to remain close to the sensual and immediate realities of life, and in what respects has she learned to transcend them? Remind them that she has been working on acquiring a deeper vision and understanding of herself and others throughout the novel. The following set of questions will help students to recount the factors that were most influential in schooling her desires.

- In what respects is Janie left with much more after Tea Cake's death than she is after Jody's?
- In what respects does Janie's story serve as an education for Pheoby and others who will hear it?
- What does Janie mean when she says that people need to go to God and find out about living for themselves? How does Janie go to God? In what respects is she advocating more than simply learning from experience?
- What account can you provide for Janie's enormous resilience and lack of bitterness in the face of tragedy? How have both pleasure and pain played a role in moral development?
- What new resources and dispositions does Janie possess at the end of the novel that she could not call upon earlier?

SUMMARY REFLECTIONS

Janie's moral progress as transcendence through trials

Unlike Elizabeth Bennet, Janie Crawford begins her journey without formal education or the clear knowledge of the ideals of a virtuous life. She has a wholly naïve understanding of marriage, yet her desire for it is great. Her ability to temper her romanticized desires stems first from obedience to her elders, rather than a principled commitment or internalized dispositions. Janie lacks the guidance of informed reason and virtue. Nonetheless, in the course of the narrative Janie matures into a self-possessed woman whose character and identity are forged in the crucible of suffering. Janie's desires are elevated from blind passion for romantic love and a naïve trust to the pursuit of genuine reciprocal love. The schooling of her desire is particularized by the suffering she experiences in the context of three marriages. It is primarily Janie's habit of assiduous reflection and realistic acceptance of the difficulties that she faces in each marriage that enable her to grow from her experiences.

Three morally pivotal points help to illustrate how her naïve and impulsive desire for marriage ultimately develops into a mature conception of love. Having conjured a sensualized image of marriage at age sixteen, her desire to marry is independent from any direct experience: her mother abandoned her when she was a baby, and she was raised by her single grandmother. Thus, her first morally pivotal point is marked by her realization that marriage itself does not necessarily give rise to love. Logan provides her with neither love nor protection; instead he makes Janie into a mule for his use. Her indignation and tangible aversion to Logan Killicks incite her to pursue a more lovable ideal. Her acquaintance with Jody prompts her to leave Logan and set about loving the man who promises to make "a wife outa" her. Janie's refined ambition, dedicating herself to a person whom she can love, does not find its fulfillment in this relationship. Jody makes Janie into an object, a topic of conversation, a trophy, a worker, but not a wife; he proves to be an egocentric and detached husband.

Seeing that she has put her faith in an ill-formed ideal, Janie's realization that her relationship with Jody is unhealthy marks her second morally pivotal point. She remains with him until his death but refines both her self-understanding and her understanding of love. From this point on she nurtures her own self-knowledge. Janie's mature desire, a desire that propels the entire novel, is not simply marriage, but "self-revelation" (6). In Janie's last and shortest marriage, she finally discovers the ideal for which she has been searching. Tea Cake treats Janie as a partner, another self, not an object. It is in her final marriage that Janie both reveals herself and liberates herself as a person.

The challenge point for Janie is her choice to embrace suffering for the sake of her refined ideal of love. Janie willingly sheds the comfort of a big house, a job, and a reputation as the widowed "mayor's wife," for life in a shanty working on the mucks in the Everglades with a gambler named Tea Cake. This choice, however, not only helps her to integrate her mature desires with her actions, but it also impels her along the path of self-sacrificing love, self-possession, and happiness. In the face of Tea Cake's sickness, Janie brings all of her talent and intelligence to bear. In the face of his death she communicates gratitude and sustains her sense of identity and happiness with the memory of his person and his love.

EXTENSION QUESTIONS

1 The introduction to *Their Eyes Were Watching God* discusses the centrality of "self-revelation" to Janie's growth and development. In a sense, the novel as a whole is a story of self-revelation. In what respects is self-revelation essential to shaping one's mature identity? In what respects is it essential to establishing healthy relationships? In what respects is it fostered in loving relationships?

2 Janie's final marriage is the shortest of the three but the most fulfilling, even after Tea Cake's death. Why?

3 Janie does not have a formal education, yet she is highly reflective about her circumstances, relationships, and beliefs. What account can you give for her self-education? That is, what enabled Janie to learn so much from both disappointment and tragedy?

4 In what respect are Janie's first two marriages important to the success of her third?

5 Why is it that the people of Eatonville may not be able to appreciate Janie's story? What do they lack that Janie has gained?

6 Discuss the significance of voice and vision in this novel.

7 In Book X of his *Nicomachean Ethics*, Aristotle discusses the significance of pleasure and pain in our moral development, arguing that growth in virtue requires and is accompanied by refinements in what we consider to be pleasant. The best and most lasting pleasure, claims Aristotle, comes from actions in pursuit of a worthy ideal. Consider Janie's experiences, particularly her evolving pursuit of pleasure in marriage, in the light of Aristotle's insights.

CONCLUSION

Janie's character is educated through far more traumatic life experiences than Elizabeth Bennet's. The pain in Janie's life is unmitigated. Her only guidance is her capacity for introspection and her ability to refine her understanding of what love means. Janie's story is one of resilience, strength, and reflection, discovering one's power beneath the pain of abuse, love-loss, and even death. In effect, Janie's desires are schooled profoundly by the power of bad example and negative experiences.

This kind of character education is important for our students to witness, especially if they have first-hand knowledge of unjust and extreme suffering. Or, if they are unacquainted with such experiences, they can learn from Janie to develop a deeper appreciation for the potential of the human spirit in the face of unrelenting adversity. Janie best illustrates Victor Frankl's insight that a person can be stripped of everything except the last of all human freedoms, the freedom to choose one's attitude no matter what the circumstances may be. Janie's story is one of liberation: her gradual liberation from ignorance about love, about her self, about each of her husbands. Her character is forged in the enormous interior strength she acquires as she deals with each personal blow and apparent defeat. Janie cultivates "her inner life," something we perhaps do not take seriously enough in a culture of consumerism, spin, and image. Janie's story challenges students to wrestle with the question of how we can cultivate our "inner life" and the resilience to meet some of life's greatest challenges more resolutely. Janie acquires the kind of character that enables her to enjoy self-possession, peace of mind, and even happiness amidst great suffering.

Chapter 6

Sydney Carton—rekindling a sense of purpose

Charles Dickens' *A Tale of Two Cities*[1] offers students a vivid perspective on the French Revolution and an engaging foray into character study. It has been said that Dickens stared long and hard into the mirror, making faces that he thought might best illustrate one of the fictional lives born of his imagination. He is also known to have spent long nights musing about the creation of new characters and to have wept at the untimely death of others. While many of Dickens' characters are amusingly stock, others are complex and warrant careful consideration. Besides introducing readers to a memorable cast of characters, *A Tale of Two Cities* is alive with haunting motifs that give relief to the various themes at work in the novel.

More importantly, *A Tale of Two Cities* has enormous resonance with young and adult readers alike. It chronicles the transformation of a man who sees his life as a failure; it brings readers face to face with bitter injustice and the ravages of war; it portrays family trauma and triumph in nuanced and wholly unexpected ways; it surprises, amuses, horrifies, and saddens. Despite its prevalence in secondary English curricula, many English teachers are apprehensive about teaching *A Tale of Two Cities*. They worry that it is too long, that the language is too Victorian, that the themes are not relevant. Some discount it as simply inaccessible to young people. Replete with suspense and mystery that rival most contemporary action-drama films, *A Tale of Two Cities* is far from dull reading. The following case study of Sydney Carton helps to focus students' attention on the protagonist, whose extraordinary story promises to capture the moral imagination of your students.

TAPPING THE MORAL IMAGINATION

One of the most poignant memories I have of teaching *A Tale of Two Cities* to tenth graders is witnessing one of my student's dramatic reading of Sydney Carton's drunken monologue after he's been left alone by Charles Darnay in a pub near the Old Bailey courthouse. This student's sensitive portrayal of Carton uncannily reflected her own struggle with feelings of worthlessness and regret and proved to be eerily prophetic. Her own trajectory through adolescence was not unlike that of Carton's adulthood. She, too, wandered aimlessly, becoming addicted to drugs and alcohol and ensnared by "low base habits" that led her to escape into sham comforts. Like Carton, she remained nostalgic for the innocence of her youth, good friendship, and the love of her family. As a young adult she was able to turn her life around. While she did not emerge from the darkness unscathed, she did rise above it with new resolve, able to chart a better course for her life ahead.

A Tale of Two Cities speaks to readers on a variety of different levels. Students can identify with Carton's sense of powerlessness and self-loathing. They are intimately familiar with what it means to regret mistakes, to feel as though they are a failure or that they missed their chance to do something worthwhile with their time or talents. Others will know exactly what it means to see great possibilities before them but to feel held back by the pull of their laziness, lack of discipline, or fear of failure. Whether it's the heartbreaking news that they didn't make the final cut for the school play or the varsity football team, or the crushing refusal after mustering the courage to ask someone to the prom, adolescents do experience the pain of feeling inadequate.

Perhaps one of the initial stumbling blocks to engaging readers in *A Tale of Two Cities* is simply making sense of Chapter One. To get this novel off the ground and spark the interest of all readers, I suggest reading the first chapter aloud. An oral reading punctuated with discussion of the context, characters, and motifs will help resistant readers through the initial confusion that sometimes prevents them from enjoying the story. You can provide a backdrop of images depicting the "king[s] with the large jaw and the queen[s] with the plain face" from both England and France. The world famous "Dickens Page" (referenced in Appendix D) provides numerous images, including that of the Dover Road and maps illustrating the various sections of London featured in the novel. A few dramatic and visual prompts will dispel fear and awaken students' curiosity about the characters they meet.

FOSTERING ETHICAL REFLECTION: SYDNEY CARTON

As you read the novel together, give students the opportunity to track the characters they find most interesting. One way to organize this approach is to assign two or three characters to small collaborative groups that you can call upon throughout your reading to make observations about these characters, to raise questions that promote authentic conversation about the novel, to offer dramatic readings and role plays, and/or to prepare illustrations with commentary. To help orient your students' study of character in *A Tale of Two Cities*, provide them with a framework for moral analysis. One useful framework is Aristotle's six states of character described in Book VII of his *Nicomachean Ethics*. The following is a summary of these stages.

1   The *brutish* are those who lack education, nurturing, and good example; they cannot be held accountable for their incivility or brutal behavior. (Think for example of children raised in an atmosphere of drug addiction or horrific domestic abuse.)
2   The *vicious* of character know right from wrong and deliberately choose and enjoy evil. (Here the Grinch, Scrooge, and Voldemort come to mind.)
3   The *weak-willed* know what is right and just, but only occasionally muster the courage to act on what they know to be good; they tend to succumb to temptations and fears. To act virtuously is almost painful. (This is where Carton fits, but Dmitri from *The Brothers Karamazov* also fits this category.)
4   The *strong-willed* are able to muster the wherewithal to do what is right, but it is still an effort for them to do so. (Anne of Green Gables and Jane Eyre most likely belong in this stage.)
5   The *virtuous*, on the other hand, find it easy and enjoyable to pursue justice in thought and action; for them right action and goodness are second nature. Living virtuously gives them pleasure. (Lucie Manette fits here, as well as Atticus Finch from *To Kill a Mockingbird*.)
6   Finally, the *heroically virtuous* choose and act in ways that are above and beyond the call of duty; they exemplify heroic magnanimity and self-sacrifice. (Mother Theresa, Gandhi, and Jesus all demonstrate heroic virtue.)

Challenge students to pay particular attention to those details that introduce us to the person of Sydney Carton: What is he like? What are his characteristic habits, dispositions, attitudes, ways of interacting with others? These constitute Carton's dispositional starting points. Is he a free moral agent? Why or why not? As they continue reading, ask them to consider how these dispositions inform his choices and commitments. The bulleted questions for reflection inserted throughout the case study provide an opportunity for students to track the experiences, events, and relationships that seem to have the greatest impact on Carton. All of these questions are designed to emphasize the four factors central to the schooling of desire (see Chapter 3), and in this specific case, Sydney Carton's moral development.

Book II, Chapters I–III

When we first meet the young attorney, Sydney Carton, in London's Old Bailey courthouse, he is simply referred to as "the wigged gentleman" noticed for little more than his persistent staring at the ceiling. As the trial of the accused Frenchman, Charles Darnay, ensues, we discover, however, that it is not the outspoken counsel, Mr. Stryver, but the unassuming genius of his co-counsel, Carton, that earns Darnay's acquittal. Carton scribbles a note to Stryver indicating that calling attention to the striking resemblance between himself and the prisoner, Mr. Darnay, would weaken the prosecution's argument suggesting that Darnay is unmistakably the man guilty of exchanging papers with French spies "that Friday night in November five years ago" (75).

While the features of the two gentlemen are shown to be remarkably similar, our attention is drawn to Mr. Carton's distinctive appearance. Mr. Stryver, before the jury, describes him as "careless and slovenly if not debauched" in contrast to the prisoner. As the trial moves to a close, Carton remains "leaning back [in his chair] with his torn gown half off him, his untidy wig put on just as it had happened to light on his head after its removal. . . . Something especially reckless in his demeanour . . . gave him a disreputable look" (77).

Sydney Carton, while hardly the picture of a gentleman and lawyer, quietly reveals his own gentility. He is the first to notice Lucie Manette, one of the witnesses, faint in the courtroom. "Officer! look to that young lady," he commands. "Help the gentleman to take her out. Don't you see that she will fall?" At the same time, however, we are reminded that "his manner was so careless as to be almost insolent." Nevertheless, his appearance belies some vestige of moral goodness.

Throughout much of the novel Carton is enshrouded in darkness. He frequently emerges from the shadows, wanders aimlessly in the night, and bears a gloomy countenance. He has no friends to speak of, except Stryver, with whom he maintains a highly utilitarian working relationship. He earns no credit for his savvy; "Nobody had made any acknowledgement of Mr. Carton's part in the day's proceedings; nobody had known of it" (83), and for the most part even he seems entirely indifferent to it.

The following questions are designed to help students to examine the narrative details that shape the readers' initial picture of Sydney Carton. As you explore these questions with your students, invite them to raise additional questions they may have about Carton and why he behaves as he does. (This is also a good time to invite students to present observations they have about some of the other characters they are tracking.)

• What are your first impressions of Carton? Why?

- Notice how Dickens describes Carton's appearance and demeanor. Catalogue the adjectives he uses to describe Carton. What characteristics and abilities stand out? What do they suggest about him?
- What do Carton's actions in the courtroom reveal about his abilities as a lawyer? About his character?
- What preliminary account can you begin to provide for this mixed portrait of Carton?

Book II, Chapters IV–V: first morally pivotal point

The first substantive speech from Carton comes after Darnay's acquittal and dramatically signals the first morally pivotal point for Carton in the novel. With an air of cynicism he invites Charles Darnay to join him for dinner and proceeds to drink himself into a stupor. Darnay cordially thanks Carton for intervening so swiftly on his behalf at the trial, but Carton responds by announcing his utter distaste for life: "I am a disappointed drudge, sir. I care for no man on earth and no man on earth cares for me." Darnay's reply cuts to the heart of Carton's misery: "Much to be regretted. You might have used your talents better" (86).

Carton is not as indifferent as he seems. He is lonely and "disappointed" with life. When Darnay leaves, Carton remains behind and offers a telling monologue as he tries to focus his drunken gaze in a mirror:

> "Do you particularly like the man?" he muttered, at his own image; "why should you particularly like a man who resembles you? There is nothing in you to like; you know that. Ah, confound you! What a change you have made in yourself! A good reason for taking to a man, that he shows you what you have fallen away from, and what you might have been! Change places with him and would you have been looked at by those blue eyes as he was, and commiserated by that agitated face as he was? Come on, have it out in plain words! You hate the fellow." (87)

Despite his impressive talent as a lawyer, Carton's interior sense of failure is awakened by his envy of Charles Darnay—the man in whom he sees not only a resemblance of himself, but also everything he "might have been." His sense of shame about what he has "fallen away from," and sense of loss about the commiseration and affection he does not—and believes he will not—enjoy, are heightened. Carton is painfully aware of what he is missing.

As a boy in school, Carton was referred to by his peers as "the old seesaw Sydney" for his mood swings. Even as a child he used his talent surreptitiously, completing the schoolwork of the other boys. While bright and academically successful, he was not a happy child. And as an adult, he is troubled by remorse.

> Waste forces within him, and desert all around, this man stood still on his way across a silent terrace, saw for a moment, lying in the wilderness before him, a mirage of honourable ambition, self-denial, and perseverance. In the fair city of this vision, there were airy galleries from which the loves and graces looked upon him, gardens in which the fruits of life hung ripening, waters of Hope that sparkled in his sight. A moment, and it was gone. Climbing to a high chamber in a well of houses, he threw himself down in his clothes on a neglected bed, and its pillow was wet with wasted tears.
>
> Sadly, sadly, the sun rose; it rose upon no sadder sight than the man of good abilities and good emotions, incapable of their directed exercise, incapable of his own help and his own happiness, sensible of the blight on him, and resigning himself to let it eat him away. (93–94)

Carton's aspiration is disclosed: to be a man of honor and goodness, everything Charles Darnay represents and Carton wishes he could have been. Carton's encounter with Darnay makes him restless; his desires are conflicted. While painfully aware of his ideal, it strikes him as ultimately unattainable.

The following questions and activities will help students to begin their moral analysis of Carton's character. They ask students to pay particular attention to Carton's habits as disclosed to date and his attitude toward those habits, as well as to the individuals who prompt him to change his focus.

- Why is Sydney Carton apparently indifferent to his victory at the Old Bailey courthouse?
- Can you think of other talented individuals who are indifferent about their successes? What are the reasons for their indifference? When is indifference healthy and natural? When is it harmful? Why?
- Present a dramatic reading of Carton's monologue in the pub. What does he seem to be saying?
- How does Carton spend his time? How do we know? What does he seem to care about?
- How would you describe the range of emotions evoked in Carton this evening? What do they suggest about his ambitions and desires up until now?
- Why is it more difficult for Carton to accept the differences between his personality and character and Darnay's when their physical appearances are so similar?

- Carton is obviously dissatisfied with his life. What prevents him from taking steps to change? Are the main obstacles internal or external?
- Which of Aristotle's six states of character best describes Carton at this point? Why?

Book II, Chapter XIII: second morally pivotal point

Carton's interior conflict—desiring to lead a life of "honourable ambition" but "incapable of their [his abilities and desires'] directed exercise"—leaves him saddened and even ashamed but not morally paralyzed. His attraction to "honourable ambition, self-denial, and perseverance" moves him to spend time with individuals whose lives, unlike his, are virtuous.

Carton begins to visit the Manette household in Soho where Lucie and her father, the former Bastille prisoner, Dr. Manette, live, and where Charles Darnay, the man indebted to him for his life, is also found visiting with the family. During Carton's infrequent visits, he is generally taciturn and removed from the others—more of an observer than a guest—"always . . . the same moody and morose lounger there. When he cared to talk, he talked well; but the cloud of caring for nothing, which overshadowed him with such a fatal darkness, was rarely pierced by the light within him" (157).

Nevertheless, his familiarity, affection, and admiration for the family increases with each visit, and it is in this small house that Carton eventually decides to open his soul to Lucie Manette. "From being irresolute and purposeless, his feet became animated by an intention, and in the working out of that intention, they took him to the doctor's door" (157). Carton sheds his air of indifference as he approaches the Manette house with the intention of speaking with Miss Manette.

The following encounter marks the second morally pivotal point prompting a change in Carton's desires and ambitions.

Lucie notices his unease upon entering the room:

> I fear you are not well, Mr. Carton!
> No. But the life I lead, Miss Manette, is not conducive to health. What is to be expected of, or by, such profligates?
> Is it not—forgive me . . . a pity to live no better life?
> God knows it is a shame!

Carton's self-disclosure to Lucie is made with more sincerity and earnest regret than it was to Darnay—a relative stranger to him at the time of their first conversation. Carton is not speaking out of drunkenness and envy, but rather from heartfelt desire to make himself known. His intention, his need to reveal himself to Lucie is only gradually made clear. He sees the vulgarity of his lifestyle and its threat to his physical and moral health.

Carton's shame is more poignant and illuminating to him than it was before, and Lucie is hopeful that this conversation could occasion a turnaround for him.

Then why not change it?

[With tears in his eyes] It is too late for that. I shall never be better than I am. I shall sink lower, and be worse. . . . I am like one who died young. All my life might have been. . . . If it had been possible, Miss Manette, that you could have returned the love of the man you see before you—self-flung away, wasted, drunken, poor creature of misuse as you know him to be—he would have been conscious this day and hour, in spite of his happiness, that he would bring you to misery, bring you to sorrow and repentance, blight you, disgrace you, pull you down with him. I know that you can have no tenderness for me; I ask for none; I am even thankful that it cannot be.

. . . Can I in no way repay your confidence? . . . Can I turn it to no good account for yourself, Mr. Carton?

To none. . . . I wish you to know that you have been the last dream of my soul. In my degradation I have not been so degraded but that the sight of you with your father, and of this home made such a home by you, has stirred old shadows that I thought had died out of me. Since I knew you, I have been troubled by a remorse that I thought would never reproach me again, and have heard whispers from old voices impelling me upward, that I thought were silent forever. I have had unformed ideas of striving afresh, beginning anew, shaking off sloth and sensuality, and fighting out the abandoned fight. A dream, all a dream, that ends in nothing and leaves the sleeper where he lay down, but I wish you to know that you inspired it.

Will nothing of it remain? O Mr. Carton, think again! Try again!

No, Miss Manette, all through it, I have known myself to be quite undeserving. And yet I . . . wish you to know with what a sudden mastery you kindled me, heap of ashes that I am, into fire—a fire, however, inseparable in its nature from myself, quickening nothing, lighting nothing, doing no service, idly burning away. . . . The utmost good I am capable of now, Miss Manette, I have come here to realize. Let me carry through the rest of my misdirected life, the remembrance that I opened my heart to you, last of all the world; and that there was something left in me at this time which you could deplore and pity.

. . . Lucie Manette wept mournfully as he stood looking back at her.

. . . I am not worth such feeling, Miss Manette. An hour or two hence, and the low companions and low habits that I scorn but yield to, will render me less worth such tears. . . . My last supplication of all, is this. . . . It is useless to say it, I know, but it rises out of my soul. For you, and for any dear to you, I would do anything. If my career were of that better kind that there was any opportunity or capacity of sacrifice in it, I would embrace any sacrifice for you and for those dear to you. (158–161)

Carton has a remarkably clear understanding of his "misdirected life" and a clear sense of purpose in speaking so forthrightly and tenderly with Lucie. His promise reveals a refined aspiration. Since he thinks that he cannot be the person he would like to be, that it is too late to lead the kind of life he admires in Lucie and Charles and Dr. Manette, he chooses to commit himself to something he can do, "the utmost good" of which he believes he is capable.

The following set of questions helps students to focus on what keeps Carton from achieving his potential as well as what motivates him to disclose his soul to Lucie. Invite students to discuss Carton's overwhelming sense of powerlessness and the conflict that is stirred up within him. Draw students' attention to the contrast between the way Carton reveals himself to Darnay and the way he reveals himself to Lucie.

- Why is Carton convinced that he is unable to change despite "old voices impelling [him] upward"? Are people's choices, mistakes, and bad habits ever really irreparable? What does the promise Carton makes suggest about him as a person?
- Note the deliberate interplay of light and dark throughout the novel thus far. Trace this motif and discuss what this imagery reveals about Carton at different dramatic junctures in the narrative.
- Sydney Carton's self-disclosure is both moving and profound. What disposes Carton, the man of indifference and profligate tendencies, to have this conversation? In other words, what has "animated" him to speak so candidly with Lucie?
- What is his intention, really? What, if anything, does he gain from this conversation? What, if anything, does Lucie gain?
- How would you characterize Carton's affection for Lucie, and Lucie's affection for Carton? Does Carton threaten to undermine Lucie's love for her husband in any way? Why or why not?
- Compare and contrast Carton's dialogue with Lucie and his earlier conversation with Darnay. Do the differences in language, tone, and attitude as conveyed through the dialogues reveal any significant moral development?
- Carton claims that he is still enslaved by his bad habits. Is he any freer now, since his conversation with Lucie, than he was before? Why or why not?

Book II, Chapters XIV–XXI

Through his relationship with Lucie Manette, Carton has come to see the importance of friendship and love. Carton is moved to self-disclosure by an enormous sense of indebtedness and love for Lucie. Her example, her affection for her father, and the home she has made together have awakened his desires to change, begin anew, and shed his "wasted, drunken" self. He is grateful to her for raising these noble ambitions to a tangible level but apologetic and ashamed about his inability to turn these ideals into practical commitments—to actually lead a kind of life different from the one to which he has become accustomed. He lacks the strength of will to escape his "low companions and low habits" despite his contempt for them. Carton's admiration and love for Lucie increases along with his desire to lead a worthwhile life. In the end, he makes the one commitment he believes he can keep: "For you and for any dear to you, I would do anything. . . . I would embrace any sacrifice for you and for those dear to you."

Carton is weak-willed, not vicious, but his conflicting desires prevent him from clearly seeing the way to a virtuous life. Carton has examined his life— he is not shallow or unreflective—nevertheless, he fails to see its worth after so much "degradation." His realization, "I am like one who died young. All my life might have been" does not move him to complete despair. Since Carton was first reminded of his shame, he has taken deliberate steps— steps he could have omitted if he lacked courage and remained envious of Darnay. By choosing to spend time in the Manette household and finally revealing his desires and regrets to Lucie, he actually moves away from the pull of self-pity and despair. He finds in the example and friendship of those who lead virtuous lives something sustaining and hopeful.

Carton's conversation with Lucie excites moral growth and prompts an animated sense of purpose in his manner. Dickens underscores this. For example, after Lucie and Darnay marry and meet again with Carton, Darnay notices for the first time "a certain rugged air of fidelity about him" (218). He is also surprised to discover that Carton seeks both his forgiveness for having insulted him during their first meeting as well as his friendship. Nevertheless, his "low habits" continue to bear down heavily upon him. Lucie asks Charles to be "very lenient on his faults when he is not by." She too remains doubtful of Carton's capacity to turn his life around. She tells her husband in confidence, "I fear he is not to be reclaimed; there is scarcely a hope that anything in his character or fortunes is reparable now. But, I am sure that he is capable of good things, gentle things, even magnanimous things" (221).

Carton, having secured permission to visit the Darnay family uninvited from time to time, "claimed his privilege . . . some half-dozen times a year, at most" and "he never came there heated with wine" (223). He manages to control his baser desires so as not to jeopardize the one source of inspiration in his life. Over time he wins a place in the hearts of Lucie and Charles Darnay's children, even in their son who died very young.

> Carton was the first stranger to whom little Lucie held out her chubby arms, and he kept his place with her as she grew. The little boy had spoken of him, almost at the last. "Poor Carton! Kiss him for me!" (223–224)

The following questions should help students to see in this second morally pivotal point how Carton's desires have been schooled from their formerly conflicted state to a clearer resolve to attain a worthy goal. While he is still unable to shed his baser desires and habits, his love for Lucie moves him to spend more of his time with the family. Encourage students to raise questions about and examine the influence of Carton's friendship with Lucie and her family.

- Why does Lucie say of Carton, "I fear he is not to be reclaimed; there is scarcely a hope that anything in his character or fortunes is reparable now. But I am sure that he is capable of good things, gentle things, even magnanimous things" (221)? What does she mean? What do you believe Carton is capable of at this point in the novel?
- How is character formed? How is it weakened and how is it strengthened? Is there a point in life after which it is too late to reclaim one's good character? Why or why not?
- Why do you suppose Lucie and Charles' children show both affection and sympathy for Carton? In what ways is their affection for Carton significant to his evolving change?
- In what ways has Carton changed since we first met him? In what ways has he remained the same?
- How would you describe his aspirations and ambitions at this point in the novel? In what ways are his actions consistent with his aspirations?

Book III, Chapters VI–IX: challenge point

As the revolution brews in France and wreaks havoc both in England and abroad, the Darnays and Dr. Manette are swept into the storm and drawn to Paris. The guillotine takes the lives of dozens of French aristocrats daily and leaves hundreds of revolutionaries thirsting for more bloodshed. Hoping to be of some assistance to his fellow citizens, particularly to one former servant, Gabelle, Charles Darnay returns to France. However, as heir to the Marquis St. Evrémonde, he is soon condemned to death for treason and imprisoned in La Force. Upon his hurried arrival in France, Dr. Manette, former prisoner of the Bastille, wins Charles' acquittal at once, but is unable to use his reputation and loyalty to the Republic to set him free after a second more condemnatory sentence. The conspiracy is too great and the situation too grave to expect any reasonable intervention or turn of events.

Nevertheless, Mr. Jarvis Lorry, Lucie's guardian and Telson's Bank manager, also arrives in Paris with a gentleman (Sydney Carton) in a "riding coat . . . who must not be seen" (299). Carton's anonymous arrival in France proves quite auspicious. His careful observations combined with a string of coincidences bring him face to face with an old familiar spy. A former informant to the English government now turned spy for the new Republic in France, John Barsad ("Sheep of the Prisons"), quickly becomes the object of Carton's blackmail and, consequently, the key to a master plan for Darnay's rescue.

By choosing to go to Paris Carton not only seizes the opportunity to keep his word, but he also embraces the challenge and risk it poses. Carton is finally able to integrate his desires and ambitions with his talents and abilities. What he now sees as most worthwhile is to secure the safety and happiness of Lucie's husband and family. His aspiration has been refined from a conception of what he might have been—a man like Charles Darnay—to a clearer sense of what his own happiness consists in. Motivated by the love and affection he has come to know through the Manette–Darnay family, he chooses to act on his promise. With a clear vision of his commitment, he is able to rise above the baser desires that leave him disappointed and to act in a way consistent with his ideal. This point serves as a defining moment for Carton, an invitation to bring his desires, talents, and abilities into intelligent harmony at the service of his promise to Lucie. He sheds his self-pity and, eventually, the "low companions" and desires which bring him down, because he now sees an opportunity to do something magnanimous in response to the needs of his friends.

Quick thought and precise action characterize Carton's unnoticed work in Paris. Now his reckless and negligent manner serves as a valuable front for the stealthy execution of his plan. A sense of purposefulness embraces all of his actions. As one character later recalls of Carton's interchange with the spy in France, "there was a braced purpose in the arm and a kind of inspiration in the eyes, which not only contradicted his light manner, but changed and raised the man" (319). Moreover, Carton carefully leads Mr. Lorry to believe that he, as a faithful guardian, is carrying the bulk of the responsibility—attending to Lucie, little Lucie, and Dr. Manette. In fact, Carton asks that Lucie not be informed of his presence in the city. Carton's intentions and full scheme remain known only to himself. Prior to his departure from Lorry the evening before Darnay's final sentencing, Carton is reflective and "wistfully" asks Lorry,

> Yours is a long life to look back upon, sir?
> I am in my seventy-eighth year.

You have been useful all your life; steadily and constantly occupied; trusted, respected, and looked up to? . . . See what a place you fill at seventy-eight. How many people will miss you when you leave it empty! . . . If you could say, with truth, to your own solitary heart tonight, "I have secured to myself the love and attachment, the gratitude or respect, of no human creature; I have won myself a tender place in no regard; I have done nothing good or serviceable to be remembered by!" your seventy-eight years would be seventy-eight heavy curses; would they not? (332)

Carton's melancholy does not keep him from assisting Mr. Lorry with his coat and seeing him to Lucie's gate. When he parts with Lorry, he leads him to believe he will spend the night recklessly, "You know my vagabond and restless habits. If I should prowl about the streets a long time, don't be uneasy; I shall reappear in the morning" (333). Carton does not sleep nor does he take a strong drink. He visits a chemist and purchases two potent drugs. Upon leaving the shop, he muses, "There is nothing more to do . . . until tomorrow. I can't sleep." We see a different man from the disreputable drudge we knew earlier. As Carton travels along the streets of Paris that night,

It was not a reckless manner, the manner in which he said these words aloud under the fast-sailing clouds, nor was it more expressive of negligence than defiance. It was the *settled manner* of a tired man, who had wandered and struggled and got lost, but who at length *struck into his road and saw its end.* (335, emphasis added)

Carton's desires are no longer conflicted. He is at peace with himself and able to move freely toward his goal. Contemplating his life as he sees it now, he recalls a childhood memory:

Long ago, when he had been famous among his earliest competitors as a youth of great promise, he had followed his father to the grave. His mother had died years before. These solemn words, which had been read at his father's grave, arose in his mind as he went down the dark streets. . . . "I am the resurrection and the life, saith the Lord: he that believeth in me, though he were dead, yet shall he live: and whosoever liveth and believeth in me, shall never die." (335–336)

Carton invokes these words repeatedly throughout the night as he contemplates the city and the horror of the 52 victims awaiting death on the guillotine the next day. Amidst his wandering he stops to help a little girl across the mud and asks her for a kiss. And by morning, "the prayer that had broken up out of his heart for a merciful consideration of all his poor blindnesses and errors, ended in the words, 'I am the resurrection and the life'" (336).

The following questions help students to attend to the change in Carton. Help them to see that Carton is freer to utilize all of his talent and savvy once this singular opportunity to perform an act of heroic nobility motivates him to shed his bad habits. Ask them to consider what sustains Carton's desire to mastermind this rescue.

- Carton is pensive but focused. Why is he now able to shed his reckless abandon? What enables him to refrain from drinking?
- What new pleasures is Carton able to enjoy?
- Carton's solitude gives rise to new reflections and insights. Compare and contrast his musings now with those disclosed earlier in the novel—in his monologue after first meeting Charles Darnay and in his heartfelt conversation with Lucie Manette. In what ways are his musings the same? In what ways do they reveal change?
- Can you think of an individual who has been able to change his or her habits and attitude radically in order to respond to a more pressing need? What motivated the person to change and why?

Book III, Chapters X–XV

During the morning's trial Darnay is condemned not only by two members of the Republic, but also by the former testimony of Dr. Manette, who in his years of imprisonment recorded the egregious deeds of Charles' father and uncle and condemned the entire line of the Evrémonde family. Lucie faints in the courtroom. And not unlike Carton's first solicitation on Lucie's behalf at the Old Bailey in England, he hurries to her aid and carries her home.

Carton urges Dr. Manette to intervene again for Charles. When the Doctor replies waveringly, "I intend to try," Carton insists, "Of little worth as life is when we misuse it, it is worth that effort. It would cost nothing to lay down if it were not" (360–361). Carton confides to Lorry, however, what he knows to be the likely outcome, "Yes, he will perish: there is no real hope." Yet Dickens invites us to note that Carton "walked with a *settled* step, downstairs" (362, emphasis added).

Carton deliberates, "But care, care, care! Let me think it out!" (363). He learns that Lucie and her child are next in line to be tried and sentenced and sets out immediately to expedite a plan for their safe return to London. He gives Lorry charge of the passes for himself and the Manettes to exit France and assures him, "Don't look so horrified. You will save them all." Lorry is so taken with Carton's "fervent and inspiring" manner that he "caught the flame and was as quick as youth" in following Carton's directives: "Wait for nothing but to have my place occupied [in the carriage], and then for England!" (370–371).

Carton's practical wisdom is fully engaged; he deliberates, understands what he has to do, discerns and chooses the proper plan of attack, and cleverly executes the task. He is not motivated by logic alone, but rather, by that unity of heart, mind, and intention that he was not able to achieve when his desires were conflicted.

Meanwhile Charles Darnay, in his prison cell, contemplates his death and composes a letter offering his love and consolation to Lucie and those who were close to them—Dr. Manette and Mr. Lorry; "[h]e never thought of Carton" (374). In the meantime, Carton secures entry to La Force by means of the "Sheep of the Prisons," John Barsad. When Carton enters the cell, "there was something so bright and remarkable in his look" that the prisoner, shocked to see anyone at all, could hardly believe it was Carton. "I come from her—your wife," Carton explains and immediately asks him to comply with him. First, he asks Darnay to exchange boots, jacket, and cravats. Then, he takes Darnay's ribbon and asks him to shake out his hair. Next, he asks him to write a letter, unaddressed and undated, as he dictates. While Darnay scribbles the words,

> If you remember the words that passed between us, long ago, you will readily comprehend this when you see it. You do remember them, I know. It is not in your nature to forget them. . . . I am thankful that the time has come when I can prove them. That I do so is no subject for regret or grief. (377–378)

Carton waves the elixir he has prepared under Darnay's nose and wearies him until, upon completing the dictation, he faints. Carton finishes their exchange of dress, and now appearing as the prisoner, he calls for the spy to carry Darnay out to the carriage waiting in the courtyard (under the pretense that Carton was weak on entering and made even more faint by his visit with the prisoner). Barsad carries Darnay to safety as planned and leaves Carton locked in the cell to face his death.

Within a short time Carton is brought from his cell to wait with the crowds being carried off in tumbrels to the guillotine. A young seamstress addresses him as the "Citizen Evrémonde" and asks if he would ride with her and hold her hand. When he agrees, she notices that he is not Evrémonde. "Are you dying for him?" she whispers.

> And his wife and child. Hush! Yes.

His final moments are spent comforting the young woman, offering his strength and inspiring hope. Before the guillotine,

> She kisses his lips; he kisses hers; they solemnly bless each other. The spare hand does not tremble as he releases it; nothing worse than a

sweet, bright constancy is in the patient face. She goes next before him—
is gone.

"I am the Resurrection and the Life saith the Lord; he that believeth in
me, though he were dead, yet shall he live; and whosoever liveth and
believeth in me shall never die."

Carton follows her.

The closing passage from this novel accounts for what we may conclude
to be the reflections of a man who achieved his aspiration—the happiness
that accompanies acting in harmony with one's ideals and commitments.
Carton faced his death with heroic virtue.

> They said of him, about the city that night, that it was the peacefullest
> man's face ever beheld there. Many added that he looked sublime and
> prophetic. . . . If he had given an utterance to his [thoughts], . . . they
> would have been these: . . .
>
> "I see a beautiful city and a brilliant people rising from this abyss, and
> in their struggles to be truly free, in their triumphs and defeats, through
> long years to come, I see the evil of this time and of the previous time of
> which this is the natural birth, gradually making expiation for itself and
> wearing out.
>
> I see the lives for which I lay down my life, peaceful, useful, pros-
> perous and happy . . .
>
> I see that I hold a sanctuary in their hearts, and in the hearts of their
> descendants, generations, hence. . . .
>
> I see that child who lay upon her bosom and who bore my name,
> a man winning his way up in that path of life which once was mine.
> I see him winning it so well, that my name is made illustrious there by
> the light of his. I see the blots I threw upon it, faded away. . . .
>
> It is a far, far better thing that I do, than I have ever done; it is a far,
> far better rest that I go to than I have ever known." (402–404)

*The following set of questions help students to examine the factors that
enable Carton to see his path so clearly and pursue it. As Carton finally
acquires the inner strength to act in accordance with his long latent noble
desires, his vision also expands and his aspirations are free to soar to new
heights. Invite students to discuss all of the images Carton "sees" before he
meets his death.*

- Why is Carton peaceful as he approaches the guillotine? How has he
  achieved this peace?
- Is Carton's last act that of a worn-out "disappointed drudge" who has
  nothing to lose by facing his death at the guillotine, or is it that of a
  hero who gives his life nobly? What determines the difference?

- What is the difference between skill and virtue? How does Carton's work in Paris reveal the combination of both?
- Sydney Carton is presented early on as a muddled portrait of an enormously capable and skilled lawyer but a socially aloof, lonely, and degraded man. Why does Dickens paint him so critically and sympathetically at the same time? What might Dickens want us to take into consideration about the hidden features of a person's soul?
- What insights does Carton's moral development offer on the interrelationship between seeing what is noble and good, loving it, and taking right action?
- What if Carton had not had this opportunity to do something great with his life? How important for moral change is *the chance*, the opportunity, to change?

SUMMARY REFLECTIONS

Carton's moral progress as harmonizing desires

Sydney Carton's desires are schooled in the crucible of shame and self-sacrifice, but they are also nurtured in the context of trust and friendship. A brilliant but lonely barrister in London, Carton appears at first glance a moral profligate who wanders aimlessly and unhappily through life with an air of apparent indifference. The schooling of Carton's desire is particularized by a gradual integration of his desires with the great ideals rendered ineffective by his bad habits. At each morally pivotal point—his encounter with Darnay, and later, his self-disclosure to Lucie—shame is present and so is an individual who treats him with respect. Shame awakens Carton's desire to change the direction of his life; respect and trust give him the impetus he needs to undergo the schooling of desire. At the challenge point, Carton chooses the guillotine, to give up his life for the sake of those he loves. Carton progresses from a state of conflicted desires, which renders him morally inert, to a state of harmonized desires that leads to fluid virtuous action and a newfound sense of freedom. He offers his life in the highest tribute of friendship and in an act of heroic virtue.

The first morally pivotal point, Carton's encounter with Darnay, draws Carton's aspirations into focus and reveals how far from indifferent he is. In Darnay, Carton is able to apprehend and appreciate the virtues of the good life—"honourable ambition, self-denial, and perseverance"—and to see what he "might have been," an insight that Gatsby never glimpses. Yet, Carton is weak-willed, unable to escape "the low companions and low habits that [he] scorn[s] but yield[s] to." Carton's knowledge of what is truly desirable and his ability to lead a noble life are in direct conflict. Dickens describes him as "the man of good abilities and good emotions, incapable of their directed exercise, incapable of his own help, and his own happiness" (94). The striking physical resemblance between Carton and Darnay is a poignant reminder of everything he could have been had he spent his life differently.

While mixed with feelings of envy and resentment, this realization does not inspire a transformation in the way Carton leads his life. This moment does, however, provoke insights about himself as well as a decision to spend more time in the company of people whose lives he finds attractive for their virtue—Lucie Manette and her elderly father, Dr. Manette. Shame also serves as a catalyst for Carton's moral growth and helps him to reflect upon the state of his own life and begin to study the lives of others. Carton's shame, awakened at the first morally pivotal point, does not paralyze him, but rather impels him to observe, surround himself with and learn from the individuals he admires. His visitations and reflections on their lives eventually prompt Carton to disclose to Lucie the aspirations that he believes he is unable to fulfill. He acknowledges his weakness and is moved by gratitude and respect to make a sincere promise.

At his *challenge point*, Carton's desires are decidedly redirected. Carton responds to the need to free Darnay from the wrath of the revolutionaries in Paris. His goal is clear: he must utilize all of his talent and abilities to keep his promise to Lucie. Thus, Sydney Carton rises to the occasion and leads the remainder of his short life with extraordinary focus and satisfaction. His desires, now harmonized with his purpose, make his profligate ways no longer a temptation. Practical wisdom kicks into gear and enables him to execute Darnay's rescue with extraordinary deftness. Carton's musings and reflections on Mr. Lorry's life, his own childhood, and the situation in Paris throughout his careful work place his newfound purpose in a wider, more meaningful context. Carton is finally able to find a purpose in the completion of every act, especially his final one.

EXTENSION QUESTIONS

1 Examine Carton's manner of speech—his language, tone, decisiveness, etc.—as the novel progresses. Discuss the insights that language provides into character.
2 Sometimes people think it is too late to make a change in the way they are leading their lives. They feel trapped by their bad habits and even their reputation and find themselves unable to break free to make a fresh start. Drawing insights from Dickens' *A Tale of Two Cities* and Aristotle, write a letter of advice to a friend or fictionalized friend in need of help. Describe what you believe he or she can realistically commit to in order to shed one or two paralyzing bad habits and develop virtues in their place.

3 Few people in life are either wholly good or wholly evil. Charles Dickens is masterful at creating stock characters and foils such as Lucie Manette and Madame Defarge. Lucie is described as the "golden thread" who knits harmony and love into all she does. At some points in the novel, her goodness is almost too much to bear. Madame Defarge, by contrast, casts a shadow of death on almost everyone she encounters. Her cold-blooded elation beside the guillotine makes her one of the darkest villains in literary history. On the other hand, Monsieur Defarge invites further reflection. He is clearly a conflicted character caught between his gratitude to Dr. Manette and his loyalty to his wife and fellow comrades. Several other characters in the novel also warrant our careful consideration because of their complexity. Choose a character other than Sydney Carton and analyze the morally pivotal points and challenge points he or she faces. At the end of your analysis, discuss whether you are ultimately sympathetic or critical of this character's choices and commitments.

4 Carton's state at the beginning of the novel is reminiscent of what Plato calls the "tyrannical soul"—"full of disorder and regret"—in his famous *Republic* (577e). How can our desires act as tyrants over our actions and choices? How does the schooling of Carton's desires parallel his growth in freedom?

5 What enables some people to be effective or skillful in certain situations such as school or work, for example, but also to maintain self-destructive habits? Think of some of your own choices and behaviors over the years—those that were born of determination to do what is right and just and those that resulted from caving in to stress or succumbing to temptation. What factors help a person to shed bad habits and acquire good ones?

6 A *Tale of Two Cities* offers a number of illustrations of power, the abuse of power, and the power of weakness. Define power, and discuss the origins and context of rightful power and its honorable uses in contrast with abuses of power. Use examples from the novel to illustrate each kind of power.

7 Read Luke's biblical narrative of the Prodigal Son (Luke 15: 11–32). Then take a look at Rembrandt's painting, "The Prodigal Son." What insights do we gain from the narrative and the painting about weakness and strength, about getting it right all the time and messing up royally? Discuss what these narrative depictions help us to understand about Sydney Carton. Are there other characters in the novel to whom these insights might also apply?

CONCLUSION

For Carton, friendship is central to his character education. We learn that he is disappointed with himself and that he experienced loss in childhood. The questions "character for what?" and "character for whom?" have been long unanswerable for Carton. He has maintained his professional skill and savvy as a lawyer, but he dedicates his non-working hours to debauchery. Carton's character education is incited by his attraction to Lucie Manette and her family. He is prompted to re-evaluate his own trajectory and choices by his observations of the Manettes and Darnay and the time spent with them. But the incident that moves him to take action and shed the habits that keep him from leading a fully flourishing life, is the opportunity he gets to rescue Lucie's husband, Charles Darnay. The chance to help Lucie and her family gives a new sense of purpose to his liing, a new-found meaning to his action, and in turn, gives him also the resoluteness he needs to abandon drinking and wanton life. His actions are not merely reckless bravado but rather the seamless and wholehearted response of friendship. He had been welcomed into the Manette household as a friend. Indeed, his love for Lucie, and her belief in his worth, inspire in him a greatness he never knew he possessed. One realizes that even as he goes to France and before he actually has the opportunity of saving Charles, that he is already a changed man. It is friendship that prompts him to reflect on his life as a whole, that makes him look more carefully at the kind of life he could lead, and finally to take action consistent with his ideals and shed those habits that hold him back from becoming the kind of person he always aspired to be.

Carton is not unlike many young people and adults who are enslaved by the shackles of addiction or regrets for past deeds they believe they cannot undo. They shut down in a kind of depression or inertia, or worse, seek a more violent recourse for their bitter disenchantment with life. Carton's story is a reminder that friendship can serve as a crucial catalyst in the schooling of desire, in re-awakening a sense of purpose. Moreover, his journey teaches us that interventions and skills alone may not provide the same impetus that admiration for what is noble, good, and attractive in human love can provide. It is important for students to note that it is not simply Carton's affection for the Manette–Darnay family that moves him, but Lucie Manette's faith and confidence in him that contributes to his transformation. All of these novels attest to the power of human relationships to educate character for better or worse. In Carton's case, his friendship with Lucie helps to elucidate a more compelling *telos* than simply doing the right thing. Carton always knew right from wrong in the abstract, but he was stuck in his bad habits, unmotivated to change his ways. Lucie and her family made the attainment of virtue personal and purposeful.

Chapter 7

Jay Gatsby—the tragedy of blind *eros*

The Great Gatsby[1] is not only a brilliant period piece bringing memorable images of the roaring twenties to life, but also a piece of literary genius that engages readers with Fitzgerald's provocative style. Below is a sampling of Fitzgerald's lilting sensuous detail from Chapter Three of the novel:

> In his blue gardens men and girls came and went like moths among the whisperings and the champagne and the stars. (39)

> Every Friday five crates of oranges and lemons arrived from a fruiterer in New York—every Monday these same oranges and lemons left his back door in a pyramid of pulpless halves. (39)

> The bar is in full swing, and floating rounds of cocktails permeate the garden outside, until the air is alive with chatter and laughter, and casual innuendo and introductions forgotten on the spot, and enthusiastic meetings between women who never knew each other's names. (40)

> The lights grow brighter as the earth lurches away from the sun, and now the orchestra is playing yellow cocktail music, and the opera of voices pitches a key higher. (40)

Students are inclined to enjoy Fitzgerald's style, to be taken in by his seductive imagery and ironic dialogue. More importantly, *The Great Gatsby* is a novel about the viability and fragility of dreams, about perceptions of reality, about desires, and about the extremes to which people will go to pursue them. It has a particular appeal to young adult readers because it challenges them to confront the meaning of friendship, love, and the pursuit of happiness in a world that at once glitters with tantalizing options and drones with an enervating barrenness. It asks them to explore what constitutes personal identity. Timely and resonant with the pulsing enticements of our own image-saturated culture, *The Great Gatsby* raises a number of important questions that appeal to students who are in the throes of developing their own sense of self: Will possessing the right "stuff" and cultivating the right image make me more attractive? Will they make my life more satisfying, exciting, and happy? Are all dreams worthy of pursuit? What makes a dream worthy of pursuit?

TAPPING THE MORAL IMAGINATION

One of the first times I taught *The Great Gatsby* to seniors in high school, I was struck by the influence of its characters on the moral imaginations of my students. They were troubled by Jordan's reputation for lying, Tom Buchanan's arrogance, and Daisy's total preoccupation with herself. They had mixed feelings toward Gatsby, torn between trying to decide if he was simply naïve and misguided or if he was dangerously obsessed, borderline insane, more of a stalker than a lover. Perhaps the most eloquent testimony to the sway these characters held over my students was given at the end of one English class, when two girls were packing their books and preparing to leave the room. They had begun discussing weekend plans and who was invited to an upcoming party, when one of them blurted out indignantly, "You are such a Daisy Buchanan." Whether or not the details of the conversation warranted such a slight I'll never know. What I do know is that the young woman accused felt the blow with full force. She was reduced to tears and a bitter quarrel ensued. Fortunately, these two young women, who had been friends for some time, reconciled their differences within the week. Perhaps their exchange was more striking to me than it was to them; it was the first time I had witnessed the invocation of a literary character nearly give rise to a fist fight. This incident remains with me as a reminder that the "company we keep" through reading can become very real to us.[2]

The Great Gatsby speaks to students on a variety of levels. Charged with romantic intrigue and boldness, the novel celebrates the allure of a glittering life replete with fancy parties, sparkling personalities, and showpiece cars, but it also points to the evanescence of it all. It illustrates the vagaries and emptiness of some people's lives despite their glamour and fortune. The novel's tragic strain challenges students to take a closer look at casual recklessness, brutal snobbery, and self-indulgent lust. While in many ways the hero remains sympathetic to readers, the tragedy of his life and dream gives them pause. Students do tend to need some guidance, however, to probe beneath the surface of this narrative.

To prepare readers for the themes they will encounter, examine Gatsby alongside a poem such as Langston Hughes' "A Dream Deferred." Alternately, you could study this poem with your students at the end of the novel. Hughes was a contemporary of Fitzgerald, writing during the Harlem Renaissance. Another way to prime students for their reading is to view a scene from a contemporary film illustrating the potential of dreams and desires to take command of a person's life. *October Sky* (Universal Pictures 1999), for example, a film about the son of coal miner whose pursuit of his dream to become a rocket scientist transforms his life, and *Quiz Show* (Hollywood Pictures 1994), a movie depicting a young academic's slip into the snare of cheating for an easy shot at fame and fortune and the life-changing consequences of his choice, offer a set of contrasting illustrations. Prompt students to look at the roles friends, teachers, family, colleagues, and society play in helping individuals to achieve their dreams.

Once you've considered the compelling nature of dreams—their potential to serve as both an impetus and stumbling block in shaping a person's course of action—ask students to describe a dream or great ambition they or someone they know would like to achieve. Ask them to explore the major obstacles to making this dream come true and what needs to be done to overcome them. Ask students to consider whether or not the dream is attainable, and encourage them to discuss whether it is worth pursuing this dream even if its attainability is uncertain. Ask them to explore any other criteria that ought to be brought to bear when thinking about the pursuit of dreams.

Then ask students to write about something they simply want or wish they had. Ask if they have ever found themselves preoccupied with this desire. Why or why not? To avoid responses that are inappropriate for the classroom, encourage the students to write about topics that they would not be embarrassed to share with a classmate or teacher. Give students the option to write about someone else's dreams and desires instead of their own. Ask students to save these reflections in order to revisit this topic after they have completed *The Great Gatsby*.

FOSTERING ETHICAL REFLECTION: JAY GATSBY

As you begin the novel, tell the students that Gatsby's neighbor, Nick Carraway, narrates Jay Gatsby's story, and explain that understanding Gatsby therefore also requires understanding a little bit about Nick. Ask them to search for passages that disclose who Nick is and what he cares about. Early on in the novel, Nick describes himself as "inclined to reserve all judgments, a habit that has opened many curious natures to me" (1). As they begin reading, ask them to collect data that will help them to determine Nick's reliability and trustworthiness as a narrator. The following passage is a helpful starting point for their consideration:

> Reserving judgments is a matter of infinite hope. . . . And after boasting this way of my tolerance, I come to the admission that it has a limit. . . . When I came back from the East last autumn I felt that I wanted the world to be in uniform and at a sort of moral attention forever; I wanted no more riotous excursions with privileged glimpses into the

human heart. Only Gatsby . . .was exempt from my reaction—Gatsby who represented everything for which I have an unaffected scorn. (1–2)

Nick's suspended judgment or tolerance of Gatsby is important for students to keep in mind as the details of Gatsby's life unfold before them. Encourage students to examine the friendship between Nick and Gatsby: *What is its basis? What do they see as the strengths of their friendship? What are the limitations?*

As the students read the first few chapters of the novel, ask them to pay attention to Gatsby's (as well as other characters') ambitions and dreams: *How are they disclosed? What do they reveal about his character? Why is Gatsby so mysterious? What does the reader want to know about him?* Invite students to pay particular attention to the factors—relationships, events, and personal dispositions—that awaken, prompt, and sustain Jay Gatsby's moral agency. That is, ask them to identify what inspires commitment, choice, and action. At each dramatic juncture in the novel, prompt students to evaluate Gatsby's conclusions and choices: *On what rationale does he draw his conclusions? To whom does he turn for advice?* Students should also consider how Gatsby's temperament and personality affect his ability to discover and pursue a worthy ideal. *In what ways does Gatsby's temperament help his moral growth? In what ways is it a hindrance?*

Chapters 1–3[3]

From the lawn of his small carriage house on the bay in West Egg, Long Island, Nick Carraway notices his neighbor Jay Gatsby for the first time. Nick hesitates "to call . . . for he [Gatsby] gave a sudden intimation that he was content to be alone—he stretched out his arms toward the dark water in a curious way, and, far as I was from him, I could have sworn that he was trembling" (21). Nick follows Gatsby's gaze to the green light across the water and turns back again to address him, but Mr. Gatsby disappears.

Gatsby's profile begins to take shape as various guests who frequent the extravagant parties in his home guess at the source of his wealth. One woman who recently visited Gatsby's home for a party asserts, "they say he's a nephew or a cousin of Kaiser Wilhelm's. That's where all his money comes from. . . . I'm scared of him. I'd hate to have him get anything on me" (33). Circulating among the guests at his first party in Gatsby's house, Nick overhears that Gatsby replaced the dress a woman tore at one of his last parties with another priced at $265. "'There's something funny about a fellow that'll do a thing like that,'" explained the woman telling the story. "'He doesn't want trouble with *anybody*.'" The whispered gossip continues: "'Somebody told me they thought he killed a man once,' . . . '[I]t's more like he was a German spy during the war'" (43–44). "'He's a bootlegger. . . . One time he killed a man who had found out that he was nephew to Von Hindenburg and second cousin to the devil'" (61).

Despite his allegedly sinister reputation, guests arrive at Gatsby's home in droves. "People were not invited—they went there" (41). When Nick finally meets Gatsby in person he describes him as warm but elusive and even bordering on absurd.

> He smiled understandingly—much more than understandingly. It was one of those rare smiles with a quality of eternal reassurance in it, that you may come across four or five times in life. It faced—or *seemed* to face—the whole external world for an instant, and then concentrated on you with an irresistible prejudice in your favor. It understood you just as far as you wanted to be understood, believed in you as you would like to believe in yourself, and assured you that it had precisely the impression of you that, at your best, you hoped to convey. *Precisely at that point it vanished—and I was looking at an elegant young roughneck, a year or two over thirty, whose elaborate formality of speech just missed being absurd. Some time before he introduced himself I'd got a strong impression that he was picking his words with care.* (48, emphasis added)

It is unclear whether Gatsby is truly understanding or extraordinarily affected. Nick continues to gather data from this emerging portrait of Gatsby, noticing that there is something sculpted and studied about him.

> Gatsby [was] standing alone on the marble steps and *looking from one group to another with approving eyes.* His tanned skin was drawn attractively tight on his face and his short hair looked as though it were trimmed every day. I could see nothing sinister about him. I wondered if the fact that he was not drinking helped to set him off from his guests, for it seemed to me that he *grew more correct* as the fraternal hilarity increased. (50, emphasis added)

As introduced through the lens of Nick's observations, an aura of mystery and unrealism hovers around Gatsby's character. Gatsby's identity itself seems akin to a surrealistic dream. This lack of realism—Gatsby's failure to check his dreams and self-image against reality and to refine them accordingly—will turn out to be one of the main obstacles to Gatsby's moral development. Call students' attention to this important theme and encourage them to keep it in mind as they learn more details about Gatsby over the course of the narrative. The following questions will help students to consider the surrealism of Gatsby's identity, priming them to see its moral effects later in the novel.

- How are reputations formed? How has Gatsby's reputation been formed thus far? Why might the author introduce us to Gatsby this way?
- A mysterious portrait of Mr. Jay Gatsby begins to unfold. Fitzgerald and the narrator attend closely to Gatsby's appearance, gestures, and demeanor. What can the reader infer about Jay Gatsby from these details? Support your conclusions.
- Can the reader adequately guess the source of Gatsby's wealth at this point, or are readers supposed to imagine multiple possibilities?
- What questions would you like to ask Jay Gatsby if you had the chance?

Chapter 4

Gatsby's unnatural propriety is further disclosed when he calls on Nick. "Good morning, old sport. You're having lunch with me today and I thought we'd ride up together."

> He was balancing himself on the dash board of his car with that resourcefulness of movement that is so particularly American—that comes I suppose with the absence of lifting work or rigid sitting in youth and, even more, with the formless grace of our nervous, sporadic games. This quality was continually breaking through his punctilious manner in the shape of restlessness. *He was never quite still; there was always a tapping foot somewhere or the impatient opening and closing of a hand.* (64, emphasis added)

Nick detects Gatsby's restless eagerness but is disappointed to learn during the course of their long drive together

> that he had little to say. So my first impression, that he was *a person of some undefined consequence*, had gradually faded and he had become simply the proprietor of an elaborate road-house next door. (64, emphasis added)

> And then came that disconcerting ride [Nick explains]. We hadn't reached West Egg village before Gatsby began leaving his elegant sentences unfinished and slapping himself indecisively on the knee of his caramel-colored suit. "Look here, old sport," he broke out surprisingly, "what's your opinion of me, anyhow?" (65)

Gatsby swiftly moves from an affected familiarity to an affected candor to relay the salient details of his background.

> "Well, I'm going to tell you something about my life," he interrupted. "I don't want you to get a wrong idea of me from all these stories you

hear. . . . *I'll tell you God's truth.*" *His right hand suddenly ordered divine retribution to stand by.* "I am the son of some wealthy people in the Middle West—all dead now. I was brought up in America but educated at Oxford, because all my ancestors have been educated there for many years. It is a family tradition." (65, emphasis added)

Over lunch in New York, Nick learns more about Gatsby from Meyer Wolfsheim, Gatsby's close friend and the gambler who "fixed the World Series in 1919." Wolfsheim's cufflinks, he brags, are "the finest specimens of human molars." When Gatsby steps away from the table, Wolfsheim remarks,

> Fine fellow isn't he? Handsome to look at and a perfect gentleman. . . . I made the pleasure of his acquaintance just after the war. But I knew I had discovered a man of fine breeding after I talked to him an hour. I said to myself: "There's *the kind of man you'd like to take home and introduce to your mother and sister. . . . Yeah, Gatsby's very careful about women. He would never so much as look at a friend's wife.*" (72, emphasis added)

Somewhat in tension with the former account, Wolfsheim also tells Nick,

> I raised him up out of nothing, right out of the gutter. I saw right away he was a fine gentlemanly young man and when he told me he was an Oggsford, I knew I could use him good. (172)

Along with providing further insight into Gatsby's still mysterious background, these passages provide ample data for reflection about the way that relationships influence Gatsby's moral development. Invite students to consider whether Gatsby seems to have any genuine friends, and to keep this point in mind as an important factor in his (failed) schooling of desire.

- We have just now begun to learn Gatsby's own story. What does he reveal about himself? What does his language and manner of speaking seem to reveal? What questions about Gatsby are still left unanswered?
- Why do you suppose he asks Nick, "What's your opinion of me, anyhow?"
- Nick never directly challenges or questions Gatsby about his background and lifestyle, despite having reasons for suspicion. Why do you think he remains silent? Does he seem to have any genuine concern for Gatsby's well-being? Does anyone provoke Gatsby to reflect about his life?
- Does Gatsby seem like an honest person? Why or why not?
- How reliable is Wolfsheim's analysis of Gatsby? Why?

- What can we tell about Wolfsheim from his short conversation with Nick?
- What does Wolfsheim mean when he says, "I knew I could use him good"? What does this reveal about the basis of Wolfsheim's relationship with Gatsby?
- In what way are Gatsby and Wolfsheim odd bedfellows? In what ways are they alike?

Chapters 5–6: first morally pivotal point

We learn eventually that Jay Gatsby has a slightly different profile. His family name is Gatz, and as a seventeen-year-old, the young Jay *Gatz* was a clam digger and salmon fisher from North Dakota. We also learn that he was full of ambition and passion and had a streak that suggests that he was not "very careful about women."

> He knew women early, and since they spoiled him he became contemptuous of them, of young virgins because they were ignorant, of the others because they were hysterical about things which in his overwhelming self-absorption he took for granted. (99)

Grandiose desires consume him, but the content of those desires do not have clear shape. Nevertheless,

> his heart was in a constant turbulent riot. The most grotesque and fantastic conceits haunted him in his bed at night. A universe of ineffable gaudiness spun itself out in his brain while the clock ticked on the washstand and the moon soaked with wet light his tangled clothes upon the floor. Each night he added to the patterns of his fancies until drowsiness closed down upon some vivid scene with an oblivious embrace. For a while these reveries provided an outlet for his imagination; they were a *satisfactory hint of the unreality of reality, a promise that the rock of the world was founded securely on a fairy's wing.* (99–100, emphasis added)

Gatz's early desires are forged in his imagination. His aspirations and ambitions gradually assume shape first, by aversion to his early experience at college, and later, by attraction to what he imagines to be a compelling incarnation of the life he would like to lead.

> An instinct toward his future glory had led him . . . to the small Lutheran college of St. Olaf in southern Minnesota. He stayed there two weeks, *dismayed at its ferocious indifference to the drums of his destiny,* to destiny itself, and despising the janitor's work with which he was to

pay his way through. Then he drifted back to Lake Superior, and he was still searching for something to do on the day that Dan Cody's yacht dropped anchor in the shallows along shore. (100, emphasis added)

The first morally pivotal point for Jay Gatz is his encounter with Dan Cody, "a product of the Nevada silver fields, of the Yukon, and of every run for metal since seventy-five," the embodiment of Gatsby's dream. The young Jay Gatz realizes his ambition

> at the specific moment that witnessed the beginning of his career—when he saw Dan Cody's yacht drop anchor over the most insidious flat on Lake Superior. It was James Gatz who had been loafing along the beach that afternoon in a torn green jersey and a pair of canvas pants, but it was already Jay Gatsby who borrowed a rowboat, pulled up to the *Tuolumne*, and informed Cody that a wind might catch him and break him up in half an hour. (98)

Jay Gatz seizes his opportunity to respond to a vocational call, to shed his working-class roots, and craft a new identity for himself.

> I suppose he'd had the name ready for a long time, even then. His parents were shiftless and unsuccessful farm people—his imagination had never really accepted them as his parents at all. *The truth was that Jay Gatsby of West Egg, Long Island, sprang from his Platonic conception of himself.* He was a son of God—a phrase which, if it means anything means just that—and he must be about His Father's business, the service of a vast, vulgar, and meretricious beauty. So he invented just the sort of Jay Gatsby that a seventeen-year-old boy would be likely to invent, and to this conception he was faithful to the end. (99, emphasis added)

This first morally pivotal point illustrates the moment Gatsby channels his adolescent desires toward realizing a specific goal. When Dan Cody's yacht drops anchor, he decidedly sets out to craft a similar life for himself—a life that he believes will make him happy. He pursues a particular kind of education.

> To young Gatz, resting his oars and looking up at the railed deck, that yacht represented all the beauty and glamour in the world. . . . At any rate, Cody asked him a few questions (one of them elicited the brand new name) and found that he was quick and extravagantly ambitious. . . . He was employed in a vague personal capacity—while he remained with Cody he was in turn steward, mate, skipper, secretary, and even jailer, for Dan Cody sober knew what lavish doings Dan Cody

drunk might soon be about, and he provided for such contingencies by reposing more and more trust in Gatsby. The arrangement lasted five years, during which the boat went three times around the Continent. It might have lasted indefinitely except for the fact that Ella Kaye came on board one night in Boston and a week later Dan Cody inhospitably died.

And it was from Cody that he inherited money—a legacy of twenty-five thousand dollars. He didn't get it. He never understood the legal device that was used against him, but what remained of the millions went intact to Ella Kaye. (101–102)

Gatsby refers to the picture of Dan Cody in his bedroom as "my best friend years ago" (94). Nick describes the image this way:

> I remember the portrait of him . . . a gray, florid man with a hard, empty face—the pioneer debauchee, who during one phase of American life brought back to the Eastern seaboard the savage violence of the frontier brothel and saloon. It was indirectly due to Cody that Gatsby drank so little. Sometimes in the course of gay parties women used to rub champagne into his hair; for himself he formed the habit of letting liquor alone. (101)

These passages are crucial for exploring the lack of realism—the lack of courage to face the truth—that leads to Gatsby's failed schooling of desire. With the following questions as a springboard, help students to see how, rather than having the courage to shape his desires in response to a reflective understanding of reality, Gatsby attempts to recreate his own reality in the image of his desires.

- Pay attention to Gatsby's early desires and passions, as well as his attitude toward his parents. Why do you think his "imagination . . . never really accepted them as his parents at all"?
- We learn that Jay Gatsby's identity is "invented." Why do people invent identities for themselves? Why is it tempting to create one's own identity? Can you think of other individuals (in literature, film, popular culture, or the media) who have invented identities?
- What is the difference between genuine identity formation and invented identity? Corporate and personal image consultants have sprouted up in major cities around the world. In what ways do image consultants help to create an individual's identity? In what ways are they limited in achieving their goal?
- Gatsby seems to have a vivid imagination. Does his imagination foster reflection, or divert him from it? How can you distinguish between reflec-

tion and daydreaming or letting one's thoughts flow in a stream of consciousness?

• Notice how Fitzgerald's narrator Nick juxtaposes allusions to high ideals — "a Platonic conception of himself" and "He was a son of God" — with references to base desires — "vulgar and meretricious beauty." What is a "Platonic conception"? How is Gatsby like "a son of God"? In what ways is he different? What might Fitzgerald be suggesting about Gatsby's self-conception?

• For further study see the passage in the New Testament where Jesus tells Mary and Joseph in the temple that he must be "about his Father's business" (Luke 2: 41–52). Compare and contrast this episode with Gatsby's decision to leave his family and join Dan Cody.

Chapters 7–8: second morally pivotal point

After five years Gatsby leaves Dan Cody's yacht penniless but having secured a "singularly appropriate education; the vague contour of Jay Gatsby had filled out to the substantiality of a man" (102). He joins the service, and as a young Lieutenant stationed in Louisville, Gatsby meets Daisy Fay, "[t]he most popular of all the girls," in October 1917 (75). Gatsby's desire is excited once again and redirected toward a new goal — winning Daisy. Daisy Fay was "the first 'nice' girl he had ever known. . . . He found her excitingly desirable" (148). It was everything about Daisy that compelled him — her beauty, her voice, her clothes, her wealth, her attractiveness to other men. Her house, in particular,

> amazed him — he had never been in such a beautiful house before. But what gave it an air of breathless intensity was that Daisy lived there. . . . There was a ripe mystery about it. . . . It excited him, too, that many men had already loved Daisy — it increased her value in his eyes. (148)

Falling in love with Daisy marks Gatsby's second morally pivotal point. His sensitivity to the power of class, fame, and fortune is heightened by his attraction to Daisy who embodies all of these and whose beauty compels his heart. While he glimpses the dramatic contrast between his own situation and Daisy's, he dismisses his true family background in order to pursue her.

> But he knew that he was in Daisy's house by a colossal accident. However glorious might be his future as Jay Gatsby, he was at present a penniless young man without a past, and at any moment the invisible cloak of his uniform might slip from his shoulders. So he made the most of his time. He took what he could get, ravenously and unscrupulously — eventually he took Daisy one still October night, took her because he had no real right to touch her hand. (149)

Moreover, the pursuit of this revised goal—winning Daisy at all costs—manifests itself in a kind of religious zeal. He "found that he had committed himself to the following of a grail. He knew that Daisy was extraordinary, but he didn't realize just how extraordinary a 'nice' girl could be. . . . He felt married to her, that was all" (149). Gatsby "had let her believe that he was a person from much the same stratum as herself—that he was fully able to take care of her" (149). Gatsby is "overwhelmingly aware of . . . Daisy, gleaming like silver, safe and proud above the hot struggles of the poor" (149–150), and he pursues his dream, confident that he can and must make it a reality. Gatsby suffers no remorse for lying or taking advantage of Daisy.

When Gatsby is called to France and Daisy attempts to visit him in New York before he goes overseas, "[s]he was effectually prevented" by her family with whom, after that, "she wasn't on speaking terms . . . for several weeks" (76). After the Armistice, Gatsby "tried frantically to get home, but some complication . . . sent him to Oxford instead" (150–151). Daisy grew impatient.

> Daisy was young and her artificial world was redolent of orchids and pleasant, cheerful snobbery and orchestras which set the rhythm of the year. . . . And all the time something within her was crying for a decision. She wanted her life shaped now, immediately—and the decision must be made by some force—of love, of money, of unquestioning practicality—that was close at hand. (151)

Despite her sadness on receiving a letter from Gatsby the night before her wedding, she goes ahead and marries Tom Buchanan of Chicago "with more pomp and circumstance than Louisville ever knew before" (77). Her friend, Jordan Baker, found Daisy drunk for the first time in her life with the letter from Gatsby clutched in her fist and the twenty thousand dollar string of pearls Tom had given her strewn on the floor. She quickly sobers up, however, and marries Tom the next day.

> [Gatsby] returned from France when Tom and Daisy were still on their wedding trip, and made a miserable but *irresistible journey to Louisville* on the last of his army pay. He stayed there a week, walking the streets where their footsteps had clicked together through the November night and visiting the out-of-the-way places to which they had driven in her white car. Just as Daisy's house had always seemed more mysterious and gay to him than other houses, so *his idea of the city itself, even though she was gone from it, was pervaded with a melancholy beauty.*
> He left feeling that if he had searched harder he might have found her—that he was leaving her behind. . . . The track curved and now it

was going away from the sun, which, as it sank lower, seemed to spread itself in benediction over the vanishing city where she had drawn her breath. (153, emphasis added)

- Review Gatsby's ambitions as revealed thus far in the novel. List all of the things that excite his imagination and desire. Then list all of the things he has deliberately parted with or discarded as useless. Divide and categorize these lists and study them to explore the patterns that emerge in Gatsby's choices to date.
- We come to understand Gatsby's rapacious desire and determination to get what he wants. However, we are provided with no rational account for his behavior. What is motivating him?
- How has Gatsby's vision of what is desirable changed since the death of Dan Cody? What do you believe he is seeking now? What evidence can you provide to support your answer?
- Has Gatsby's relationship with Daisy been a catalyst for his moral growth? Why or why not?

Having lost Daisy, Gatsby's fervor and desire for her do not subside. Gatsby's ambition to marry Daisy has been met with a challenge, and he makes a choice. He remains determined in his quest despite Daisy's marriage to Tom Buchanan. He does not pivot, change direction, or evaluate the worthiness of his pursuit. He does not refine his aspirations. Instead, his desire to possess Daisy consumes him and moves him to hold relentlessly to his dream. For three years Gatsby involves himself in bootlegging and various kinds of fraud to secure enough money to purchase a mansion: "Gatsby bought that house so that Daisy would be right across the bay" (79). He is fully convinced that once Daisy sees his house, she will want to come back to him. The mystery of Jay Gatsby gesturing that night begins to unfold for Nick—"Then it had not been merely the stars to which he had aspired on that June night. He came alive to me, delivered suddenly from *the womb of his purposeless splendor*" (79, emphasis added).

- How does Gatsby finally "come alive" to Nick? How does he come alive to the reader in this scene? What do we learn about him?
- What do you think Nick means when he refers to "the womb of his purposeless splendor"? Do you believe that Gatsby's aspirations are purposeless? Why or why not?
- So far, Gatsby has met with success in every endeavor—reinventing his identity, winning Daisy's affections, securing enormous wealth—except getting Daisy to marry him. How have these successes had an impact on Gatsby's capacity for moral reflection?

- Do you think there would have been a significant change in Gatsby's character and the trajectory of his life if he had encountered more difficulties and setbacks in his pursuits? Why or why not? How might he have been a different person if he had won Daisy the first time around?

Without having seen or spoken with Daisy in five years, Gatsby faithfully attends to the green light on her dock across the bay. He sets out to recreate the past as he imagines it should have been, building an empire to woo Daisy back. Sustained by blind passion, Gatsby moves further and further from reality. Nick tells us that Gatsby "talked a lot about the past" as if he

> wanted to recover something, some idea of himself perhaps, that had gone into loving Daisy. *His life had been confused and disordered since then, but if he could once return to a certain starting place and go over it all slowly, he could find out what that thing was. . . .* (111–112, emphasis added)

Challenge point

When Daisy does not show up at any of his parties, thrown with the sole purpose that she just might happen to attend, Gatsby orchestrates a plan. Jordan, Daisy's friend, explains the scheme to Nick. "He wants to know . . . if you'll invite Daisy to your house some afternoon and then let him come over. . . . He wants her to see his house. . . . And your house is right next door" (80). Nick agrees and facilitates the meeting between Daisy and Gatsby.

On the morning of Daisy's scheduled visit the rain pours incessantly. In the meantime, Gatsby fills Nick's house with flowers and sends someone to cut the grass. Gatsby arrives "nervously . . . in a white flannel suit, silver shirt, and gold-colored tie. . . . He was pale, and there were dark signs of sleeplessness beneath his eyes" (84–85). When Daisy finally arrives and the two meet again, Gatsby is pained and awkward.

> [H]is hands still in his pockets, [he] was reclining against the mantelpiece in a *strained counterfeit of perfect ease, even boredom.* His head leaned back so far that it rested against the face of a defunct mantelpiece clock, and from this position his distraught eyes stared down at Daisy, who was sitting, frightened but graceful, on the edge of her stiff chair. (87, emphasis added)

For the first time, Gatsby experiences reservations about his whole enterprise and rushes into the kitchen to confess to Nick, "This is a terrible mistake" (88). His panic seems to stem more from nervous energy than conscience.

Gatsby quickly regains composure and focuses on the object of the visit: to have Daisy see his house. Nick describes Gatsby's state of mind as follows:

> there was a change in Gatsby that was simply confounding. He literally glowed; without a word or a gesture of exultation a new well-being radiated from him and filled the little room. (90)

Then, getting right to the point, Gatsby announces,

> "I want you and Daisy to come over to my house . . . I'd like to show her around. . . . My house looks well, doesn't it?" he demanded. "See how the whole front of it catches the light." . . . His eyes went over it, every arched door and square tower. . . . "I keep it always full of interesting people, night and day. People who do interesting things. Celebrated people." (90–91)

Gatsby is passionately consumed with his mission. He is wholly absorbed by Daisy and the interest she takes in his palatial home and possessions.

> He hadn't once ceased looking at Daisy, and I think he revalued everything in his house according to the measure of response it drew from her well-loved eyes. Sometimes, too, he stared around at his possessions in a dazed way, as though in her actual and astounding presence none of it was any longer real. Once he nearly toppled down a flight of stairs. . . . He had passed visibly through two states and was entering upon a third. After his embarrassment and his unreasoning joy he was consumed with wonder at her presence. He had been full of the idea so long, dreamed it right through to the end, waited with his teeth set, so to speak, at an inconceivable pitch of intensity. Now, in the reaction, he was running down like an over-wound clock. (92)

With a certain exhilaration, Gatsby announces, "I've got a man in England who buys me clothes," and he begins tossing shirts of various colors from his closet (93). And "Suddenly, with a strained sound, Daisy bent her head into the shirts and began to cry stormily. 'They're such beautiful shirts . . . It makes me sad because I've never seen such—such beautiful shirts before'" (94). The absurdity of the scene is lost to Gatsby who is wholly consumed by Daisy.

- Notice the way Gatsby attends to Daisy. What seems to interest him the most? How can you tell?
- What new side of Gatsby is revealed in this scene? Are you more or less sympathetic toward him at this point in the novel? Why or why not?

- Have you ever "re-valued" an object or a possession because of the regard someone else has for it? What motivates people to do this?
- Read Robert Browning's dramatic monologue, "My Last Duchess." What parallels can you draw between the Duke and Gatsby? How are they different?
- Why do you think Daisy cries over Gatsby's shirts?
- What is revealed about Daisy in this encounter with Gatsby? Do we gain any new insights into her character? If so, what are they?

As the visit draws to a close Nick notices Gatsby trying to make sense of it all.

> I saw the expression of *bewilderment* had come back into Gatsby's face, as though *a faint doubt had occurred to him as to the quality of his present happiness*. Almost five years! There must have been moments even that afternoon when Daisy tumbled short of his dreams—not through her own fault, but because of the colossal vitality of his illusion. It had gone beyond her, beyond everything. He had thrown himself into it with a *creative passion*, adding to it all the time, decking it out with every bright feather that drifted his way. No amount of fire or freshness can challenge what a man will store up in his ghostly heart. (97, emphasis added)

- Why is Gatsby's dream so "colossal"?
- Do you think Gatsby is happy with his visit from Daisy? Why or why not?
- Why might Gatsby be bewildered right now?

Gatsby has achieved his preliminary goal and is reasonably confident that the rest of his dream will follow as he has imagined it: Daisy will agree to divorce Tom and marry him back in Louisville just the way it should have been five years ago. "I'm going to fix everything just the way it was before," Gatsby tells Nick. "She'll see." Nick cautions him, "I wouldn't ask too much of her. . . .You can't repeat the past." Gatsby is incredulous. "Can't repeat the past? . . .Why, of course you can!" (111).

- Nick advises Gatsby for the first time, when he tells him, "You can't repeat the past." How would you advise Gatsby after witnessing this encounter?
- Why is Gatsby so confident about his ability to repeat the past? How is his attitude consistent with what we know of him thus far?

Failing to detect the fragility of his dream, Gatsby attends a dinner in New York with Daisy, Tom, Nick, and Jordan, and speaks straight to his point. Daisy is not as receptive as he had expected.

"Oh, you want too much!" [Daisy] cried to Gatsby. "I love you now—isn't that enough? I can't help what's past." She began to sob helplessly. "I did love [Tom] once—but I loved you too." (133)

Tom launches a string of bitter accusations against Gatsby—insults mixed with accusations pointing to the corruption and scandal from which he has built his fortune.

It passed, and [Gatsby] began to talk excitedly to Daisy, denying everything, defending his name against accusations that had not been made. But with every word she was drawing further and further into herself, so that he gave that up, and only the *dead dream fought on as the afternoon slipped away, trying to touch what was no longer tangible, struggling unhappily, undespairingly, toward that lost voice across the room.* (135, emphasis added)

- Conduct a dramatic reading of this climactic scene in which Gatsby renders his unwavering love for Daisy. Be sure to assume each character's persona and capture the interpersonal tensions among the characters at each dramatic turn in the dialogue. What is going through Tom's mind? What is Daisy feeling? What is Gatsby convinced of at this point in the narrative? Begin your dramatization with Gatsby telling Tom, "I've got something to tell *you*, old sport" (131), and end with Tom's insistence that Daisy ride home with Gatsby in his car, "Go on. He won't annoy you. I think he realizes that his presumptuous flirtation is over" (136).
- Discuss the evolution in each of the character's (Tom, Daisy, Gatsby, and Nick) assessment of Gatsby and Daisy's love for one another.
- Has Gatsby come to realize anything new? How do you know?

Because he is no longer threatened by Gatsby's "presumptuous flirtation," Tom insists that Daisy drive back to West Egg with Gatsby. When they get to Gatsby's magnificent yellow car, Daisy, unnerved by the afternoon's events, asks Gatsby if she can take the wheel and distract herself by driving. Gatsby is not derailed by the events of the afternoon. He remains wholly absorbed by Daisy. As she speeds along the highway past Wilson's gas station, Myrtle Wilson, the woman with whom Tom Buchanan has been having an affair, rushes into the street to flag down the car. Daisy swerves but kills her. She never stops the car.

Nick, Tom and Jordan arrive at the scene of the accident momentarily and learn from a bystander that a big yellow car killed Mrs. Wilson. Tom assumes Gatsby was driving and his hatred for him becomes more vitriolic. When they return to Daisy and Tom's house, Nick, dazed and sickened by the tragedy, encounters Gatsby hiding in the bushes. Gatsby inquires as to whether or not the woman was killed and then says, "I thought so" (144). For the first time, Nick is shocked by Gatsby's indifference. "He spoke as if Daisy's reaction was the only thing that mattered. . . . I disliked him so much by this time that I didn't find it necessary to tell him that he was wrong [about assuming that no one had noticed his car]" (144).

Gatsby turns his attention immediately to Daisy, referring to his concern about the "unpleasantness this afternoon" and then assuring himself that "she'll be all right tomorrow" (145). His reason for keeping vigil over the house, he claims, is his fear that Tom will do something to Daisy. "I don't trust him, old sport" (145). Nick departs from the increasingly pathetic figure of Gatsby in his pink suit illuminated by the light of the moon.

> [Gatsby] put his hands in his coat pockets and turned back eagerly to his scrutiny of the house, as though my presence marred the sacredness of the vigil. So I walked away and left him standing there in the moon-light—*watching over nothing*. (146, emphasis added)

Nick takes pity on Gatsby and grows concerned for his safety. He visits him the next morning and learns that Gatsby is convinced Daisy will be calling sometime. His assessment of the previous day has been recreated to suit his imagined reality. Gatsby remains convinced of Daisy's love for him. He tells Nick,

> [Tom] told her those things in a way that frightened her—that made it look as if I was some kind of cheap sharper. And the result was that she hardly knew what she was saying. . . . Of course she might have loved him just for a minute, when they were first married—and loved me even more then. (152)

- How has Gatsby changed at this point in the novel? How has he remained the same?
- How does the reality of Daisy's relationship with Gatsby conflict with Gatsby's idealized notion of it? Why is Gatsby incapable of recognizing the truth?
- Nick associates liking Gatsby with caring enough to tell him the truth. Has Nick spoken truthfully to Gatsby up to this point? Where has he missed opportunities to tell Gatsby what he truly thought? What is the connection between liking a person and caring enough to tell the truth? What motivates people to do just the opposite—to keep the truth from a person they like very much?

Chapter 9

Shortly after Nick leaves Gatsby to go to work, a disturbed and grief-stricken George Wilson, Myrtle's husband, breaks into Gatsby's home by stealth and shoots the owner of the yellow car that killed his wife. Gatsby was floating on a raft in his pool. Wilson then takes his own life. Gatsby dies never having received a call from Daisy. Nick, overwrought by the tragedy, attempts to muster together friends and family for a wake at the house. No one comes except a few servants, an aging Mr. Gatz from Minnesota, and the Lutheran minister. Even Wolfsheim wires his regrets and later explains, "I can't do it—I can't get mixed up in it. . . . Let us learn to show our friendship for a man when he is alive and not after he is dead. . . . After that, my own rule is to let everything alone" (173). Gatsby's father carries two mementos of his son with him: the photograph Gatsby had sent him of his house and a copy of *Hopalong Cassidy*, a book from his childhood. Inscribed in the back of the book are Gatsby's daily "Schedule" and "General Resolves." Here he detailed, among other things, his commitment to bathe regularly, read "one improving book or magazine per week" and to "be better to parents."

- Wolfsheim makes the following observations about friendship: "Let us learn to show our friendship for a man when he is alive and not after he is dead. . . . After that, my own rule is to let everything alone." Discuss both the truthfulness and irony of his words. Compare and contrast Wolfsheim and Nick in terms of their friendship with Gatsby.
- While Gatsby's parties draw enormous crowds of "friends," his death summons few people to pay their respects. What is the difference between being alone and being lonely? How can a person be lonely even in the midst of a boisterous party? Do you think Gatsby led a lonely life? Why or why not?
- What do the mementos Mr. Gatz has of his son further reveal about Gatsby and his aspirations?

Nick and Mr. Gatz were accompanied to the cemetery by the "minister . . . four or five servants and the postman from West Egg," and later, arrived the "man with the owl-eyed glasses" who Nick had seen at several of Gatsby's parties (175). The most sympathetic words come from this man who apologizes for not getting to the house for the wake. When Nick tells him no one else made it either, he exclaims, "Why, my God! they used to go there by the hundreds. . . . The poor son-of-a-bitch" (176).

If Gatsby did realize before he died that Daisy was not going to call, Nick muses, he may have had a rude awakening. Gatsby's imagined world had been so fantastic that reality must have been a dismal disappointment.

I have an idea that Gatsby himself didn't believe [the call] would come, and perhaps he no longer cared. If that was true he must have felt he had lost the old warm world, paid a high price for living too long with a single dream. He must have looked up at an unfamiliar sky through the frightening leaves and shivered as he found what a grotesque thing a rose is and how raw the sunlight was upon the scarcely created grass. A new world, material without being real, where poor ghosts, breathing dreams like air, drifted fortuitously about . . . like that ashen, fantastic figure gliding toward him through the amorphous trees. (162)

Saddened, Nick explains, "I had tried to think about Gatsby then for a moment, but he was already too far away, and I could only remember, without resentment, that Daisy hadn't sent a message or a flower" (176). When he finally meets Tom again, Nick refuses to shake his hand knowing that he told Wilson that Gatsby was responsible for Myrtle Wilson's death.

I couldn't forgive him or like him. . . . It was all very careless and confused. They were careless people, Tom and Daisy—they smashed up things and creatures and then retreated back into their money or their vast carelessness, or whatever it was that kept them together and let other people clean up the mess they had made. (181)

- Why do you suppose that Nick was "without resentment" about Daisy's failure to send "a message or a flower"?
- In what ways did Tom and Daisy "smash things up"? Revisit earlier passages in the novel about Tom and Daisy. Is Nick's assessment accurate? Why or why not?
- What is it about people's upbringing, experiences, or education that leads them to become "careless people," as Nick describes Tom and Daisy?
- What about Nick? He knows what has happened and becomes angry with Tom and Daisy for covering up the truth of the tragedy. Why doesn't he tell anyone? In effect, Nick meets his challenge point when he encounters Gatsby keeping vigil over Daisy. What choices does he have before him?
- Can someone be guilty for not taking right action even when they did not do something wrong in the first place?

Nick's reflections about Gatsby, however, reveal a kind of reverence, an inability to hold him morally accountable for any of his own misdeeds and misjudgments. He is sympathetic to Gatsby, as if his unfailing belief in his dream somehow legitimized it.

I thought of Gatsby's wonder when he first picked out the green light at the end of Daisy's dock. He had come a long way to this blue lawn, and his dream must have seemed so close that he could hardly fail to grasp it. He did not know that it was already behind him, somewhere back in that vast obscurity. . . . Gatsby believed in the green light, the orgastic future that year by year recedes before us. (182)

His trunk packed and ready to move from West Egg, Nick "went over and looked at that huge incoherent failure of a house once more" as if the house were more to blame than anything else (181). Gatsby has become for Nick the incarnation of an aesthetic ideal, a compelling and attractive embodiment of the promise of imagination and hope.

If personality is a series of unbroken gestures then there was something gorgeous about him, some heightened sensitivity to the promises of life, as if he were related to one of those intricate machines that register earthquakes ten thousand miles away. This responsiveness had nothing to do with that flabby impressionability which is dignified under the name of the "creative temperament"—it was an extraordinary gift for hope, a romantic readiness such as I have never found in any other person and which it is not likely I shall ever find again. (2)

Taken with a kind of aesthetic awe of Gatsby's life, by the beauty of his *eros*, Nick seems to overlook his moral bankruptcy and concludes, "No—Gatsby turned out all right at the end; it is what preyed on Gatsby, what foul dust floated in the wake of his dreams that temporarily closed out my interest in the abortive sorrows and short-winded elations of men" (2). Nick finds in Gatsby's dream something both beautiful and absurd. He is sympathetic yet fully aware of how unreal and unattainable it is.

Before exploring the next set of questions about the text, ask students what they think about Nick's transformation. Gatsby's indifference to Myrtle's death and the events that led up to it anger Nick at first. How is it that he now assumes an attitude of awe?

- What does the narrator mean by "hope," when he says Gatsby had "an extraordinary gift for hope"? Look up the definition of "hope" in the *Oxford English Dictionary*. How would you distinguish hope from blind optimism? Which quality does Gatsby possess? Why? Is there any evidence to suggest that Gatsby ever succumbs to despair?
- Those who pursue dreams despite seemingly insurmountable obstacles are often acclaimed for their courage and perseverance. Consider, for example, Helen Keller, Sojourner Truth, or Nelson Mandela. How is Gatsby's determination different?
- What is the "foul dust that floated in the wake of Gatsby's dream"? Do you agree with Nick's final analysis of Gatsby? Why or why not? Is Gatsby exonerated, free from blame in this tragedy?

- What makes Gatsby "gorgeous"? Do you find him to be a sympathetic or reprehensible character in the end? Why? Does Gatsby strike you as stalker or an undying romantic?
- Does Nick learn anything from Gatsby's demise? Will he be a better or wiser person for what he has experienced, or has this tragedy been "wasted" on him, so to speak? How does Nick's ability to remain a detached observer help or hinder him? Are his assessments of Gatsby really objective?
- What factors, internal or external to Gatsby, keep him from examining the recklessness of his dream?

SUMMARY REFLECTIONS

Gatsby's moral regression as the tyranny of blind eros

Gatsby's story is one of moral decline borne out through his imagined rather than rational apprehension of truth and reality. Gatsby's desire to be happy is informed by blind ambition to possess an idealized love, based on pretense and sustained by wishful thinking. As the narrator aptly points out, Jay Gatsby "sprang from his Platonic conception of himself" (99). Gatsby is loyal to the image he conceives of for himself, as perverted as it may seem. A strain of tragic optimism runs through the novel as a whole. We are invited to revel in Gatsby's "heightened sensitivity to the promises of life" and to mourn their lack of fulfillment, to be carried along by his imaginative and erotic impulses, but to remain unsatisfied. Gatsby is not a contemptible materialist, eager to amass wealth for his own glory; he is a formal materialist. That is, material wealth and possession are a means to achieve the ideal form he desires. It is not so much Dan Cody, the man, who is enviable to the young Jay Gatz; rather, the lifestyle, freedom, and reputation Cody enjoys are what Gatsby seeks to possess. Money and reputation ultimately serve as the means for Gatsby to impress Daisy; they are not in fact the primary object of his desire.

Gatsby is awakened to his ideal, his conception of happiness, through the lives of those individuals with whom he pursues a relationship, the most influential being Dan Cody and Daisy Fay. The only evidence of Gatsby's moral virtue or desire to lead a noble life comes from the "Schedule" and "List of Resolves" (174) printed in the back of his childhood copy of *Hopalong Cassidy*. He is certainly resolved to pursue the goals he sets for himself in adulthood, but nowhere in his education and experience does he learn to evaluate the moral worthiness of his aspirations. Moreover, his relationships with others never challenge him to do this either. The poles of his moral compass are skewed; they do not allow him to evaluate the path he charts for himself. Jay Gatsby's unbridled passion and blind ambition are unsuccessfully schooled because he is not subject to any of the four factors in the schooling of desire. He lacks the habit of reflection and the meaningful relationships that could challenge and correct his idealized self-conception. And even when faced with setbacks like Daisy's marriage to Tom, which could have enabled Gatsby to reorient his desires toward a more realistic *telos*, Gatsby continues to live in a world of illusions because he has neither the courage nor the will to face the truth.

Thus Jay Gatz-turned-Gatsby at age seventeen willingly commits himself to training in artifice and fraud. While enormously savvy and able to pursue his own interests with great alacrity, Gatsby lacks practical wisdom, what Aristotle calls the "eye of the soul" that enables it to determine the course of action in each situation that is most conducive to one's genuine flourishing as a human being. Gatsby's difficulty is not an inability to judge the means appropriate to his ends or to carry out his plans skillfully, but rather an unwillingness to evaluate the worthiness and reality of his chosen *telos*. It is impossible to have practical wisdom "without the aid of virtue," that is, without a habitual moral disposition to seek and pursue genuinely good courses of action. (*Nicomachean Ethics* VI.12 1144a 26–36). And at the same time, pursuit of an ill-conceived *telos* leads to overall moral degradation, as exemplified by Gatsby's indifference to Myrtle Wilson's tragic death and the complete absence of any hint of guilt for the role he played in the accident. While the mature Jay Gatsby is charming, cordial, and ostensibly sincere, he lacks the capacity and the desire to see and discern what is good and right. He has been wholly misguided by the reign of his blind desires over reason.

The first morally pivotal moment signals the young Jay Gatz's surrender of his true identity and background and the fashioning of a new created identity. Gatsby is unreflectively determined to respond to the "drums of his destiny" by joining Dan Cody. When Dan Cody's yacht drops anchor, Jay Gatz seeks no counsel, and no Socrates comes along to interrogate him about the kind of education he expects to get from Dan Cody. No one challenges him as to whether or not his future on the yacht will help him to achieve the "best possible state of his soul." His goal is decidedly disclosed. Gatsby sees what he imagines to be his "future glory" and "the beginning of his career." He is impelled by his vainglorious ambitions and sets out fervently in "the service of a vast, vulgar, and meretricious beauty." Gatsby is not interested in Cody's yacht or becoming like Cody himself. He is interested in acquiring the ideal image of being wealthy, free, and able to take the world by storm.

Five years later Jay Gatsby, thoroughly trained in worldliness but penniless, deceives Daisy Fay into believing he is of her "same stratum," seduces her, and falls madly in love. While this second morally pivotal point represents something apparently positive—Gatsby's love for someone beyond himself—he corrupts its potentially transforming power by founding his relationship on pretense rather than truth. Daisy is the wealthiest and most popular girl in Louisville; even her "voice is full of money." Gatsby's desire for her is driven in large part by her wealth and beauty. Daisy represents all that Gatsby did not have growing up and all that he has been seeking since joining up with Dan Cody, all wrapped up in one beautiful package. Gatsby idealizes his goal. Gatsby believes he can achieve happiness and fulfill his ambitions by possessing Daisy. When this plan is foiled, a saddened and sentimental Gatsby sets out determinedly to earn enough money to build an empire and win her back. The details of how Gatsby earns his income are never fully disclosed. We are left to infer that it is primarily through his illegal dealings with Wolfsheim and his associates. When Gatsby acquires enough money to purchase his great mansion across the Sound from Daisy, he is convinced that he has everything in place to win her back. He obsesses over a way to orchestrate their meeting again.

Gatsby is met with a challenge. At what *could* be a morally pivotal point in his life, Gatsby chooses to turn a blind eye to the truth and continue to live within his own imagined reality. Gatsby's identity is wrapped up in recovering "some idea of himself . . . that had gone into loving Daisy" (111). After he finally shows Daisy his house, he is convinced that his dream will materialize. He believes that he can, in fact, "change the past" and marry Daisy. Thus, his ambition is clear—"he wanted nothing less of Daisy than that she should go to Tom and say: 'I never loved you.' After she had obliterated four years with that sentence they could decide upon the more practical measures to be taken" (111).

At each juncture, each morally pivotal moment of refined purpose for Gatsby, there is a lack of ethical reflection—of deliberation about the worth of his goal. He blindly follows his dominant desire and engages in fraud, subterfuge, and even total denial of reality to help him attain it. With each morally pivotal point, Gatsby relinquishes a part of himself. When he allies himself with Dan Cody, he abandons his family and his identity as Jay Gatz from North Dakota. When he falls in love with Daisy and loses Daisy, he loses not only his heart but also any remnant of the truth of who he is. Finally, in blindly pursuing Daisy despite her four-year marriage to Tom, he becomes morally indifferent and intellectually closed to the truth. This moral and intellectual indifference is epitomized at the end of the story when he ignores Daisy's refusal to leave Tom and marry him. And later, after letting Daisy drive recklessly and kill Myrtle Wilson, he fails to take responsibility or to show remorse.

Gatsby has no true friends to speak of. The people who come to his parties "were not invited—they went there." Most of his guests simply "paid him the subtle tribute of knowing nothing whatever about him" (61). Nick cannot secure the presence of any of these guests or even alleged friends like Wolfsheim to attend his wake or funeral. And perhaps the most telling testimony to the emptiness of his dream is Daisy's failure to call, write, or inquire about the funeral.

Nick's friendship with Gatsby, while stemming from mutual regard, is essentially utilitarian. Gatsby needs Nick to secure Daisy. If Nick had "wanted what was best" for Gatsby and vice versa, he would have confronted him about the folly of his dream. There are two moments when Nick calls Gatsby's enterprise into question—when he tells him that he cannot change the past (which Gatsby flatly denies) and when he is disgusted with him after Myrtle is killed. Nevertheless, Nick's sympathy for Gatsby triumphs in the end; he chooses to overlook Gatsby's self-deception and not to hold him accountable. It would seem as though he, too, is seduced by Gatsby's dream. Gatsby ends up living his short life guided by blind ambition and unchecked *eros* in pursuit of an impoverished yet glittering ideal of happiness.

EXTENSION QUESTIONS

1 Examine the language and manner of speech Gatsby uses throughout the novel. How does Fitzgerald use choice of words and ways of speaking to disclose character? Contrast this analysis of Gatsby's character through language with the analysis of one other minor character's speech.

2 Compare and contrast Gatsby with a tragic hero.

3 Examine Nietzsche's idea of the "superman," who creates values for himself and is "beyond good and evil." In what ways is Gatsby like a Nietzschean superman?

4 Identify and describe one or two other well-known individuals from literature, film, popular culture, or current events who have blindly embraced an untenable dream. Describe the results of their pursuits.

5 Trace the biblical allusions and religious imagery throughout the novel. What effect does Fitzgerald create by invoking religious language? In what contexts is this imagery most prevalent? Why?

6 Trace the references to "value" and money in this novel. Daisy's "voice is filled with money," for example. What effect does this imagery create? In what ways does Fitzgerald help us to understand Gatsby better by employing this imagery?

7 Research Fitzgerald's life (*The Great Gatsby* was first published when he was only 29), and write a paper analyzing some of the major resonances between *The Great Gatsby* and Fitzgerald's own experience.

8 Imagine you are a childhood friend of Jay Gatz who encounters him at one of his parties on West Egg, Long Island. You are troubled by the new Jay Gatsby you meet and moved to write a letter expressing your earnest concerns about the direction his life has taken. What would you challenge him to think about and evaluate? Why?

9   What does Gatsby's story teach us about how the goals we strive for influence the choices we make and the kind of person we become?

CONCLUSION

Jay Gatsby's case study reveals a lack of character education. Unlike Elizabeth, he is not interested in pursuing the truth or reflecting on the new information disclosed to him about people. Unlike Janie, in the course of his second pursuit of Daisy, he remains relatively free from disappointment, trauma, and pain, or if he does experience it, there is little evidence of introspection or learning that results from it. Finally, unlike Carton, Gatsby never enjoys the kind of friendship that awakens admiration or the desire for noble love. Nor does he receive the kind of support or confidence needed to change. He is single-minded and morally one-dimensional. Gatsby fails to question the worth of his *telos*. His narrow, self-centered approach to his pursuits prevents him from being open to learning, moral growth, or change.

Gatsby is not unlike some people whose goal orientation knows no limits—what they want is what they want. Gatsby is savvy; he is charming; he has a cultivated image that attracts others. His apparent friendship and ostensible kindness to Nick, his guests, and Daisy illustrate a form of care that might pass for character today. His story is both mysterious and seductive. But despite his sparkle, despite our sympathy for his grand but reckless schemes, Gatsby is empty. No greater purpose ever surfaces in this narrative. The love between Daisy and Gatsby is never developed beyond mere attraction and possession. His wanton detachment from Myrtle's death and his inability to accept responsibility reveal a kind of moral emptiness. His life invites us to reflect on character, on the motivations for human love and choices. They ask us to consider how our desires in fact can be schooled negatively, how our character can be malformed over time, if we don't get our *telos* straight.

Chapter 8

Final considerations

A book can be a life-changing experience: for Augustine it was the New Testament, for Alexander the Great it was Homer's *Iliad* and *Odyssey*.[1] Abraham Lincoln read and reread *Macbeth* several times over to contemplate the power of ambition.[2] My own students' essays and observations offer testimony to the insights they gained about the darker side of human nature from reading Shakespeare's *Hamlet* or Golding's *Lord of the Flies*. In fact, it is difficult to track the ways in which students are morally enlightened by the novels they read. As Wayne Booth observes, it is "always difficult to demonstrate" the "moral effects" of literature on the reader.

> When I ask people, "Name fictions that changed your character or made you want to change your conduct," I almost always get a quick response and the responses range all over the moral landscape. . . . Such dramatic reports . . . are of course inherently untrustworthy. No doubt every one of these changes, for good or ill, occurred in a medium—*the reporter's soul*—already richly prepared. The reader must have to some degree "*desired to desire*" the new *desires*, good or bad; otherwise the particular book would not have been read and *new desires* would not have taken root. (1988: 279, emphasis added)

Booth reminds us that stories alone do not account for the schooling of desire in a reader's soul. The locus of desire and moral growth (or decline, as desires can be bad or unhealthy) is the individual soul that has been "richly prepared" by a variety of influences. What does this preparation involve? What kinds of experiences, learning, and relationships help a person "desire to desire"? A fruitful analysis of this "medium"—the human soul—how it is prepared and how new desire effectively takes root, has not been sufficiently explored in moral education.

As literature study is only a thin slice of our students' experience and novel study an even thinner slice, this book has not aimed to uncover the "moral effect" of narratives on student readers. Many factors influence young people's moral development. A complex web of experiences helps to shape their desires and aspirations. Students may be undergoing rigors that make greater psychological, emotional, or moral demands on them than the narratives they read in school. One student may be dealing with a parent dying of cancer, another with a divorce in the family. For some, the experience of making the school play or being kicked off the soccer team may serve as a defining moment. Nonetheless, the habits of ethical reflection that students acquire through thoughtful reading and guided analysis may help students to respond better to and learn from the challenges they face in their own lives. I have chosen in this book, therefore, not to explore the entire range of students' responses to literature or the reader's soul as Booth puts it. Instead, this book has sought to examine the ways in which we can awaken students' moral imaginations as they analyze the moral paths of souls that have been writ large and immortalized in novels.

In the 1936 story of her adventures, *West With the Night*, Beryl Markham, a female African Bush pilot and the first person to fly solo across the Atlantic ocean from East to West, wrote, "If a man has any greatness in him, it comes to light not in one flamboyant hour, but in the ledger of his daily work" (1983: 153). An analysis of morally pivotal points in the lives of characters in literature is instructive to students and teachers in that it reminds us that the moral life is very much like a story—that we do experience morally pivotal points and that the way we respond to them has a profound impact on the direction of our lives.

For the most part, the characters in the four novels examined in this book lived ordinary, unexceptional lives from an external point of view. They are exceptional and present themselves to us as worthy of emulation because of the dispositions and virtues they develop. Even the heroic self-sacrifice of Carton at the end of *A Tale of Two Cities* is prepared and made possible by the new habits and interests he has begun to foster through his relationship with the Darnays.

The characters' reactions at morally pivotal moments—most of which were not extraordinary occurrences—decisively prepared them to act well at the challenge point (or, in Gatsby's case, poor choices at morally pivotal moments paved the way to a self-destructive choice at his challenge point). The way characters react at morally pivotal moments likewise flows from the dispositions they fostered through even smaller decisions and daily actions. As such, ethical reflection on these novels enables us to see how seemingly small choices and actions profoundly shape the person we become and help to determine whether or not we will be prepared to act well in the face of a challenge. This lesson is especially crucial for students, who may not see how the choices they make on a daily basis—between doing homework and watching TV, between joining in gossip or changing the subject, between getting to class on time or socializing in the halls—affect their ability to choose well when the stakes are higher.

This final chapter focuses on comparative data from the four protagonists. My hope is that the case studies, combined with a cross-analysis of factors and outcomes, will raise additional insights about the schooling of desire. I also hope that this final set of considerations prompts a whole new set of questions to be taken up in the high school literature classroom.

COMMON FACTORS

The four factors that contribute to the schooling of desire in the characters' lives resemble what moral philosophers since Aristotle have called the cardinal virtues: relationships (justice/responsibility); pleasure and pain (temperance); courage to face the truth about oneself (fortitude); capacity for reflection (wisdom/prudence). This connection only serves to emphasize how virtue helps each character to live a fully flourishing human life and to respond well to the challenges life presents them.

Relationships

To illustrate the point in the negative, Gatsby—despite surrounding himself with people—has no true friends. He engages with others primarily for motives that Aristotle would characterize as utilitarian. Even his relationship with Daisy is essentially motivated by sentimentality. While one could argue that Gatsby seeks to love more than to be loved, his relationship with Daisy does not prompt him to lead a better life because it is developed on pretense, and because Daisy herself does not lead a virtuous life. Gatsby strives to win Daisy back after five years of separation, but he blindly disregards her husband, her daughter, and Daisy's direct cues that she is no longer interested in marrying him. Gatsby's relationship is one-sided, sustained primarily by his imagination and romanticized ideal. His blind obsession is never corrected in part because Gatsby does not seek out or allow himself to develop any trusting friendships. Gatsby is not interested in seeking what is best for others nor are any of his acquaintances eager to help him achieve a virtuous life. Despite his savvy and charm, Gatsby is essentially detached, revealing details of his life to others only to the extent necessary for them to be instrumental in executing his plan. The individuals he claims to admire—Dan Cody, Wolfsheim, and even Daisy Buchanan—turn out to be shallow and even corrupt, leaving him without any exemplars of a noble life. Gatsby offers empty praise and displays an affected familiarity toward Nick, but there is little evidence of an honest and substantive friendship between them. Nick is more of an anthropological observer, taken with Gatsby's life and story, than a genuine friend concerned enough to challenge or help him reconsider his *telos*. The tragedy of Gatsby's life is revealed when no one shows up at his funeral except Nick Carraway, his estranged father, and a few servants.

On the other hand, Carton, while apparently "lonely" and without immediate friends and family, is moved to change by a chance encounter with Charles Darnay and the Manette family. Both admiration and envy of Charles Darnay awaken Carton's shame and dissatisfaction with his own life. He sees in Darnay everything he could have been and is not. Despite his own affection for Lucie Manette, Carton regards Darnay as a much worthier match for Lucie than he could ever be. He never descends to bitter resentment or seething envy, nor does he wallow in self-pity. Instead, Carton chooses to become a close observer and friend of the Manette family he admires; he effectively submits himself to an apprenticeship of virtue. Taken with their evident solicitude and love for one another, Carton comes to see in all the individuals who make up the Manette–Darnay family the kind of happiness he could have enjoyed, had he employed his time, energy, and talents differently. Most influential in Carton's schooling is Lucie. In her, Carton finds both the embodiment of his ideal and a source of much-needed encouragement. And in the affection he receives from her children, he draws new hope, a new aspiration to begin again. Although his encounter with Darnay sparks Carton's initial dissatisfaction with his life, it is Lucie's trust in Carton — her belief that there is something good in him — that renews his sense of worth and purpose. Her children's affection for Carton strengthens that confidence even more, offering him new possibilities for securing love and trust. Thus, it is Carton's willingness to entrust himself — to reveal his own shame and degradation — to Lucie and make a promise to her that perhaps serves as the greatest catalyst for moral growth in his life. In the end, he is driven more by loving than by being loved. Carton attains the "best possible state of soul" in an act of perfect friendship toward Lucie and her family.

Several relationships help to prompt the schooling of Janie's desire. It is both her respect for her grandmother and her eventual rejection of her grandmother's vision of happiness that help Janie to refine her own understanding of love and marriage. Janie forges her identity in breaking from her tradition (MacIntyre 1984). More importantly, her three husbands help to shape her experience and provide her with data for reflection on the nature of love and marriage. Her first husband, Logan Killicks, represents everything Janie finds loathsome; thus, her desire for higher love is schooled by her aversion to him. Joe Starks, a more attractive candidate, and the husband who provides her with the most material comfort, security and social recognition, helps Janie to see ultimately that love does not thrive on utility and one-sided dedication alone. Communication and mutual respect are necessary. Through the loneliness and disappointment she experiences in her marriage to Joe, Janie's desire is awakened to the need for self-love and reciprocity. In both marriages Janie learns what it is like to be treated as an object. Logan turns her into a mule to pull his plow; Jodie keeps her busy as a shop manager and displays her like a trophy bride. In both instances her voice and her personhood are reduced to something merely instrumental. In her third and final marriage to Tea Cake (Vergible Woods), Janie experiences love, trust, and reciprocity for the first time. It is in the context of this last relationship that Janie finds someone who embodies what she has come to value, and with whom she is finally able to flourish and find happiness despite the material poverty and even bitter tragedy that accompany her short marriage to him. Even though she loses Tea Cake, she attains the best possible state of her soul in the context of loving him.

In contrast to Janie, Elizabeth Bennet, as a young single woman, has a much richer first-hand experience with married couples and their relative happiness. Several relationships school her understanding of love and marriage. As Janie learns from Logan, Elizabeth learns from her aversion to Mr. Collins precisely what she does not want in a husband. Moreover, when her best friend Charlotte willingly accepts Mr. Collins' hand, Elizabeth witnesses what a marriage based on social utility looks like. She rejects Charlotte's philosophy that "happiness in marriage is entirely a matter of chance." From her parents as well as from Lydia and Wickham, Elizabeth also comes to see the results of a marriage based on immature and blind passion. From her aunt and uncle, the Gardiners, she learns by contrast what a marriage of love and virtue involves. Jane's naïveté helps Elizabeth to see the dangers of allowing oneself to be too naïve about romance and men in general. From her mother and Lydia, Elizabeth acquires a keen sense of disdain for frivolity and irrationality. Although the list of characters is long and few escape Elizabeth's thoughtful examination and judgment, the person who has the most impact on the schooling of her desire is Darcy, her intellectual match. While humiliated by his first proposal of marriage, she eventually discovers that his character is not as haughty as she had presumed. From his letter she realizes the blinding prejudices behind her misconceptions and judgments. As she learns more about Darcy through her visit to Pemberley and her discovery of his intercession on behalf of Lydia, Elizabeth comes to see him as a model of virtue, a true gentleman and friend. Elizabeth takes the risk of loving Darcy and finds true friendship and happiness in return.

Response to pleasure and pain

The schooling of desire ameliorates some of the psychological intensity of pain by helping an individual to embrace that pain in a larger context—the pursuit of one's revised *telos*. Carton's desires are schooled in the crucible of self-loathing and shame, Janie's in the context of lifelong suffering and disappointment, and Elizabeth's through stinging humiliations. One could argue that Gatsby endures the pain of losing Daisy to Tom Buchanan and then undergoes tremendous anxiety in his effort to win her back. However, in Gatsby's tenacious pursuit of Daisy, his firm embrace of an idealized dream anesthetizes him from the painful truth of reality. He remains in denial about the untenable nature of his dream. His blind ambition keeps him from attaining a superior perspective on his own life or a greater understanding of the world around him. He remains a slave to an unattainable ideal. Pain is a catalyst for moral growth, then, only insofar as it provokes reflection and fortitude in the face of difficulties.

Carton, "the man of good abilities and good emotions, incapable of their directed exercise, incapable of his own help and his own happiness," cries himself to sleep at night because he is so keenly attuned to his moral misery (94). When he reveals himself to Lucie, he shamefully admits the wastefulness of his life. He describes himself "like one who died young. All my life might have been." He is "troubled by a remorse" at his misdeeds yet feels painfully trapped by "the low habits" he "scorn[s] but yield[s] to" (161). Carton's willingness both to face and to reveal himself is excruciating but integral to awakening his self-knowledge and his capacity to turn his life around. In fact, there is nothing easy or painless about Carton's scheme to save Darnay. Keeping his promise involves the ultimate self-sacrifice, but he is impelled by a purposeful vision.

Janie's life is fraught with suffering. While she enjoys a childhood relatively free from pain, at sixteen she learns of the legacy of suffering she has inherited from her mother and grandmother. Subsequently, two of her three marriages involve physical and emotional abuse. In the second, her expectations of happiness and love are shattered. She is not only beaten and ridiculed by Jody, but also controlled, shut up and shut out of conversation and community life. Janie is nearly stripped of her identity before she finally realizes the need to foster a healthier self-love and independence in order to retain any sense of dignity. Even in her third, and finally happy, marriage to Tea Cake, Janie endures the pain of economic hardship, natural disaster, the premature death of her husband, and murder charges. After these bitter trials, however, Janie emerges confident, settled, happy, and even triumphant. The pain involved in Janie's first two marriages provokes her to refine her goals and arms her with the strength necessary to pursue her *telos* in the third marriage despite the pain involved.

Elizabeth Bennet does not experience pain on the same scale as Janie and Carton. She does, nonetheless, endure pain at each morally pivotal point, a pain that moves her to revisit her *telos*. Surprised by the absurdity of Mr. Collins' proposal of marriage, she rejects him, but she is more shocked and even pained to learn that her friend Charlotte, whom she regards so highly, has agreed to take his hand. Charlotte's choice represents an egregious departure from what she anticipated for her friend. This blow is compounded by Darcy's first proposal of marriage in which he disparages her family and connections. At the height of her pride, Elizabeth angrily dismisses Darcy's proposal and laments the scourge of a man who haughtily expects that class and reputation will guarantee him a wife. At the second morally pivotal point, Elizabeth is humiliated again, but this time her humiliation gives rise to shame and sorrow. Elizabeth sees the truth of her own mistaken judgment and her family's impropriety. She acknowledges that she has been "blind" and wrong all of this time—"She grew absolutely ashamed of herself. . . . 'I who have prided myself on my discernment!— I, who have valued myself on my abilities! . . . Till this moment, I never knew myself'" (159).

While the proper response to pain is presented here as one of the four main factors, I do not mean to suggest that pain and pleasure are mutually exclusive in the schooling of desire. At each morally pivotal point there is some pleasure that helps to evoke a turn: Carton takes pleasure in spending time with Lucie and her family; Janie enjoys keeping a home with Tea Cake; and Elizabeth delights in the prospect of becoming "mistress of Pemberley" (185). Both classical philosophers and contemporary psychologists affirm that learning to take pleasure in what is truly good—"to delight in what is right" as Plato put it, "and to be pained by what is bad"—is central to the schooling of desire. As evidenced by these characters' experiences, however, pain can often be a more dramatic catalyst for growth than pleasure.

Reflection

Carton's hyper-reflection is almost paralyzing at first. Nevertheless, it is apparent that Carton's knowledge of what the good life consists in is in part what sustains his desire to lead one despite his weakness of will. Knowledge alone, however, is not sufficient for Carton to change. He needs the love of Lucie and her children.

Janie is more introspective and emotional than Carton, and we witness her reflections throughout the novel. She is initially carried along more by feeling and blind obedience than by deliberation. While she has not received a formal education, she subjects her life experience to thoughtful examination. She "deliberates" before leaving Logan. She cultivates her "inside" life after she realizes that Jody is not an ideal husband. She assesses and reflects upon her relationship with Tea Cake so as to avoid another bad marriage.

Elizabeth Bennet, by contrast, is highly educated, articulate, and the daughter of a gentleman. Like Janie, she is also highly reflective, although her prejudice and presumptuousness tend to skew her judgment. She ponders all the circumstances of her life as well as the decisions of others; Darcy challenges her to reflect upon and reassess her judgments. Unlike Carton, she has the habits and the strength of character to lead a morally upright life, but she needs a clearer perspective on reality before she can truly flourish.

Gatsby is wholly unreflective. While the others have relationships with individuals who challenge or provoke them to reflect in one way or another, there is no Socrates to question Gatsby about whether or not he is pursuing "the best possible state of his soul." From his youth Gatsby has been highly imaginative: "each night he added to the patterns of his fancies. . . . These reveries provided an outlet for his imagination; . . . a satisfactory hint of the unreality of reality, a promise that the rock of the world was founded securely on a fairy's wing"(100). His unbridled imagination eventually eclipses reality: "Jay Gatsby of West Egg, Long Island, sprang from his Platonic conception of himself. . . . He invented just that sort of Jay Gatsby that a seventeen-year-old boy would like to invent, and to his conception he was faithful to the end" (99). Neither Gatsby nor any of his companions subject his claims and pursuits to investigation. While Nick's narration itself calls into question the worth of Gatsby's self-propelled mission, he never invites Gatsby to do the same. Rather, Nick manages with amazing sophistication to present what is reprehensible about Gatsby's choices and commitments, to illustrate his "meretriciousness" and to remain at the same time in awe of his "purposeless splendor." Gatsby unreflectively pursues his illusory goal, while Nick stands by wondering at the unrelenting power of his blind *eros*.

Courage to face the truth about oneself

At each pivotal point courage is required to move ahead in a morally salutary way, and for all of the characters, except Gatsby, the courage to face the truth about themselves helps to sustain the schooling of desire. Carton, Janie, and Elizabeth do not allow themselves to become victims, blaming others and circumstances for the trials they must endure. Admittedly, Elizabeth does accuse Darcy of arrogance and snobbery; Carton is downright envious of Darnay at first; and Janie comes to resent and reject her grandmother's view of marriage. Yet none of them allows this anger to thwart their own moral progress or to lessen their own personal accountability for their choices and actions. In short, they have courage to face and accept their mistaken judgment or misplaced trust.

Without courage, Sydney Carton would have caved in to a desperate suicide or allowed himself to become paralyzed by inertia instead of setting off to Paris and modestly executing a master plan to save Charles Darnay. Without courage Janie could have devolved into a victim of circumstance, blaming her mother and her first two husbands for the misery of her life. Despite the socio-cultural limitations of her status as an uneducated mulatto woman in the post-Civil War South, Janie does not complain. She makes deliberate choices (to leave Logan, for example, and to stay with

Jody despite his cruelty) and accepts responsibility for the consequences. Elizabeth Bennet demonstrates courage in humbling herself before Darcy and disclosing the scandal of her family, and in seeking forgiveness for her cruel misjudgment of his character. Gatsby, by contrast, shows no courage. He denies the truth of his own life, masking his family background, his source of income, and his relationships with others. He fails to accept Daisy's rejection of his ambitions for marriage. Moreover, he blatantly ignores his responsibility in Myrtle's tragic death.

OUTCOMES: BEST POSSIBLE STATE OF ONE'S SOUL

> The only freedom that is of enduring importance is the freedom of intelligence, that is to say, freedom of observation and judgment, exercised in behalf of purposes that are intrinsically worthwhile.
>
> (Dewey 1938: 61)

An analysis of these four cases indicates that flourishing is not achieved by a single heroic choice; instead, it results from a pattern of action and choices integrated with one's aspirations or refined *telos*, with "purposes that are intrinsically worthwhile." Having examined the dispositions and factors that lead to successful schooling of desire, we are now ready to consider how characters' choices and actions subsequent to their challenge point are constitutive of their flourishing. In these four novels the reader has the vantage point of seeing what each character chooses in the end, and glimpsing the effects on the overall state of each character's soul at the end of the narratives.

Gatsby has schooled his desires in the wrong things; we could say that they are misschooled, misdirected by his ambition to create a vision of himself and the world that is out of sync with reality. He is a moral imposter, a charlatan, a pathetic testimony to the way dreams can run amok, destroy a person's life and render them incapable of flourishing. What miseducated Gatsby's capacity to choose his *telos*? Selfishness, impulsiveness, superficiality, and an unreflective attitude toward life.

Carton's knowledge of what is worthwhile has been schooled from childhood. He has a clear vision of what is good and right. He knows what he should take pleasure in and be pained by, but he is weak-willed and unable to sustain the behavior needed to act in accord with what he understands. His challenge is to bring his moral dispositions into sync with his clear vision of what is good.

Elizabeth Bennet's challenge is different from Carton's. She has strong moral dispositions and habits but a slightly misguided vision of her *telos*. Elizabeth needs to correct her vision and bring this refined vision into line with her good moral dispositions.

When we first meet Janie, she delights in the sensuous pleasures as well as naïve ideas about love and marriage. Neither her dispositions nor her desires have been adequately schooled. She needs both a refined vision and educated moral dispositions. While her dispositions are not bad in and of themselves, they do lack orientation.

In the three positive case studies, the results of successfully schooled desires are virtuous dispositions. After the challenge point each character's actions are consistent with the criteria Aristotle identified as requisite for virtuous action. Each one "has knowledge," "choose[s] acts and choose[s] them for their own sake," and "proceed[s] from a firm and unchangeable character" (*Nicomachean Ethics* II.4, 1105a29). Moreover, at the end of their schooling, Carton, Janie, and Elizabeth evidence a set of virtuous dispositions:

- self-possession;
- vision or perspective on one's life as a whole;
- gratitude;
- heightened capacity for self-giving;
- practical wisdom.

In her book, *Happiness*, Elizabeth Telfer reminds us that happiness has more to do with self-respect and pursuing what is worthwhile than with "enslavement to caprice or drifting along without an overall plan." The dispositions internalized by the three characters whose desires are successfully schooled illustrate precisely this kind of happiness, this "integratedness of life" (1980: 121).

Gatsby, on the other hand, internalizes each of these dispositions in the negative. He lacks self-possession and healthy self-love or care for the best possible state of his soul. He remains unsettled, awkward, and insecure in manner. Moreover, Gatsby flatly denies the truth about himself and fails to see it in others. With respect to gratitude, Gatsby demonstrates a thankless sense of entitlement. He is indebted to no one because he has no substantive relationships. Gatsby has not acquired a greater capacity to give. In the end, Gatsby never attains the practical wisdom needed to choose well. He fails to recognize the truth and act accordingly. Instead, he allows the world of his imagination to dominate reality. Thus, Gatsby remains mistaken about what is truly excellent and desirable in life. He commits himself to an "empty," "purposeless," and "dead dream."

Independent of their circumstances—in the end, Janie moves from material comfort to poverty, Carton goes to the guillotine, and Elizabeth, by contrast, enjoys a much improved material and social status—each of these characters acquires an internalized strength of character and sense of fulfillment never achieved by Gatsby. The four characters help to illustrate that the schooling of desire transcends class, education, cultural, and family backgrounds.

Let us look in more detail at the virtuous dispositions mentioned above.

Self-possession

Carton's self-possession and sense of freedom are perhaps most evident in the equanimity with which he faces his death; "They said of him, about the city that night, that it was the peacefullest man's face ever beheld there. Many added that he looked sublime and prophetic" (402). Janie, too, faces tragedy with peace. Returning to her home town widowed again, she is no longer restless for love. She sustains herself with the memory of love lost:

> The kiss of his [Tea Cake's] memory made pictures of love and light against the wall. *Here was peace.* She pulled in her horizon like a great fish-net. Pulled it from around the waist of the world and draped it over her shoulder. So much of life in its meshes! *She called in her soul to come and see.* (183–184, emphasis added)

Although Elizabeth has not experienced the extreme trials with which Carton and Janie have contended, her schooling is imbued with the pain of personal humiliation and leads to greater self-possession. We see Elizabeth's renewed sense of self through the eyes of her new sister-in-law who at first "listened with astonishment bordering on alarm, at her [Elizabeth's] lively, sportive manner of talking to her brother." Soon, however, "by Elizabeth's instructions she began to comprehend that a woman may take liberties with her husband, which a brother will not always allow in a sister more than ten years younger than himself" (297). Elizabeth's tendency to "deliberately misunderstand" and hastily censure has been corrected. Her spirited manner is more deliberately channeled toward good humor, honesty, and a generous understanding toward others.

Heightened capacity for self-giving

Carton's progression from self-hate and envy of Darnay to trust in and affection for Lucie and her family reveals his moral growth. His final choice is the most supreme act of self-giving—to lay down one's life for one's friend. Similarly, Janie progresses from a preoccupation with her own limited and romanticized image of marriage to a healthy reciprocal love in which she flourishes. She tells Pheoby, "Ah wants to utilize mahself all over again" (107). Her desires are energized. It is Janie's experience of true love—albeit short-lived—that moves her to dedicate herself "in loving service" to her husband, and eventually to share her experience with those who will benefit from her story. In sharing her story with Pheoby and trusting that she will transmit it honestly and well, Janie seizes the opportunity to give back to the community everything she has learned about love and life. Elizabeth not only gives of herself to Darcy, she also forgives and welcomes into her home the condescending Lady Catherine de Bourgh, and weaves several relations—from the most absurdly hypocritical to the most genuine—into a web of family connectedness. She includes her estranged sister and brother-in-law, Lydia and Wickham, in her web of family love despite the havoc they have both wrought on the family. Moreover, she frequently draws her young sister Kitty into her home and watches her mature into a more thoughtful and responsible young woman as a consequence.

Refined vision or perspective on life

The successful schooling of desire results in genuine understanding. At the end of Carton's life, his manner changes: "It was a settled manner of a tired man, who had wandered and struggled and got lost, but who at length struck into his road and saw its end" (335). His parting words to Dr. Manette reveal his refined perspective: "Of little worth as life is when we misuse it, it is worth that effort. It would cost nothing to lay it down if it were not" (361). Carton walks "with settled step" to the prison where he exchanges places with Darnay (362). Before he dies he articulates a revised understanding of the meaning of both his life and death:

> I see a beautiful city and a brilliant people rising from this abyss . . . I see the lives for which I lay down my life, peaceful, useful, prosperous, and happy. . . . It is a far, far better thing that I do, than I have ever done; it is a far, far better rest that I go to than I have ever known. (403–404)

Similarly, Janie acquires a new perspective from the tragedy of her life and shares her insights with Pheoby: "Ah'd done been to de horizon and back and now Ah kin set heah in ma house and live by comparisons." She knows people will not understand her experience with love, so she offers Pheoby the following wisdom:

> Dey gointuh make 'miration 'cause ma love didn't work lak they love, if dey ever had any. Then you must tell 'em dat love ain't somethin' lak uh grindstone dats de same thing everywhere and do de same thing tuh everything it touch. Love is lak de sea. It's uh movin' thing, but still and all, it takes its shape from de shore it meets, and it's different with every shore. (182)

Janie's mature vision can be summarized in her final words to her friend:

> It's a known fact, Pheoby, you got tuh *go* there tuh *know* there. Yo' papa and yo' mama and nobody else can't tell yuh and show yuh. Two things everybody's got tuh do for theyselves. They got tuh go tuh God, and they got tuh find out about livin' fuh theyselves. (183)

Elizabeth Bennet's refined vision and perspective is not portrayed as dramatically as Carton and Janie's. Nevertheless, it is evident from the narrative that she has acquired penetrating insight into both reality and people. As a consequence of her schooled desires, Elizabeth is able to see for the first time the contempt with which her father holds her mother and his abnegation of responsibility in raising her younger sisters. She also sees more clearly the integrity and goodness of the Gardiners; she understands Darcy and the reasons for his past behavior; she regains perspective on each of her sisters and their prospects for happiness.

For each character, a refined perspective gives rise to a profound sense of freedom. This is especially poignant when considering the stark contrast between Janie and Elizabeth's opportunity and experience. Janie, a young mulatto woman raised by her former slave grandmother, knows that the black woman has been regarded as the "mule of the world" and has few friends and examples of marital happiness from whom to learn or on whom to lean for help. Elizabeth Bennet, while enjoying better friendships and opportunities from the outset, stands outside of convention, holding tight to her principled definition of love and not willing to marry for "security" or "advantage" despite her family's economic difficulties. Yet both women ultimately enjoy a tremendous freedom of spirit in the end, acting in accordance with their refined vision of happiness without regard for the critical opinions of others. Sydney Carton, who as a student was regarded as "famous among his competitors as a youth of great promise," matures into an unhappy "disappointed drudge." Through the schooling of desire, however, he turns his life around and sacrifices it altogether for the sake of those he loves. Moreover, like Janie and Elizabeth, Carton's actions at the end of the novel are free and consistent with his revised *telos*; consequently, he achieves peace and happiness.

Gratitude

Janie dedicates much of her conversation with Tea Cake to expressing her gratitude for his generous love—and Tea Cake responds in kind. There are several exchanges motivated by Janie's heartfelt thanks to Tea Cake (or vice versa). And in the end, holding her dead husband in her arms, Janie's final disposition toward him is one of gratitude: "Janie held his head tightly to her breast and wept and thanked him wordlessly for giving her the chance for loving service" (175).

Similarly, Carton is grateful to Lucie Manette for "the remembrance that I opened my heart to you." Before exchanging places with Darnay, he has him scribble a letter to Lucie, saying "I am thankful the time has come when I can prove [the words of his promise to her]" (377–378). Carton is indebted as he goes to his death, because he sees this occasion as not simply as an opportunity to save Darnay but as a chance to give back to Lucie and her family all the hope they have given to him. Finally, Carton is grateful for the opportunity to wipe out "the blots" of his life on the world with an act of generosity and reparation.

Elizabeth is indebted to Darcy for his kindness to her and her family despite her cruel refusal of him. She is grateful on behalf of her family for his discreet intervention to help rectify the situation between Lydia and Wickham. When he proposes to her a second time she explains that, "Her sentiments had undergone so material a change . . . as to make her receive with gratitude and pleasure his present assurances." Moreover, both she and Darcy find themselves especially indebted to the Gardiners, "ever sensible of the warmest gratitude towards the persons who, by bringing her into Derbyshire, had been the means of uniting them" (298).

The gratitude that Carton, Janie, and Elizabeth possess, in the end, captures their indebtedness. These characters are thankful for both the persons and experiences that helped to school their desires. They see themselves not as simply as finished projects, but rather as part of a larger set of interdependent relationships.

Practical wisdom

In Ross's translation of the *Nicomachean Ethics* choice is described as "*deliberate desire*, therefore both reasoning must be true and desire right. . . . This kind of intellect and truth is practical" (1944: 1023, emphasis added). The achievement of moral maturity that Aristotle calls practical wisdom— "a true and reasoned capacity to act with regard to the things that are good or bad for man"—stems both from early habituation and moral virtue. As Aristotle explains, both clear moral vision and strong moral dispositions are needed: "This eye of the soul acquires its formed state not without the aid of virtue . . . it is impossible to be practically wise without being good" (*Nicomachean Ethics*, VI.12, 1144a 26–36). In his commentary on the *Ethics* Urmson summarizes Aristotle this way,

> Without wisdom excellent character would be like a man groping in the dark and not knowing where to go; without the desires of an excellent character, wisdom would have nothing to do. (Urmson 1988: 84)

Practical wisdom is the mark of mature character. Practical wisdom requires the development of a full range of moral desires, including love for what is good and contempt for what is evil. It calls for a capacity to take an interest in and empathize with others, to set worthy goals and pursue them with deftness and determination. Being virtuous involves the ability to take right action after thoughtful consideration of the circumstances and relevant facts; it entails good judgment and volition—the will to act on one's better judgment. Finally, mature character is informed by an understanding of what is good and evil, true and false, right and wrong, while being able to discern the complex gradations in between. A person of good character has the ability to assess a situation, deliberate, and choose the best course of action. Aristotle called this *practical wisdom*; today we call it good judgment.

Each of the characters in the three positive case studies has acquired moral maturity or practical wisdom. Their actions are purposive and "consistent with [their] ideals" (Blasi 1993). After Carton's desires have been harmonized, he overcomes his inertia and executes his plan in Paris intelligently and purposefully. He deliberates: "But care, care, care! Let me think it out!" (363). He sheds his past vices and takes no "strong drink." His manner of action becomes both "fervent and inspiring." He is able to size up the problem swiftly, navigate the obstacles, and carries out his plan without a flaw.

Janie, like Carton, is transformed from feeling trapped in her marriage to Jody, to being liberated and fulfilled in her marriage to Tea Cake. While Janie loses all the amenities and material comforts of being the mayor's wife and settles into a more impoverished lifestyle, she flourishes. She acquires and cultivates her talents, becoming a better marksman than Tea Cake, learning how to plant, and creating a home that becomes the center of community life.

Elizabeth also acquires the practical wisdom she needs to help Lydia and Wickham pay off their debts through "economy in her own private expenses." She handles her condescending and overbearing aunt, Lady Catherine de Bourgh, and she serves as mistress of Pemberley, an estate well beyond her class and experience, with great aplomb.

Gatsby, on the other hand, remains imprisoned in the cave, content with his self-fashioned image of himself and his world and their shadows of reality. He eventually dies a victim to his circumstances. The incarnation of what he creatively wills himself to be, Gatsby is rich, popular, and fraudulent. He is a compelling image of what MacIntyre (1984) describes as "the outward appearance of morality" which, in fact, belies "uneducated passion." In definitively rejecting his parents who in his mind were "shiftless and unsuccessful farm people," he rejects his class and climbs swiftly to economic prosperity through bootlegging. He exaggerates his "education" at Oxford and sustains his hopes on an empty dream. Gatsby acquires not self-possession but nervous anxiety, not practical wisdom but affectation, not a heightened capacity for self-giving but an increased egotism, not a sense of gratitude but a blind sense of entitlement.

A REASON TO BE HAPPY

As the late Viktor Frankl, concentration camp survivor and renowned twentieth-century psychologist, explained in his seminal work, *Man's Search for Meaning* (1984: 135), it is not simply happiness that individuals aspire to but rather a "reason to be happy." This reason, he illustrates, can be disclosed through suffering, the sense of achievement that accompanies hard work, or the experience of love. One way to remember the importance of an ideal in contemporary moral education is to remind educators that students are always in pursuit of a "reason to be happy," not simply good grades, parties, popularity, or a new compact disc player. An analysis of morally pivotal points in the lives of characters in literature helps to illuminate an individual's "reason to be happy." What this book yields as a whole, then, is a set of dramatic testimonies that illustrate the pursuit of this ideal or reason to be happy. The reasons disclosed through the gradual unfolding of morally pivotal points in the lives of Fitzgerald's Jay Gatsby, Dickens' Sydney Carton, Hurston's Janie Crawford, and Austen's Elizabeth Bennet reveal the nature, complexity, and results of each character's schooling and remind teachers and readers of these texts that desire is determined by what it aims at achieving.

These four case studies do not distill a list of exemplified virtues or a moral doctrine of the right thing to do. They do not reveal one-dimensional characters caught in a moral dilemma, nor do they generate a set of controversial moral issues and questions for discussion and debate. Rather, they yield a set of moral-psychological profiles of individuals who, having been awakened to some compelling *telos*, gradually develop certain character dispositions (among which we can also find the four cardinal virtues of justice, self-mastery, wisdom, and fortitude). These narrative profiles draw into focus the internal, highly personalized dimension of moral development: the schooling of desire. The virtuous dispositions that result from the successful schooling—those "loves, tastes, and habits" Lewis (1961) speaks of—are actually constitutive of a flourishing, meaningful life, not tacked on moral appendages or mechanical skills.

An analysis of morally pivotal points in fictional life narratives helps to disclose the complexity and meaning of character study without reducing it to an empirical science. The moral life is neither monolithic nor black and white. Sometimes the paths that unfold in individual lives are deliberate and clearly paved; others are more accidental and incidental, and even surprising. The complexity of each life path cannot be underestimated. The four case studies in this book cannot possibly address all the nuances of each character's life journey. However, they can help us make more sense of the unfolding direction of a character's life in light of his or her (best possible) overriding *telos*. They demonstrate that a closer examination of the schooling of desire—and the subsequent progression of each character toward an overarching *telos*—invite readers and teachers to consider how these characters are motivated and even impelled by an evolving "reason to be happy."

CONCLUSION

Character education is hardly a neat or short-term enterprise; it is a lifelong and often messy project. Examining character education through literature awakens students' moral imaginations to the possibilities for their own lives. Instead of focusing merely on good behavior and the practical consequences of bad behavior, narrative lives challenge students to grapple with the reasons for developing virtue anyway. They confront them with the questions, "Character for what?" "Character for whom?" When given the opportunity to both experience a fictional life journey and examine his or her choices and commitments, students can develop habits of ethical reflection in the literature classroom that will last them a lifetime.

Definitions and distinctions

DESIRE

As I am using the term desire, it has both motive force and direction; it can be base or noble, and it moves a person toward a goal. Emotions and feelings, on the other hand, are blind insofar as they have no volitional power. They are neither good nor bad; it is choosing that makes them so. For example, we know the feeling of panic or even rage that can overcome us when we are trapped in rush hour traffic and late for an appointment. We can feel attracted to someone who is not our spouse; we can feel loathing toward everything from Brussels sprouts to calculus problems and people who mispronounce our name. These feelings, however, have no volitional content unless we intentionally grant it to them. Desire is both rational and affective; it animates intelligent choice and action. Pascal's sage observation comes to mind here, "The heart hath reasons of which reason understands little" (*Pensées*, section IV: 277). The heart's reasons do not amount to the suppression of emotion but rather the wise guidance provided by an intelligent desire, wise guidance that enables individuals to freely choose and invest themselves in worthy plans and purposes.

VIRTUE

The word virtue itself comes from the Latin *vir*, which has a root meaning of "force" or "agency." In Latin, the expression *virtus moralis* became the established equivalent of the Greek expression *arete ethike*, "moral excellence." Virtue contributes to one's connoisseurship of life—living excellently. Virtues are dispositions rooted in the ability to make good choices (*Nicomachean Ethics* II.1 1103a25), and learning to choose well among a range of options is essential to moral growth. Here it is important to distinguish between intellectual virtue, such as practical wisdom, and moral virtue, such as justice or fortitude. The two types of virtue are cultivated differently—intellectual virtue through teaching and experience, moral virtue through habit—but in tandem (*Nicomachean Ethics* II.1 1103a33–b25). The schooling of desire involves both intellectual and moral virtue: through experience or advice a person learns to choose certain paths and avoid others (intellectual virtue), while the habitual disposition to do what is good despite internal or external difficulty (moral virtue) enables a person to act in accordance with sound judgment and fosters the desire to know what is good. Desires must first be schooled by good habits. Burnyeat (1980) suggests that this habituation guided by someone wiser and more experienced than a child is an "interfering factor" which acts as a catalyst for the eventual development of practical wisdom. These early, "unreasoned responses," he explains, are later "integrated with" and "corrected by" a "reasoned scheme of values" (81).

Moral virtue disposes a person to practical wisdom. Difficult to attain, moral virtue lies in the challenge of habitually choosing "what is best and right." As moral virtues guide our appetites and desires by directing them toward the person's overall good, they lie between two extremes, a vice of excess and a vice of deficiency. For example, temperance moderates desires for food, sleep, comfort, etc., and is the mean between self-indulgence and self-neglect; courage requires having the appropriate amount of fear in any situation, and is the mean between cowardice and recklessness (*Nicomachean Ethics* II.6, 1106b36–1107a8).[1] Practical wisdom (the intellectual virtue most closely intertwined with moral virtue) enables a person to locate that mean, discerning the best course of action for a specific person in a given situation.

MORAL

I use the adjective "moral" in the categorical sense, of or pertaining to our human capacity to distinguish right from wrong action, good from bad character, and/or praiseworthy from blameworthy agency. We are moral beings in this sense, whether acting rightly or wrongly, whether of good character or bad character, whether acting in a praiseworthy or blameworthy fashion on this or that occasion. Moral development can be good or bad. I am using the term *moral* imagination to highlight the imagination's capacity to see and make sense of these distinctions as they are presented in fictional characters' lives. The moral imagination is fed with images of the schooling of desire and the negative schooling of desire.

ETHICS

Ethics is essentially rational thinking about morality. It is a branch of philosophy that examines the morality of human choice and action. I am deliberately using the expression *ethical* reflection on literature because this kind of reflection is rooted in an intelligent study of the narrative data presented in each novel rather than subjective response or opinion.

CHARACTER

Character comes from the Greek word, *kharaseein*, meaning to engrave a distinctive mark or impression on a tablet, soft wax, or a precious gem. Character is that distinctive mark of our person; the combination of these distinguishing qualities that make us *who we are*. Character is deeper than appearance and reputation and constitutes more than our personality or temperament. Temperament is something we are born with, hard-wired inclinations such as whether we are a morning person or a night person, outgoing or introverted, cheerful by nature or more melancholic. We can mostly blame our parents for our temperament. Character, however, is something we build, something we can call our own because we are free to modify our habits and have the power to choose our attitude and dispositions. But this building project needs a guiding vision—a clear *telos* to orient its sound development.

Extending reflection across novels

Several topics for study and discussion cut across all four novels. A few ideas for comparative analysis and reflection are given below.

1 Each author has a fascinating life story, which has echoes in his or her fictional work. Fitzgerald once said, "I began to bawl because I had everything I wanted and knew I would never be so happy again" (Fitzgerald, *My Lost City*, 1932). Take a look at the background of one of the authors we have read. See if you can determine morally pivotal points or a dramatic challenge point in the author's life. In what respects is the author's biography evident in his or her writing?

2 What do habituation and experience have to do with learning to distinguish a good *telos* (worthy goal) from a bad one (an unworthy one). How do these habits and experiences contribute to the development of mature reflection—practical wisdom that guides us to do what is called for and right in each moment?

3 At the beginning of the novels, both Janie Crawford and Jay Gatsby are young idealists with unrealistic dreams and ambitions. Why does Janie, who is less educated and more limited economically and socially, come to acquire a more mature understanding of reality and of herself than Gatsby does?

4 Sydney Carton and Jay Gatsby are both disenchanted with their youth. Both have enormous difficulty realizing their dreams. Both die before their time, and both can be described as disappointed and lonely at different points in their lives. Write an essay comparing and contrasting these two characters.

5 Recreate a description of Gatsby the night of Myrtle's death, writing as if you were Charles Dickens.

6 Recreate a description of Carton as if you were F. Scott Fitzgerald. Select a scene that you think will lend to the best use of Fitzgerald's style (Carton's drunken monologue, his conversation with Lucie, or his attitude before the guillotine).

7   Rewrite the scene where Elizabeth Bennet gets snubbed by Darcy at the ball or the scene where she reads and rereads his letter as if you were Zora Neale Hurston.

8   Rewrite a scene from *Their Eyes Were Watching God* as if you were Jane Austen.

9   Friendship is essential to each character's growth in self-knowledge (Janie, Elizabeth, and Sydney). In many ways friendship is noticeably absent in *The Great Gatsby*. How does the absence of true friendship among any of the characters in the novel contribute to Gatsby's demise?

10   Courtship, love, and marriage are themes that run across all four novels. What insights have you gained about the characteristics of healthy relationships? Divide and categorize the different types of relationships. Draw data from each novel to develop your essay.

11   Self-knowledge (and lack thereof) is another motif that can be traced across each novel. Imagine you must deliver a speech to your peers on the importance of self-knowledge. What insights have you gained about the importance of self-knowledge to happiness and the ability to make good choices? Use illustrations from each character's development to present these insights in a compelling way.

12   Each one of these novels provides us with an array of images of how individuals lead their lives. Divide and categorize the characteristics of human degradation or flourishing as evidenced in at least three of the four novels.

13   Classical philosophers argue that true human freedom is exercised in the pursuit of noble and worthy goals. To what extent does the moral journey of each of the protagonists illustrate this understanding of freedom?

14   Aristotle defines happiness as "activity of the soul in accordance with human excellence" (*Nicomachean Ethics* I.7, 1177a2). With this definition in mind, consider to what extent the protagonists of the four novels achieve happiness.

Character tables

Elizabeth Bennet

| | The schooling of desire leads to a character's refined understanding and pursuit of an ideal that is both worthwhile and compelling | |
| | Example/illustration | Telos/object of desire |

Mapping pivotal points	Definition	Example/illustration	Telos/object of desire
Moral starting points Habits, dispositions, and context	What we know about the character's habitual behavior, attitudes, dispositions as well as initial aspirations and goals (tele).		
1st morally pivotal point	Shake-up, realization that character is not pursuing the best possible telos.		
2nd morally pivotal point	Leap in self-knowledge, clearer perspective on a worthy path.		
Challenge point	Meets a challenge that imposes stress or pressure; telos becomes clear but it is difficult to pursue. The character chooses a course of action and exercises practical wisdom in achieving that goal.		
Change: new dispositions			

Note: this handout includes a summary of definitions for review.

Janie Crawford		The schooling of desire leads to a character's refined understanding and pursuit of an ideal that is both worthwhile and compelling	
Mapping pivotal points	**Definition**	**Example/illustration**	**Telos/object of desire**
Moral starting points Habits, dispositions, and context			
1st morally pivotal point			
2nd morally pivotal point			
Challenge point			
Change: new dispositions			

Sydney Carton		*The schooling of desire leads to a character's refined understanding and pursuit of an ideal that is both worthwhile and compelling*	
Mapping pivotal points	**Definition**	**Example/illustration**	**Telos/object of desire**
Moral starting points Habits, dispositions, and context			
1st morally pivotal point			
2nd morally pivotal point			
Challenge point			
Change: new dispositions			

Jay Gatsby		The schooling of desire leads to a character's refined understanding and pursuit of an ideal that is both worthwhile and compelling	
Mapping pivotal points	Definition	Example/illustration	Telos/object of desire
Moral starting points Habits, dispositions, and context			
1st morally pivotal point			
2nd morally pivotal point			
Challenge point			
Change: new dispositions			

Hotlist of teaching resources

Jane Austen Biography: Life and Family
http://www.pemberley.com/janeinfo/janelife.html

This link provides the biographical and informational portion of the main website, which includes the annotated hypertext edtion of *Pride and Prejudice*. The text is embedded with related links to other relevant people, characters, or topics. In addition to biography, this site also includes information about Victorian culture, politics, and women's issues. This is an excellent resource.

The Jane Austen Society of North America
http://www.jasna.org/

This site, published by the Jane Austen Society of North America, contains information on Victorian England, a yearly essay contest for high school and college students, and links to the society's scholarly journal, *Persuasions*. Full text for many articles can be found online.

Zora Neale Hurston
http://i.am/zora

This site, a strange mix of the formal and very informal contains biographical information, excerpts from Hurston's novels and short stories, and a collection of critical essays written by a variety of authors, from high school students to doctoral students and scholars.

Voices from the Gap: Zora Neale Hurston
http://voices.cla.umn.edu/authors/HURSTONzoraneale.html

This site contains a short but informative biography of Hurston, and links to information about many other black women writers.

Zora Neale Hurston
http://www.dclibrary.org/blkren/bios/hurstonzn.html

Another short but interesting biography of Hurston detailing important personal and literary events in her life.

David Purdue's Charles Dickens page
http://www.fidnet.com/~dap1955/dickens/index.html

An amazing resource on all things relating to Dickens. This excellent site contains listings and descriptions of all Dickens major characters (with links in each description to related characters or facts), a glossary of nineteenth-century terms, information on the original publication and illustration of Dickens' novels, a biography, information and a map of Dickens' London, and much more.

Charles Dickens Gad's Hill Place
http://www.perryweb.com/Dickens/index.html

After David Purdue's page, everything looks bleak, but this site has some interesting information about Dickens' life, the inspirations for his novels, and most interestingly, a searchable database of quotes. Here you can search for quotes by novel, topic, word or phrase, or just scroll through an unending list of related material.

Tale of Two Cities
http://www.hti.umich.edu/cgi/p/pd-modeng/pd-modeng-idx?type=header&idno=Dicke TalTC

A complete online text of *A Tale of Two Cities*.

F. Scott Fitzgerald Centenary
http://www.sc.edu/fitzgerald/

This website, from the University of South Carolina contains a wealth of biographical and literary information about the life and times of Fitzgerald. Quotes about and from Fitzgerald, as well as from his characters, and links to photographs from his life are also included.

Biographies: F. Scott Fitzgerald and the American Dream
http://www.pbs.org/kteh/amstorytellers/bios.html

This PBS site contains brief but excellent biographies of Fitzgerald and his wife Zelda, an artist in her own right. The format is excellent, information is concise, clear, and well written, and the 1920s photographs make excellent additions. Brief but highly recommended.

F. Scott Fitzgerald
http://www.kirjasto.sci.fi/fsfitzg.htm

Another brief biography of the author, longer than the PBS one.

Notes

Introduction

1 See also Hartshorne's previous studies that gave momentum to the American character education movement of the 1920s: *Studies in the Nature of Character* Volumes 1–3 published in 1928, 1929, and 1930.

2 Consider, for example, James Arthur's *Education With Character* (2003), William Damon's *Bringing in a New Era of Character Education* (2002), Nel Noddings' *Educating Moral People* (2002), James Hunter's *The Death of Character* (2000), Kevin Ryan and Karen Bohlin's *Building Character in Schools* (1999), R. J. Nash's *Answering the Virtuecrats* (1997), Alfie Kohn's "How Not to Teach Values: A Critical Look at Character Education" (1997), William Damon's *Greater Expectations* (1996), M. Glendon and D. Blankenhorn's (eds) *Seedbeds of Virtue: Sources of Character, Competence, and Citizenship in American Society* (1995),William Kilpatrick's *Why Johnny Can't Tell Right From Wrong* (1992), James Leming's "In Search of Effective Character Education" (1993) and "Whither Goes Character Education?" (1997), James Q. Wilson's *The Moral Sense* (1993), and Thomas Lickona's *Educating for Character* (1991).

3 While this book does not provide a comprehensive analysis of character education, it seeks to familiarize English teachers with the various theoretical perspectives informing it, as this background can be useful in evaluating new curricula or pedagogical approaches presented at professional development training workshops. The National Council of Teachers of English (NCTE) in the United States and the National Association for the Teaching of English (NATE) in the UK have addressed the relationship between literature study and moral development only tangentially. This book focuses on the ways secondary and post-secondary English teachers can awaken and educate the moral imagination of their students through their study of novels.

4 The National Schools of Character Awards Program is sponsored by the Character Education Partnership (CEP) in Washington DC (www.character.org).

5 See, for example, the data cited in William Damon's *Greater Expectations*, James Hunter's *Death of Character*, and James Arthur's *Education with Character*.

6 Albeit in complex and overlapping ways, these various perspectives find their philosophical roots among three principal approaches to ethics in the Western tradition: 1) duty-based ethics that focuses on rules and originates in the philosophy of Immanuel Kant (1785); 2) utilitarian or consequence-based ethics inspired by Bentham (1823) and John Stuart Mill (1861); and 3) virtue- or character-based ethics stemming from the tradition of Socrates, Plato, and

Aristotle and revived in the contemporary scholarship of Alasdair MacIntyre (1984) and Charles Taylor (1989 and 1992).

7 Howard Kirschenbaum (1976) has attempted to redefine values clarification and refute its value neutrality. The pedagogy associated with values clarification continues to tend toward moral neutrality; see, for example, Simon, Howe, and Kirschenbaum's *Values Clarification* (1972).

8 For more on the social and emotional learning movement in the United States, see the Collaborative for Academic, Social, and Emotional Learning (CASEL): www.casel.org.

9 In his *Sources of the Self* (1989) Charles Taylor reminds us that modern philosophy has focused almost exclusively on the content of obligation rather than the nature of the good life. Yet, he argues, in order to make sense of our lives orienting ourselves toward the good and determining our place in relation to it is "an inescapable requirement of human agency" (52).

10 From *Specimens of Table Talk* of Samuel Taylor Coleridge, a collection of notes jotted down as records of conversation. They were published one year after his death by his nephew, Henry Nelson Coleridge.

11 You will notice that I refer to *students* throughout the text. In the United States, we do not make the distinction between pupils and students as is typically made in the UK. The students referred to here are secondary and post-secondary students of literature.

12 The actual words of Kafka are as follows: "The books we read are the kind that act upon us like a misfortune, that make us suffer like the death of someone we love more than ourselves, that make us feel as though we were on the verge of suicide, or lost in a forest remote from all human habitation—a book should serve as the ax for the frozen sea within us." (From a letter of Franz Kafka to Oskar Pollak.)

13 I do not make any distinctions between the national English curriculum in Great Britain and the national and state standards for English education in the United States. Instead I am drawing on works and curricular objectives common to both.

14 This book began as an academic study; I set out to discover the practical insights literature could shed on a long tradition of moral theory. After reading each novel several times, I carefully coded passages that signaled moral change and growth and looked for patterns both within each character's development and across the four protagonists.

1 The schooling of desire

1 I have changed the name to mask her identity.

2 This story is part of the anecdotal research data I collected for the 1998 National Schools of Character Awards. *Schools of Character: Reclaiming America's Values for Tomorrow's Workforce* (1998: 14–15). A publication sponsored by *Business Week* and McGraw-Hill Educational and Professional Publishing Group in collaboration with the Character Education Partnership and the Boston University Center for the Advancement of Ethics and Character.

3 Sir John Templeton of the Templeton Foundation also speaks of the importance of tapping into the noble purpose of young people. To this end, his foundation inaugurated the Templeton Laws of Life Essay Contest, which invites adolescents from all over the world to write about experiences, individuals, and events that have helped to shape their noble purpose, the inspiration for the laws of life by which they live. The essay contest dovetails nicely with the study of literature,

language, and writing in secondary English. For more information on content and planning, please visit www.lawsoflife.org.

4 Gangsta rap is a genre of rap music that tends to direct anger at authority and depict the emotional and psychological angst of disenfranchised youth. The student in this anecdote was soon after taken to the emergency room and then admitted for psychological treatment.

5 In Steven S. Tigner's "Homer, Teacher of Teachers" (1993), he provides a fuller discussion of the three-part soul and the implications of Plato's Analysis for teachers. I am indebted to Professor Tigner for his lectures on the relevance of Plato and Aristotle to teaching and learning. His teaching has inspired my references to these seminal works.

6 Arthur Schwartz (1997) offers a compelling overview of Blasi's moral ideals concept and its link to considerations about the moral education of adolescents.

7 For a more comprehensive discussion of this topic, see journalist Neil Postman's *Amusing Ourselves to Death*.

8 Alasdair MacIntyre (1984) explains the history of the Enlightenment's breach with virtue. By focusing on human nature as it *is*, rather than on what "it-could-be-if-it-realized-its-*telos*," Enlightenment philosophers have broken with Classical and Christian tradition. They have reduced morality to that which is intelligible through scientific method—the *is*, not the *ought*, of man (53). Once the concept of an overriding *telos* is abandoned, MacIntyre argues, we are left without any clear understanding of man's purpose. As a consequence, he concludes that "there are and can be *no* valid rational justifications for any claims that objective and impersonal moral standards exist and hence, that there are no such standards" (19). And once objective moral standards are rendered null and void, the Classical understanding of virtue and the virtuous life are rendered meaningless. The pursuit of what is good is transformed into the pursuit of what I *feel* is good for me. Immersed in this level of subjectivism, we lack a common language and shared vision with which to engage in moral discourse or make sense of the schooling of desire. We have no means for discerning why some goals are more worthy of pursuit than others. James Davison Hunter expands this argument from a sociological perspective in his groundbreaking discourse, *The Death of Character* (2000).

9 *Nicomachean Ethics* I.8, 1098b5–28. Happiness or flourishing, then, is "the activity of soul exhibiting excellence, and if there are more than one excellence, in accordance with the best and most complete" (*Nicomachean Ethics* I.7, 1098a15).

10 Aristotle identifies three types of friendship ordered hierarchically according to their objects (*Nicomachean Ethics* VIII): friendship of virtue, friendship of utility, and friendship of pleasure. Virtuous friendship is highest because it is motivated by the most noble desires for oneself and others. While it incorporates pleasure and utility, friendship of virtue is concerned with wanting the best for one's friends.

11 See also *Republic* X590d–591a. Adults have a responsibility to foster dispositions in children that will enable them to govern their own souls well: "[W]e don't allow [children] to be free until we establish a constitution in them, just as in a city, and—by fostering their best part with our own—equip them with a guardian and ruler similar to our own to take our place. Then, and only then, we set them free." Similarly, we are inclined by nature, Aristotle reminds us, to pursue what is pleasurable and useful, but our desires and dispositions must be trained to pursue what is noble. Therefore, he advises, our desires must be schooled "by means of habit for noble joy and noble hatred" (*Nicomachean Ethics* X, 1179b4–31).

2 Literature and the moral imagination

1 In his essay, "Art and Contemplation," Josef Pieper (1990) asserts that "man's ability to see is in decline" (31). That is, our capacity for contemplation, reflection, thoughtfulness, and even careful observation has been weakened by an era that places emphasis on utility and technology over friendship and the arts, and producing and consuming over thinking and being.

2 This student is referring to Jane Austen's *Pride and Prejudice*

3 In this book I do not address the research and theory on the power of students' storytelling in their own voice. For a more thorough discussion of this view of narrative see, for example, Tappan and Brown (1989) and P. Rabinowitz and M. Smith (1998) *Authorizing Readers: Resistance and Respect in the Teaching of Literature*. The theory, data, and framework used in this book deal primarily with the use of literary narrative to distill insights about moral education.

3 Fostering ethical reflection in our classrooms

1 Teachers Academies sponsored by the Center for the Advancement of Ethics and Character (CAEC) at Boston University are five- to ten-day humanities-based retreats for educators. For more information on Teachers Academies, visit www.bu.edu/education/caec.

2 Narrative is perhaps the longest standing means of education and communication in our culture. In his book, *Actual Minds, Possible Worlds* (1986), Jerome Bruner introduced the concept of "narrative thinking" as one of two modes of learning and making sense of reality. We tend to order our thoughts, he explained, by way of "propositional thinking" and "narrative thinking." The former has more to do with logical deductive reasoning whereas the latter is more context specific, engaged with people, events, happenings and the intentions that inform them. While we know that the development of propositional thinking, rigorous logic, and sound judgment are crucial, narrative thinking offers us a more penetrating lens on life.

3 Similarly, in his book, *Psychological Seduction* (1983), William Kilpatrick asserts, "Knowing the stories to which one belongs is not a matter of narcissistic self-authoring but having a direction, a point . . . as well as a sense of origin and history" (107–108).

4 See also Elridge's *On Moral Personhood* (1989).

5 To borrow from J. A. Jacobs, *Virtue and Self-Knowledge* (1989), *tele* are "motivational self-conceptions" that "express ends which one (a) desires for their own sake, and (b) judges to be worthwhile. . . . Their joint satisfaction specifies the sense in which we identify with these conceptions; in which they are conceptions of self and not just ends" (17 and 22).

6 Aristotle, *Nicomachean Ethics* II.6.

Part II Case studies in character

1 Louise Rosenblatt made a pioneering contribution to our understanding of aesthetic reading in her seminal works, *The Reader, the Text, and the Poem: The Transactional Theory of the Literary Work* (1978) and *Literature as Exploration* (1938, 1995 5th edn). In *Reader, the Text, and the Poem* she describes aesthetic reading as reading in which "the reader's attention is centered directly on what he is living through during his relationship with that particular text" (25). In her first work, Rosenblatt describes the power of literature on

readers this way: "The students valued literature as a means of enlarging their knowledge of the world, because through literature they acquire not so much additional information as additional experience. . . . Literature provides a living through, not simply knowledge about" (37–38).

2 Aristotle also explains that moral and intellectual virtue are cultivated differently—intellectual virtue through teaching and moral virtue through habit—but in tandem: "Virtue, then being of two kinds, intellectual and moral, intellectual virtue in the main owes both its birth and growth to teaching (for which reason it requires experience and time), while moral virtue comes about as a result of habit" (*Nicomachean Ethics* II.1, 1103a33–b25).

3 William Bennett's *Book of Virtues* (1993) and *Moral Compass* (1994) have been widely criticized for reducing stories to a simplistic moral lesson. The stories in both anthologies, however, appeal to a wide range of ages and readers. It is not the stories themselves but the teaching of these stories that can become reductionistic. For a good example of teaching literature effectively at university level, see Susan Resnik Parr's *The Moral of the Story* (1982) and see Vigen Guroian's *Teaching the Heart of Virtue* (1998) for insights on the power of fairy tales on the moral imagination of younger children.

4 Elizabeth Bennet—humbled heroine

1 All of the passages in this case study are taken from the Oxford World's Classics edition of the novel (1980) based on the 1813 edition of Austen's *Pride and Prejudice*.

2 The parallels between Darcy and Elizabeth's moral growth merit further study. As this case study focuses more narrowly on Elizabeth, it does not explore the parallels and contrast between these two protagonists as carefully as is warranted by the text.

5 Janie Crawford—trial and transcendence

1 All of the passages in this case study are taken from the Harper and Row edition of the novel (1937/1990).

6 Sydney Carton—rekindling a sense of purpose

1 All of the passages in this case study are taken from the Everyman's Library edition of the novel (1993) based on the 1859 edition of Dickens' *A Tale of Two Cities*.

7 Jay Gatsby—the tragedy of blind eros

1 All the passages in this case study are taken from the Macmillan edition of the novel.

2 Wayne Booth, *The Company We Keep*.

3 You will note that excerpts from *The Great Gatsby* do not always follow a neat chapter sequence as the other case studies do. Because of the novel's plot structure, some passages are drawn from chapters before or after those designated in the sub-heading.

8 Final considerations

1 See Steven S. Tigner's "Homer: Teacher of Teachers" (1993).
2 See M. Knox Beran (1998) "Lincoln, Macbeth, and the Moral Imagination" in *HUMANITAS*, Volume XI, No. 2, National Humanities Institute, Washington, DC.

Appendix A Definitions and distinctions

1 It lies in making a habit of "find[ing] and choos[ing] that which is intermediate . . . between excess . . . and defect." Aristotle explains the requisite criteria for virtuous action. First, "the agent must have knowledge." Second, "he must choose acts and choose them for their own sake." Third, "his action must proceed from a firm and unchangeable character" (*Nicomachean Ethics* II.4, 1105a29).

Bibliography

Albom, M. (1997) *Tuesdays with Morrie*, New York: Broadway Books.

Annas, J. (1993) *The Morality of Happiness*, New York: Oxford University Press.

Applebee, A.N., Burroughs, R. and Stevens, A. (Feb 2000) "Creating Continuity and Coherence in High School Literature Curricula," *Research in the Teaching of English*, 34: 397–423.

Appleyard, J.A. (1991) *Becoming a Reader: The Experience of Fiction from Childhood to Adulthood*, Cambridge: Cambridge University Press.

Aristotle, *Nicomachean Ethics*, David Ross (trans.) (1992) New York: Oxford University Press.

Aristotle, *The Politics*, Carnes Lord (trans.) (1984) Chicago: University of Chicago Press.

Arthur, J. (2003) *Education with Character: The Moral Economy of Schooling*, London and New York: RoutledgeFalmer.

Austen, J. (1813/1980) *Pride and Prejudice*, Oxford: Oxford University Press.

Bennett, W.J. (1993) *The Book of Virtues: A Treasury of Great Moral Stories*, New York: Simon & Schuster.

Bennett, W.J. (1994) *The Moral Compass: Stories for a Life's Journey*, New York: Simon & Schuster.

Bentham, J. (1823) *An Introduction to the Principles of Morals and Legislation*, L.J. Lafleur (ed.) (1948) New York: Haffner Press.

Blasi, A. (1993) "The development of identity: Some implications for moral functioning," in G.G. Noam and T. Wren (eds), *The Moral Self: Building a Better Paradigm*, Cambridge: MIT Press.

Bohlin, K. (Summer 2001) "Perseverance in Character Education: Aiming Higher," in Boston University's Center for the Advancement of Ethics and Character and ASCD's newsletter, *CHARACTER*, 9(1): 1–11.

Booth, W.C. (1988) *The Company We Keep: An Ethics of Fiction*, Los Angeles: University of California Press.

Booth, W.C. (Sept 1998) "The ethics of teaching literature," *College English*, 61(1): 41–55.

Booth, W.C. (2001) "Literary criticism and the pursuit of character," *Literature and Medicine*, 20(2): 97–108.

Bruner, J. (1986) *Actual Minds, Possible Worlds*, Cambridge: Harvard University Press.

Burnyeat, M.F. (1980) "On learning to be good," in A.O. Rorty (ed.) *Essays on Aristotle's Ethics*, Berkeley: University of California Press.

Coles, R. (1989) *The Call of Stories: Teaching and the Moral Imagination*, Boston: Houghton Mifflin.

Damon, W. (1996) *Greater Expectations: Overcoming the Culture of Indulgence in America's Homes and Schools*, New York: The Free Press.

Damon, W. (ed.) (2002) *Bringing in a New Era of Character Education*, Stanford: Hoover Institute Press.

Denby, D. (1996) *Great Books*, New York: Touchstone.

Denby, D. (4 September 1996) "A movie critic's classical odyssey," *The Boston Globe:* F1, F7–F8.

DeVries, R. (1998) "Implications of Piaget's constructivist theory for character education," *Action in Teacher Education*, Vol. 20: 4, 39–47.

Dewey, J. (1933) *How We Think*, in Jo Ann Boydston (ed.), *The Later Works, 1925–1953*. Vol. 8, Carbondale: Southern Illinois University Press.

Dewey, J. (1938) *Experience and Education*, New York: Touchstone.

Dewey, J. (1944) *Democracy and Education*, New York: The Free Press.

Dickens, C. (1859/1993) *A Tale of Two Cities*, London: David Campbell Publishers Ltd.

Dorsett, L.W. and Mead, M.L. (eds) (1985) *C.S. Lewis' Letters to Children*, New York: Simon & Schuster.

Dostoevsky, F. (1991) *The Brothers Karamazov*, R. Pevear and L. Volokhonsky (trans.), New York: Vintage Books.

Edson, M. (1999) *Wit*, New York: Farrar, Straus & Giroux.

Elridge, R. (1989) *On Moral Personhood*, Chicago: University of Chicago Press.

Fesmire, S. (2003) *John Dewey and Moral Imagination: Pragmatism in Ethic*, Indiana University Press.

Fitzgerald, F.S. (1925/1980) *The Great Gatsby*, New York: Macmillan.

Fitzgerald, F.S. (1932) "My lost city," in K. Norris (1995) *Leaving New York: Writers Look Back*, Saint Paul: Hungry Mind Press.

Frankl, V.E. (1984) *Man's Search for Meaning*, 3rd edn, New York: Simon & Schuster.

Garrison, J. (1997) *Dewey and Eros: Wisdom and Desire in the Art of Teaching*, New York: Teachers College Press.

Glendon, M. and Blankenhorn, D. (eds) (1995) *Seedbeds of Virtue: Sources of Character, Competence, and Citizenship in American Society*, New York: Madison Books.

Guroian, V. (1998) *Teaching the Heart of Virtue*, Oxford: Oxford University Press.

Hartshorne, H. (1932) *Character in Human Relations*, New York: Charles Scribner's Sons.

Hartshorne, H. and May, M. (1928) *Studies in the Nature of Character*, Vol. 1, New York: Macmillan.

Hartshorne, H. and May, M. (1929) *Studies in the Nature of Character*, Vol. 2, New York: Macmillan.

Hartshorne, H. and May, M. (1930) *Studies in the Nature of Character*, Vol. 3, New York: Macmillan.

Hoff-Sommers, C. (1984) "Ethics without virtue: Moral education in America," *American Scholar*, 53(3): 381–389.

Hoff-Sommers, C. (Fall 1992) "Teaching the virtues," *Letters from Santa Fe*: 12–17.

Hunter, J.D. (2000) *The Death of Character: Moral Education in an Age Without Good or Evil*, New York: Basic Books.

Hurston, Z.N. (1937/1990) *Their Eyes Were Watching God*, New York: Harper & Row.

Jacobs, J.A. (1989) *Virtue and Self-knowledge*, Englewood Cliffs: Prentice-Hall.

Jarvis, F.W. (1993) "Beyond ethics," *Journal of Education*, 175(2).

Johnson, M. (1993) *Moral Imagination: Implications of Cognitive Science for Ethics*, Chicago: University of Chicago Press.

Kafka, F. (1948) *The Diaries of Franz Kafka*, J. Kresh (trans.), M. Brod (ed.), London: Secker & Warburg.

Kilpatrick, W.K. (1983) *Psychological Seduction: The Failure of Modern Psychology*, New York: Thomas Nelson.

Kilpatrick, W.K. (1992) *Why Johnny Can't Tell Right from Wrong*, New York: Simon & Schuster.

Kilpatrick, W.K., Wolfe, G. and Wolfe, S.M. (1994) *Books that Build Character: A Guide to Teaching Your Child Moral Values through Stories*, New York: Touchstone Books.

Kirschenbaum, H. (1976) "Clarifying values clarification: Some theoretical issues," in D. Purpel and K. Ryan (eds), *Moral Education: It Comes with the Territory*, Berkeley: McCutchon.

Kiyosaki, R.T. and Lechter, S.L. (1998) *Rich Dad, Poor Dad: What the Rich Teach Their Kids About Money—That the Poor and Middle Class Do Not!* New York: Warner Books.

Knox Beran, M. (1998) "Lincoln, Macbeth, and the Moral Imagination," in *HUMANITAS*, Volume XI, No. 2, National Humanities Institute, Washington, DC.

Kohn, A. (1996) *Beyond Discipline: From Compliance to Community*, Alexandria: Association for Supervision and Curriculum Development.

Kohn, A. (1997) "How not to teach values: A critical look at character education," *Phi Delta Kappa*, 78(6): 429–439.

Leming, J.S. (1993) "In search of effective character education," *Educational Leadership*, 51(3): 63–71.

Leming, J.S. (1997) "Whither goes character education? Objectives, pedagogy, and research in contemporary character education programs," *Journal of Education*, 179(2): 11–34.

Lewis, C.S. (1961) *An Experiment in Criticism*, Cambridge: Cambridge University Press.

Lewis, C.S. (1975) *The Abolition of Man*, New York: Touchstone.

Lickona, T. (1991) *Educating for Character: How Our Schools Can Teach Respect and Responsibility*, New York: Bantam Books.

MacIntyre, A. (1984) *After Virtue: A Study in Moral Theory*, Notre Dame: University of Notre Dame Press.

Markham, B. (1983) *West With the Night*, New York: North Point Press. (Original edition 1942.)

Milburn, M. (2001) "Lighting the flame: teaching high school students to love, not loathe literature," *English Journal* 91(2): 90–95.

Mill, J.S. (1861) *Utilitarianism*, Oskar Piest (ed.) (1957) Indianapolis: Bobbs-Merrill Company, Inc.

Nanfeldt, S. (1996) *Plus Style*, New York: Penguin Books.

Nash, R.J. (1997) *Answering the Virtuecrats: A Moral Conversation on Character Education*, New York: Teachers College Press.

Noddings, N. (1992) *The Challenge to Care in Schools: An Alternative Approach to Education*, New York: Teachers College Press.

Noddings, N. (2002) *Educating Moral People: A Caring Alternative to Character Education*, New York: Teachers College Press.

Nussbaum, M.C. (1990) *Love's Knowledge: Essays on Philosophy and Literature*, New York: Oxford University Press.

O'Brien, T. (1990) *The Things They Carried*, New York: Penguin Books.

O'Connor, F. (1962) "The nature and aim of fiction," in S. Fitzgerald and R. Fitzgerald (eds), *Mystery and Manners*, New York: Farrar, Straus & Giroux.

Palmer, P.J. (1998) *The Courage to Teach: Exploring the Inner Landscape of a Teacher's Life*, San Francisco: Jossey-Bass.

Parr, S.R. (1982) *The Moral of the Story: Literature, Values, and American Education*, New York: Teachers College Press.

Patterson, K. (1995) *A Sense of Wonder: On Reading and Writing Books for Children*, New York: Plume.

Pieper, J. (1990) *Only the Lover Sings: Art and Contemplation*, San Francisco: Ignatius Press.

Plato, *Apology*, G.M.A. Grube (trans.) (1981) Indianapolis: Hackett Publishing.

Plato, *Meno*, G.M.A. Grube (trans.) (1981) Indianapolis: Hackett Publishing.

Plato, *Protagoras*, Stanley Lombardo and Karen Bell (trans.) (1992) Indianapolis: Hackett Publishing.

Plato, *Republic*, G.M.A. Grube (trans.), revised by C.D.C. Reeve (1992) Indianapolis: Hackett Publishing.

Plato, *Symposium*, A. Nehamas and P. Woodruff (trans.) (1989) Indianapolis: Hackett Publishing.

Postman, N. (1986) *Amusing Ourselves to Death*, New York: Viking Penguin.

Rabinowitz, P and Smith, M. (1998) *Authorizing Readers: Resistance and Respect in the Teaching of Literature*, New York: Teachers College Press.

Raths, L., Harmin, M. and Simon, S. (1978) *Values and Teaching*, Columbus: Merrill.

Rosenblatt, L. (1978) *The Reader, the Text and the Poem: The Transactional Theory of the Literary Work*, Carbondale: Southern Illinois Press.

Rosenblatt, L. (1995, 5th edn) *Literature as Exploration*, New York: The Modern Language Association.

Ross, W.D. (1930) *The Right and the Good*, Oxford: Oxford University Press.

Ross, W.D. (ed.) (1944) *The Works of Aristotle*, Oxford: Oxford University Press.

Rowling, J.K. (1999) *Harry Potter and the Chamber of Secrets*, New York: Scholastic.

Ryan, K. and Bohlin, K.E. (1999) *Building Character in Schools: Practical Ways to Bring Moral Instruction to Life*, San Francisco: Jossey-Bass.

Ryan, K. and Bohlin, K.E. (1999, March 3) "Educating for character: Values, views, or virtues?" *Education Week*, 18(25): 72 and 49.

Safire, W. (25 May 2003) "On Language," *The New York Times Magazine*.

Schapps, E. (1998) "Risks and rewards of community building," *Thrust for Educational Leadership*, Sep/Oct 98, Vol. 28, Issue 1, 6–10.

Schwartz, A.J. (1997) "A philosophical inquiry into the structure and function of the moral ideals concept: implications for character education strategies during adolescence," Unpublished doctoral dissertation, Harvard University Graduate School of Education.

Simon, S., Howe, L. and Kirschenbaum, H. (1972) *Values Clarification*, New York: Hart Publishers.

Tappan, M.B. and Brown, L.M. (1989) "Stories told as lessons learned: Toward a narrative approach to moral development and moral education," *Harvard Educational Review*, 59(2): 182–205.

Taylor, C. (1989) *Sources of the Self: The Making of Modern Identity*, Cambridge, MA: Harvard University Press.

Taylor, C. (1992) *The Ethics of Authenticity*, Cambridge, MA: Harvard University Press.

Telfer, E. (1980) *Happiness*, New York: St. Martin's Press.

Tigner, S. (1993) "Homer, teacher of teachers," *Journal of Education*, 175(3): 43–64.

Tigner, S. (1995) "Signs of the Soul," in G.S. Fain (ed.), *Leisure and Ethics: Reflections on the Philosophy of Leisure* (Vol. II, pp. 9–24), Reston, VA: American Association for Leisure and Recreation.

Tigner, S. (1996) *Plato's Republic: An Outline Guide for Educators*, Boston: Boston University.

Urmson, J.O. (1988) *Aristotle's Ethics*, Oxford: Basil Blackwell.

Vitz, P. (1990) "The use of stories in moral development: new psychological reasons for an old education method," *American Psychologist*, 45(6): 709–720.

Wilson, J.Q. (1993) *The Moral Sense*, New York: The Free Press.

Woodring, C. (ed.) (1990) *The Collected Works of Samuel Taylor Coleridge: Table Talk*, Vol. 14, Princeton, NJ: Princeton University Press. (Original edition 1836.)

Wynne, E. and Ryan, K. (1996) *Reclaiming Our Schools: Teaching Character Academics and Discipline*, New York: Macmillan.

Further reading

Applebee, A.N. (1993) *Literature in the Secondary School: Studies of Curriculum and Instruction in the United States*, Urbana: National Council of Teachers of English.

Bergmann, F. (1977) *On Being Free*, Notre Dame: University of Notre Dame Press.

Berman, J. (February 15, 2002) "Syllabuses of risk," *The Chronicle Review*, B7–9.

Bettleheim, B. (1977) *The Uses of Enchantment*, New York: Vintage.

Campbell, J. (1971) *Hero With a Thousand Faces*, New York: Meridian Books.

Carlyle, T. (Spring 1999) "Literature is the thought of thinking souls," *Curriculum Update*, Alexandria: Association for Supervision and Curriculum Development.

Carr, D. and Steutal, J. (eds) (1999) *Virtue Ethics and Moral Education*, London: Routledge.

Chazan, B. (1985) *Contemporary Approaches to Moral Education*, New York: Teachers College Press.

Crisp, R. and Slote, M. (eds) (1997) *Virtue Ethics*, Oxford: Oxford University Press.

Cunningham, A. (2001) *The Heart of What Matters: The Role of Literature in Moral Philosophy*, Berkeley: University of California Press.

Davison, J. and Dowson, J. (eds) (1998) *Learning to Teach English in the Secondary School*, London: Routledge.

Davison, J. and Moss, J. (eds) (2000) *Issues in English Teaching*, London: Routledge.

De Saint-Exupéry, A. (1971) *The Little Prince*, New York: Harcourt Brace.

Dewey, J. (1909) *Moral Principles in Education*, in Jo Ann Boydston (ed.), *The Middle Works, 1899–1924*, Vol. 4, Carbondale: Southern Illinois University Press.

Ellenwood, S. and McLaren, N. (1994) "Literature-based character education," *Middle School Journal*, 11: 42–47.

Foot, P. (ed.) (1978) *Virtue and Vices and Other Essays in Moral Philosophy*, Berkeley: University of California Press.

Gibbon, P. (2002) *A Call to Heroism*, New York: Atlantic Monthly Press.

Ingall, C.K. (1997) *Metaphors, Maps, and Mirrors: Moral Education in Middle School*, Greenwich: Ablex.

Jones, E., Ryan, K. and Bohlin, K. (1999) "Character Education and Teacher Education," *Action in Teacher Education*, 20(4): 11–28.

Kekes, J. (April 1991) "Moral imagination, freedom and the humanities," *American Philosophical Quarterly*, 28(2): 101–111.

Kennedy, L. (28 April 2003) "Lighting the way: Lois Lowry's books help children understand life, but parents don't always like the dark themes," *Boston Globe*, B7.

Kohlberg, L. (1985) "The just community approach to moral education in theory and practice," in M. Berkowtiz and F. Oser (eds), *Moral Education: Theory and Application*, Hillsdale: Lawrence Erlbaum.

Lewis, C.S. (1951) *English Literature in the Sixteenth Century, Excluding Drama*, Oxford: Clarendon.

Lockwood, A.L. (1993) "A letter to character educators," *Educational Leadership*, 51(3): 6–11.

Lopez, B. (1990) *Crow and Weasel*, New York: HarperCollins.

Losin, P. (1996) "Education and Plato's parable of the cave," *Journal of Education*, 178(3): 49–66.

Marnane, M. and Heinen, J.R.K. (1993) "Fostering moral growth through literature," *The Clearinghouse*, 67(2): 80–82.

Midgley, M. (1984) *Wickedness: A Philosophical Essay*, Boston: Routledge & Kegan Paul.

Nabakov, V. (1999) "Literature and butterflies are the two sweetest passions known to man," *Curriculum Update*, Alexandria: Association for Supervision and Curriculum Development.

Parry, R.D. (1996) "Morality and happiness: Book IV of Plato's *Republic*," *Journal of Education*, 178(3): 31–48.

Piaget, J. (1965) *The Moral Judgment of the Child*, New York: The Free Press.

Ricoer, P. (1986) *Time and Narrative*, Chicago: University of Chicago Press.

Roberts, D.F., Foehr, U.G., Rideout, V.J. and Brodie, M. (1999) *Kids and the Media at the New Millennium*: A Kaiser Family Foundation Report.

Rosenstand, N. (1997) *The Moral of the Story: An Introduction to Ethics*, 2nd edn, Mountain View: Mayfield Publishing Company.

Rule, P.C. (1984) "Something of Great Constancy: Uses of Imagination," Paper presented at the Nash lecture series, University of Regina, Canada.

Schools of Character: Reclaiming America's Values for Tomorrow's Workforce (1998) A publication sponsored by *Business Week* and McGraw-Hill Educational and Professional Publishing Group in collaboration with the Character Education Partnership and the Boston University Center for the Advancement of Ethics and Character.

Scruton, R. (1993) *On Humane Education*, An inaugural lecture for the University Professors Program at Boston University, Boston, MA.

Showalter, E. (January 17, 2003) "What teaching literature should really mean," *The Chronicle Review*, B7–B9.

Stutz, C.K. (1995) "The Soul of Life: Literature, Teaching, and Moral Awareness," Unpublished doctoral dissertation, Boston University School of Education, Boston.

"Teaching the Teachers: A Special Report" (1985) *The Literary Classics: Literature as a Mode of Knowledge*, Dallas: Dallas Institute of Humanities and Culture.

Teloh, H. (1986) *Socratic Education in Plato's Early Dialogues*, Notre Dame: University of Notre Dame Press.

Tigner, S. (1993) "Character education: Outline of a seven-point program," *Journal of Education*, 175(2): 13–22. Reprinted in Ryan and Bohlin (1999).

Walsh, M. (Oct 1997) "Aristotle's conception of freedom," *Journal of the History of Philosophy*, 35(4): 495–507.

Weiner, N. (1993) *The Harmony of Soul: Mental Health and Moral Virtue Reconsidered*, Albany: State University of New York Press.

Weisberg, M. and Duffin, J. (1995) "Evoking the moral imagination: Using stories to teach ethics and professionalism to nursing, medical, and law students," *Change*, (27)1: 21–27.

Zedler, B.H. (1956) "John Dewey in context," in D. Gallagher (ed.), *Some Philosophers on Education*, Milwaukee: Marquette University Press.

Forthcoming National Report: *Smart and Good High Schools: Developing Excellence and Ethics for Success in School, Work and Beyond*. This research conducted by Thomas Lickona, PhD and Mathew Davidson, PhD has been funded by a grant from the John Templeton Foundation. To pre-order a Free Digital Copy of *Smart and Good High Schools*, visit http://www.cortland.edu/templeton.

Index